Dr Judith Locke is a registered clinical psychologist, former teacher and school counsellor. She speaks to parents, teachers and students throughout Australia and internationally on topics related to modern parenting, family wellbeing and academic environments. Judith is the author of two bestselling parenting books, *The Bonsai Child* and *The Bonsai Student*, the first of which has also been published in China. She has a clinical practice and consults with families in Australasia. Judith wrote a weekly parenting column for *The Sunday Mail* for five years and her psychological commentary continues to feature regularly in the media.

Dr Danielle Einstein is a clinical psychologist and Adjunct Fellow at Macquarie University. She was head of Westmead Hospital's Anxiety Clinic before establishing her private practice. She has published research into prevention and treatment of anxiety, tolerance of uncertainty, emotional health and social media use. Danielle's book, *The Dip*, gives students and parents a step-by-step guide for positively managing their device use. She was the first Australian clinical psychologist to call for a phone ban in schools and her research findings and practical advice are regularly quoted in the media. Based on her work, Danielle has pioneered an innovative approach to taming worry.

Raising Anxiety

Why our good intentions are backfiring on children
(and how to fix it)

Judith Y Locke, PhD
Danielle A Einstein, PhD

First published by Dr Judith Locke and Dr Danielle Einstein (Australia), 2024
Copyright © Judith Locke & Danielle Einstein 2024
Judith Locke and Danielle Einstein assert their right to be identified as the co-authors of this work.

This book is copyright. Apart from any fair dealing for the purpose of private study, research, criticism or review, as permitted under the Copyright Act, no part of this book may be reproduced, stored in a retrieval system, or transmitted in any form or by any means without prior written permission. Email enquiries can be directed to either author. Specifically, for the anxiety components, contact Dr Danielle Einstein (at deinstein@danielleeinstein.com) and for the parenting components, contact Dr Judith Locke (at judith@confidentandcapable.com).

Design by Tess McCabe
Cover design by Tess McCabe
Authors' images by Jamie Hanson (Judith) and Giselle Haber (Danielle)
Typesetting by Sunset Publishing Service Pty Ltd
Printed in Australia by Ingram Spark

Disclaimer
The contents of this book are intended for information purposes only. The information contained in this book is not a substitute for, and is not intended to replace, independent professional, legal, or medical advice. Readers should consider the need to obtain any appropriate professional advice relevant to their own particular circumstances.
Every effort has been made to ensure the information is correct at the time of publication. As psychological advice can change with new research on best practice treatment, you may be best to consult with a professional to ensure you have the latest advice for your child's or your own psychological or other concerns.
This book draws on cases the authors have treated or been informed about over the years; however, the cases mentioned are composites of typical cases, rather than particular people or particular situations. Any information that may identify a particular person has been altered or omitted.

A catalogue record for this book is available from the National Library of Australia

ISBN 978-0-9943692-6-0
eISBN 978-0-9943692-5-3

Suggested citation: Locke JY and Einstein DA 2024. *Raising anxiety: why our good intentions are backfiring on children (and how to fix it)* Judith Locke and Danielle Einstein

Contents

Introduction		vii

PART A

Chapter 1	All about anxiety	3
Chapter 2	Parenting, schooling and anxiety	15
Chapter 3	Technology and anxiety	37
Chapter 4	Friendships and anxiety	53
Chapter 5	Sensitive children and anxiety	65
Chapter 6	Envy, FoMO and anxiety	73
Chapter 7	Self-regard and anxiety	81
Chapter 8	The subtle benefits of anxiety	95

PART B

Chapter 9	Climbing out of the anxiety hole	125
Chapter 10	Getting your child on the right track	127
Chapter 11	Getting technology right	159
Chapter 12	Getting your child friendship ready	193
Chapter 13	Helping your child face day-to-day challenges	217
Chapter 14	Dealing with persistent worries	251
Chapter 15	Seeking professional assistance	287
Chapter 16	Frequently asked questions	305
Chapter 17	Embrace life's uncertainty	325

Further reading	329
Acknowledgements	343

Introduction

Shelby was always a shy child. When she was a toddler, she would hide behind her mother's or father's legs when she met anyone new. At the park, her parents would encourage her to join games with other children, but Shelby liked to insist that her mother or father sit next to her in the sandpit. At birthday parties, she would rather spend time with the adults in the kitchen than play with the children outside.

Starting school was a huge worry for Shelby. She kept asking her parents for reassurance in the months leading up to the first day: 'Am I going to make friends?' and 'Will my teacher like me?' And even though her parents told her they were sure she would love her teacher and that she would make lots of new friends, she remained worried about what would happen.

When she went to school, her mother faced a daily challenge to get Shelby to separate from her. In Prep, she would cling to her parent's leg, gazing up with tears streaming down her little face. It took weeks before she would reluctantly go into her classroom on her own. Every now and then she would tell her parents at the dinner table that no one in her class liked her as much as they liked the others, and she hadn't known who to sit with at lunch. She sometimes claimed to have a sore throat or a sick feeling in her tummy and asked if she could stay home from school, particularly when she found out that one of her parents was working from home that day.

Shelby found certain school tasks particularly difficult. She was uncomfortable doing oral presentations in front of the rest of the class, as she was concerned the others might laugh at her. Her nervousness was so obvious that her Year One teacher started to let Shelby do a special show-and-tell by herself at lunch time, so she wasn't overwhelmed by the rest of the class and at risk of crying. Shelby also worried about sports days: what if she came last in her races and looked silly in front of the whole school? Her parents tried to get her to participate by offering special lunches on those days, or taking turns to attend the carnival and cheer Shelby on, but eventually they gave up and simply let her stay at home on sports days.

Shelby often declined to participate in activities her parents thought she would enjoy. They worked so hard to prepare her costume exactly as she wanted for Book Week in Year Three, and she seemed excited about turning up as Harry Potter. But that morning, when she didn't think the lightning bolt her father had drawn on her forehead looked exactly like Harry's scar, she ran to her bedroom and refused to go to school.

Her parents became so worried about her that they consulted a psychologist. After a formal assessment, Shelby was diagnosed with anxiety. The psychologist wrote a letter to the school requesting Shelby be allowed to opt out of activities which might cause her to worry excessively.

Shelby's parents look back on those times as far easier than the situation they face now. Shelby is in Year 8 and attends school only occasionally. It has become harder and harder to get her to go to school, attend events she is invited to, or participate in her team's sports matches. Distraught, her parents have taken her to different psychologists over the years, but Shelby tends to meet them once or twice before refusing to return, saying that she doesn't like them, or they don't understand how she feels.

Shelby's parents are at their wits' end. They tell her that she needs to go to school, participate in extra-curricular events and meet up with her schoolmates, but every time Shelby says, 'I can't do those things because I have anxiety.' Bit by bit, their daughter's world and her future potential seem to be shrinking.

William's parents are also at their wits' end. Until he was around five, their son was full of energy and fun. At family get-togethers, he loved playing with all the cousins, even the little ones, and he often looked out for his younger sister.

He was certainly a strong-willed child (his parents used to joke that he was living up to the first part of his name), and always insisted things be done the way he liked them.

There was a 'right' way to cut sandwiches, and if the bread was cut diagonally, he refused to eat it. There was also a 'right' person to put him to bed each time even when he was young – 'Not Mummy, Daddy do it' – and regardless of who had the job, William would sometimes insist on a last-minute change. He always needed to know what was going to happen that day, often wanted the schedule changed to suit him, and was quite prepared to throw a tantrum unless the family complied with his demands. If they tried to go to the playground after – not before – they went to Grandma and Grandpa's, then William's defiant mood often soured the visit.

Sometimes he was sweet, coming in for a special cuddle with his parents while sitting on the sofa, or being extremely helpful to his sister when she was having difficulty putting on her shoes. But these flashes of 'kind William' were brief.

His parents discussed their concerns with a friend who was a teacher. The friend suggested William might be a little anxious and that a sense of control might make him feel better. So William's parents started to give him more choices, such as which restaurant they would go to and where they would sit at the table – 'Daddy sits next to me, Mummy goes over there'. They complied, thinking this would make him feel better and more comfortable in new situations.

But it didn't seem to work. No matter how much they catered to William's wishes and allowed him to make decisions, he didn't seem to appreciate the family's adjustments. He didn't like to comply with his parents' instructions, and his younger sister often simply allowed her brother to have his way. More and more the family seemed to walk on eggshells around him. It was Wilful William they usually saw; Sweet William made only rare appearances.

Since he turned nine, his behaviour has become more intense. William now expects the whole family to do exactly as he says and if things don't go the way he wants, he becomes furious. The other day when his sister didn't want to have the first shower, he slapped her arm so hard it left a mark. He has started to scream or hit things when he becomes frustrated. Yesterday, when told he had to stop his gaming session, he slammed his door and a treasured wedding photo fell off the sideboard in the next room, smashing the glass in the frame. He seems to be constantly close to rage and takes his feelings out on everyone.

William can still turn sweet after arguments, and sometimes he even expresses remorse. But it seems like only moments before the wilful part of him takes hold again.

What happened to their lovely boy?

As clinical psychologists, we have helped many families who have come to us describing scenarios like these. Shelby and William show variations of anxious behaviours – the need to be in control of situations, excessive fear of what *might* happen, extreme self-consciousness which reduces daily enjoyment, or a belief they cannot cope with certain circumstances. Many parents in our clinics would describe their children as fearful, shy or anxious – and often they are not wrong.

Nearly every one of the stories we hear begins with instances of minor shyness or occasional concerns about not being in control of the day's schedule. By the time families seek our help, these tendencies have often turned into fully formed problems for the child and for the people around them who love them but have become exasperated with their behaviour.

We believe it is far preferable to deal with these tendencies when they are more easily solved. Timely intervention is more helpful than providing treatment when the child is older and behaviours are much harder to change. So we decided to write a book to help families identify and resolve anxious behaviours early, before gusts of worry or wilfulness are able to transform into tempests of anxiety or rage.

In this book, we have combined our individual areas of knowledge and expertise. We are both clinical psychologists who have been interested in anxiety prevention and management for some time – we even met when we were working at an anxiety clinic. Since then, we have each gone on to specialise in particular psychological and treatment fields.

Danielle is an expert on anxiety, having been the director of said anxiety clinic. She is internationally known for her work on obsessive-compulsive disorder, worry and social media. In 2014, Danielle's theory on uncertainty was published, and following that she championed research trials targeting uncertainty in secondary schools. During the pandemic, she co-authored the Chilled and Considerate programs that helped thousands of teachers, parents and students around the world. She was the first Australian clinical psychologist to call for school phone bans. Danielle's work on mental health and device use has influenced many through her 2019 book and video *The Dip*, lectures to clinical psychologists, media interviews, podcasts and her contribution to the 2023 Australian documentary, *Disconnect Me*.

Judith is an expert in modern parenting, family wellbeing and academic environments. Her practical strategies help parents and teachers assist children to become confident and capable as they develop their maturity and independence. Judith primarily works with schools around Australia and internationally, delivering keynotes, training and information sessions about the best ways to improve children's wellbeing in a time when parenting has changed significantly from previous generations. She's also written the bestselling books for parents, *The Bonsai Child* and *The Bonsai Student*. Both give practical and effective strategies to build children's resilience, confidence and capability in the home and in their schooling. Judith also wrote a weekly parenting column for *The Sunday Mail* in Australia for over five years.

For some time, we have both been aware that to truly treat a child's anxiety, the whole family needs to be involved to encourage them to step out of their comfort zone and be brave and resilient, both at home and at school. We knew that by combining each other's areas of expertise, we could further help the many students, parents and teachers we both work with. We also knew that the optimal time for parents to start supporting their child to overcome anxious thoughts is when the child is still young, particularly in their kindergarten, prep or primary years. But we were also aware that anxiety problems may only become apparent to parents when children are older, so we wanted to help these families as well. That's how this book was born.

Before we go further, we want to check that this is the right book for you. The fact that you are investigating a parenting book indicates that being a good parent is important to you. We assume you show your child you love them through time spent together, physical affection and positive attention. No doubt you work hard to give them a happy childhood and a good educational start in life. And it is likely that your child knows they matter to their family and that they feel listened to and loved, even though they might occasionally think life is unfair when things don't go their way – much like every other child out there!

Despite this, you may feel that your child is experiencing some anxiety or heightened sensitivity. The following behaviours are cues that anxious thoughts may be present. None are necessarily a cause for concern – most children occasionally show signs of them. But if these behaviours are affecting your family and reducing the quality of life for your child or for you, reading this book will help.

Your child may be exhibiting anxious behaviour if:

- Their worries dominate family activities to the extent that your priorities are centred on making your child feel better, sometimes at the expense of spending quality time with other family members, including the other parent.
- They resist separating from you to go to school or day care, or to go to sleep on their own at night.
- They behave badly when asked to do things they don't want to do, prompting you to provide lengthy explanations and justifications of what is happening or why you want them to do something.
- They are extremely strong willed and need to feel they are in charge; exerting your authority as their parent is becoming much more challenging than when they were younger.
- They dislike change and become upset when their day doesn't go exactly to plan, and they have to follow someone else's directions.
- They insist on certain aspects of their appearance or their clothing being exactly as they wish. If you don't braid their hair in a certain way, or the particular t-shirt they feel they must wear is in the wash, they find it hard to cope.
- They are overtly sweet and attentive toward you, to the extent of providing you with loving notes and wanting frequent hugs and kisses from you, especially after you have both had a big argument. At other times, they might insist to be always on your lap or become upset when you turn your attention to others, even if only briefly. Without your focused attention, they become upset, even when you are on the phone to the plumber.
- They seem addicted to certain material things. As a child, they are inseparable from their blankie or favourite toy; as a tween, they constantly check their phone, take selfies, or are unable to stop playing Fortnite – or whichever game is currently popular – when asked.

We are confident that reading this book will help parents of anxious children, including those with clinically diagnosed anxiety, by showing them ways to react to their child's concerns which validate their fears without inadvertently increasing their worries or reducing their resilience.

Even if you do not see these particular behaviours in your child, this book will help. Most of the strategies we suggest can assist any child to develop their confidence and resilience, regardless of the presence of fearful behaviours.

We hope that by reading this book, parents will realise that some of their child's worries are perfectly normal. Indeed, many parents will read this book and apply its strategies to their family to prevent anxiety developing in their children.

A few caveats. If there are complicating factors in your child's life, such as abuse or family violence, the behavioural concerns we mention in this book might be caused by trauma, not anxiety. If these situations could be affecting your child, in their past or present, we urge you to seek individual professional advice rather than relying on this book. Similarly, if your child is neurodiverse (for example, if they have been diagnosed with autism or ADHD), we think it would be more beneficial for you to see a specialist for specific strategies to help them reach their full potential. We believe you will find useful strategies in this book for many of these diagnoses, but to receive targeted assistance, you are best to go to a professional specialising in your child's particular situation.

Reading this book may also help you with your anxiety. Anxious parents frequently have anxious children – not always, but often. Research shows there is a genetic basis for this, but it is also likely that parental anxiety rubs off on children. The strategies we give here can improve your confidence alongside your child's.

This book is written in two parts.

In Part A, we look at the nature of anxiety and the main factors that contribute to people becoming anxious, particularly children and teens. We look at how some popular parenting beliefs and caring approaches, our use of technology, and today's schooling environment can inadvertently set up the perfect environment for anxiety to grow.

Then we show why some efforts to overcome worry can accidentally start a cycle of actions that maintains it. We examine how factors like envy and social media can accentuate and contribute to unhealthy ways of thinking. We look at some of the unintended 'benefits' of anxiety that help make it difficult to overcome. Many of the examples we give reflect the sorts of clinical presentations we see regularly.

Part B is perhaps the most important part of the book because this is where we give you ways to turn your situation around. We show you how to set up your home environment so that it won't inadvertently 'grow' anxiety. These prevention strategies first draw on Judith's work to ensure you have the most helpful goals and the right mix of care and age-appropriate demands for your child to reach their true potential. We then draw on our joint expertise to help you make sure your child is ready to develop lasting and sustaining friendships and able to deal with occasional challenges while building and maintaining good social support among their peers. We show you how to help your child navigate their everyday difficulties in a way that acknowledges their feelings without inadvertently amplifying any unhelpful emotional reactions to life events. We also include strategies to carefully introduce technology such as phones and social media, so that these help rather than hinder your child's and your family's wellbeing.

We look at ways to resolve anxiety – be it your anxiety rubbing off on your child, or your child's anxiety affecting you. This section focuses on you as a parent and how you can provide something of a protective barrier to keep your family's anxiety at bay. We demonstrate some ground-breaking strategies from Danielle to better manage your fears and coach your child to deal with their worries using the same techniques.

We discuss ways to get the best out of psychological treatment should your child be one who would benefit from personalised, professional help, or if they are already receiving therapeutic assistance. Our Q and A section covers answers to questions that are often asked in our sessions with parents and teachers. To finish, we offer a suggestion that will put the wind in your sails and inspire you to keep going with the strategies in the book.

We can't wait any longer to share our knowledge with you. So let's get started!

Part A

CHAPTER 1

All about anxiety

Everybody gets worried, but some people worry a lot more than others. And some of us worry to the point where we feel overwhelmed by anxiety. In this chapter we explore the nature of anxiety, and why some of us are more affected by it than others.

What is anxiety?

Anxiety describes a range of cognitive, behavioural and emotional responses to fear. Our experience of anxiety can be intensely physical, such as the racing pulse, shallow breathing and dizziness we feel during a panic attack. At other times, it is more subtle: we appear to be our usual selves yet are so consumed by worries that we lose sleep, tense our muscles until they ache, and crave release through any distraction we can find.

We tend to view anxiety as a problematic feeling, but that isn't always the case. When anxiety isn't causing unnecessary discomfort, it is a clever response that we developed to keep us focused on goals and help us avoid danger. If we face physical danger, anxiety prepares our bodily systems to act. Humans have had this ability forever. When one of our ancestors encountered something big and scary like a grizzly bear, they would feel afraid, and their bodies would simultaneously react in the following ways:

- Their blood would rush to their legs and arms to be ready to run away or fight.
- Their heart rate would increase to prepare for the physical exertion required to run from or take on the bear.
- Their brain would narrow its focus to what really mattered, like quickly creating an escape route through the forest or trying to remember if bears can climb trees.
- Their digestion would be put on hold to conserve energy for more important things, such as running as long as it takes to get very far away from an angry bear.

These are known as panic responses. Feeling this way is problematic only if these panic responses repeatedly kick in when there is no objective danger. If this happens, we become fearful of the response itself and noticing panic symptoms can set off further anxiety. We start to think the butterflies in our tummy and heart beating fast are telling us there *is* danger. The physical responses of our body *perceiving* something scary – be it a truly dangerous situation we face, or simply one we have made up about what might happen at school today – amplify our fear to the point where we unintentionally become hyperalert to signs of anxiety in ourselves.

Rational worry vs debilitating anxiety

Most of us worry from time to time and our worries are often rational given the circumstances. If your child was worried that they might get in trouble at school for not doing their French homework well enough, and they actually *hadn't* put their best into their homework, we would say their worry was warranted. Indeed, you would almost hope their worry had kicked in earlier when they should have been doing their homework to a decent standard instead of doing the bare minimum so they could get back to their video game.

But if your child had spent hours diligently doing their homework, yet was still worried it wasn't good enough, we would call this debilitating worry. In this scenario, their worry can work against them because it might make them so nervous that they think more about potentially failing to reach the mark they aim for than the questions in front of them. Becoming less focused on the task at hand may cause them to not do as well as they could. Their anxiety might also lead them to overthink about the task afterward, to the point where they toss and turn at night and miss out on important sleep. For some, the fear might become so overwhelming or unpleasant that they give up trying to do their homework and choose to watch YouTube videos instead.

What separates diagnosable anxiety from normal anxiety is its persistence, the level of distress it causes or the degree to which it interferes with daily life. Let's consider someone with a fear of snakes. Concern about snakes when bushwalking is understandable, particularly in dense bushland known for their presence. But if the person's concern were so great that they didn't bushwalk with friends, even in an area where the incidence of snake bites was low and the chance of survival if bitten was high, they would have forfeited an enjoyable and social activity for fear of an unlikely outcome.

Fears about situations can be so unwarranted that some people stop living a normal life. A person might be so scared of snakes that they refuse to walk with their friends through the well-manicured lawn of an inner-city park. A person who is so fearful of their cats escaping their home that they constantly check their windows are closed may be unable to sleep at night or leave the house during the day. This would be considered an extreme level of anxiety because their undue worry is making them unable to carry out daily functions in life, which would be reason enough to seek psychological treatment.

Anxiety disorders refer to life-altering problems which emerge from a range of fears. Psychiatrists and psychologists have labelled these problems according to the subject of their fear. *Social anxiety* is a fear of what a person imagines others might think of them. *Panic disorder* is a fear of the panic symptoms we listed earlier. *Separation anxiety* is a fear of being apart from someone trusted and depended on – usually one's parents. *Generalised anxiety disorder* (GAD) occurs when people worry incessantly about a wide range of concerns. Their muscles tense, they feel irritable, and they can't ever fully get their worries out of their mind.

One last distinction to make is between rumination and worry. Ruminating is a type of repetitive thinking in which someone tries to analyse the cause, meaning and implications of *past* events. A student might replay in their mind the comment they made to their friends at morning tea or their answer in class that was corrected by their teacher. This is rumination if they continue to replay the incident over and over to the point where they cannot participate in or enjoy the handball game at lunch.

In contrast, a child (or adult) is worrying when they spend too long thinking about a potential *future* event. But the two actions aren't unrelated.

Worrying often goes hand in hand with ruminating. Still thinking about a silly off-the-cuff joke that you made at the drycleaners days ago is rumination. But when it makes you think too hard about conversations you'll have with the new team at work and leads you to imagine them complaining to your boss, or become nervous that a colleague will be asked to take over the account because you're not quick-witted enough? That's worry.

Worry is directly related to your fears. Checking the door is locked before you go to bed is a normal protective action. But double and triple checking and still worrying that someone could break in to the extent that you can't get to sleep night after night becomes a behaviour that interferes with your quality of life. You are thinking too much about something that *might* happen (although it isn't really likely to happen), particularly if you have such fears when you live in a safe community.

Helpful vs unhelpful anxiety

Everyone feels anxious at times in their life. While it is not a pleasant emotion, it is essential. It helps us to anticipate danger and stops us from doing something potentially unsafe or unhelpful. 'This side of the road is dark and the neighbourhood is considered dangerous, perhaps I should take the well-lit side as I walk to the bus stop.' Or, 'The traffic is usually bad on a Thursday afternoon, so I'd better leave early to be sure to get to the interview on time.'

When we experience the anxiety response to perceived threats, it can feel uncomfortable and sometimes overwhelming. And to stop it, we may react in ways that are not helpful.

An anxiety response makes us zero in on our fears and focus on how to neutralise them. It's why our ancestors would have used some of their energy to think about bears' climbing abilities and whether further energy was best used hoisting themselves into the branches or running away from the fast-approaching mass of brown fur. But when we are continually anxious, we can concentrate on our concerns to the point that we don't really take in anything else that's going on around us. This makes us less likely to be fully aware of what's happening in the present moment and magnifies our own thoughts while minimising our awareness of everything around us.

This can be detrimental to us in a range of situations. For example, when we attend a professional networking event, we may feel nervous about making a good impression. Our nerves might lead us to focus so much on our contributions to the conversations we join that we lose touch with the direction of the broader discussion. Ironically, this makes it more likely that we will not come across to others as socially adept. Our extreme focus might make our worst fears come true because we dwell on our own concerns rather than the conversation we should be actively participating in.

Anxiety also encourages us to shift into avoidance mode.

> *Rather than facing a situation which concerns us*
> *and learning that we can cope,*
> *or that our feared outcome isn't so bad,*
> *we sometimes do everything in our power to avoid it.*

A person might be so concerned about their appearance that they feel their Target jeans and jacket are not special enough for the hip inner-city bar where their friend's party is being held, so they decline the invitation. Had they turned up, they might have found that others had chosen a range of clothing styles, and that the group was more welcoming than they expected.

Sometimes people try to reduce their anxiety by taking actions that are not actually connected to their fears. Someone may feel they need to clean out every drawer in their house before going on holiday, a tween might insist they have their uniform and hair ribbons perfectly ironed for school, or a child might carry their blankie, favourite toy or expensive water bottle with them everywhere to feel they can face situations safely. These are all responses which might be believed to calm anxiety, but are essentially unhelpful and involve wasted time or energy, particularly if the family has to endure a long drive home to retrieve a forgotten blankie before heading to a picnic. These actions undermine our ability to overcome anxiety because they give us a false sense of what we need to do to feel safe. Instead of facing the feared event or outcome and finding we can endure it, deep down we believe we have safely survived it because of our blankie, our perfectly ironed ribbons, or our extremely tidy drawers back home.

If anxiety is left untreated and allowed to prosper, it can easily intensify over time and become a full-blown disorder. Once present, untreated anxiety disorders all tend to move in a similar direction. A person has one or several fears and their response to these fears involves refusing to face them. This avoidance means they don't learn to get over their fears and live their life uncurtailed by them.

Why some people are prone to problematic anxiety

While everyone feels fear, only some people become avoidant and experience problems with anxiety or go on to develop anxiety disorders. There are three characteristics that make some of us more vulnerable than others to experiencing problems with anxiety. They are interrelated, but psychologists have identified each one as a predictor of the likelihood that someone will develop problematic anxiety.

Anxiety sensitivity

The first characteristic is a person's *anxiety sensitivity*. People who have anxiety sensitivity are particularly attentive to the physical changes that occur when they feel fear. They are probably more in tune with noticing sensations in their body than other people. They might become acutely aware of physical reactions such as their heart beating fast, or their digestion slowing down and an accompanying odd feeling of discomfort.

People who are less sensitive might feel a butterfly or two in their stomach prior to their first day in a new job and simply put it down to normal nerves. But people who react more to bodily sensations fear both the physical effects of the feeling and the consequence of others noticing. Before going into a job interview, they might feel fearful, notice their body trembling, and then worry that others will see how nervous they are.

Unfortunately, these reactions increase their fear in what is already an anxiety-producing situation for them. Not only are they worried about starting their new job, they are also fearful they will tremble or blush excessively in front of their new workmates. This makes their fear even worse and their bodily symptoms more acute, and so sets up a vicious cycle.

People with high anxiety sensitivity are quick to detect their internal cues and believe these will be associated with poor outcomes. They notice even the slightest panic symptoms, think this means something bad is about to happen, and do everything in their power to avoid it. This avoidance determines whether anxiety becomes problematic for a person because it causes them to restrict the way they live their life. A bushwalk that involves crossing a creek by jumping from rock to rock will bring on stomach flutters for most of us, but while some will find this thrilling, others may find this temporary feeling so distressing they forgo bushwalking altogether.

Do you ever feel this way? Let's look at your anxiety sensitivity.

- Do you quickly notice when your heart beats fast? Do you ever think you are about to have a heart attack?
- Do you catch yourself sweating and worry whether anyone else is aware of it?
- Do you sometimes feel tightness in your throat? Does it frighten you? Do you think it signals something bad is about to happen for you?
- Have you ever wanted to avoid an event because you think others will notice your physical symptoms of anxiety, such as blushing, stammering or perspiring?
- Do you think others can see if you tremble? Do you think they are judging you when it happens?
- When your thoughts race, do you ever fear you may be going crazy or that you have ADHD – even on days when you have a lot on your mind?

Behavioural inhibition

The second characteristic influencing anxiety is *behavioural inhibition*. Behavioural inhibition is often described as being shy. People who are behaviourally inhibited mostly prefer to avoid new situations or people and stick with things they know well. They often need to experience a situation several times before they develop confidence.

Some children appear to be born with a degree of shyness. These children may hold back while their less behaviourally inhibited friends eagerly approach challenging situations. This type of wariness is not unusual in a child; research shows that about 40% of people would be described as shy. But, normal as it is, your child hiding behind you in unfamiliar situations likely indicates they have a propensity to develop anxiety.

Shyness gives a person a greater chance of developing behaviours that could potentially reduce their social skills and increase their anxiety. Do you feel you might have a level of behavioural inhibition? You may recognise some of the following tendencies in yourself.

- Do you get 'worked up' when you think something unpleasant may happen, like imagining that you won't find anyone to talk to at a party? Does this ever make you want to avoid an event?
- Does it take you a long time to settle into a new crowd? Do you

sometimes hold back in a conversation rather than make what would be a perfectly relevant point?
- Do you notice negative social cues, such as a person you are talking to crossing their arms or looking away, long before anyone else would? Are you always on the lookout for these? Do you ever act immediately and move away from that person, rather than continuing the conversation and seeing what happens?
- Do you really dislike being criticised?
- Do you worry a lot about making mistakes? Does this fear hold you back from speaking up or trying new experiences which may be embarrassing, like a Zumba class or stand-up paddle boarding?

Discomfort with uncertainty

The third characteristic that influences the likelihood of someone developing anxiety is their *discomfort with uncertainty*. Discomfort with uncertainty refers to difficulty coping with the fact that you do not know what will happen in the future. People who have discomfort with uncertainty feel a need to control situations and avoid surprises, and tend to believe they can only feel comfortable in predictable circumstances. Faced with an imminent situation which is important to them and which has an uncertain outcome, these people fear a terrible result, even if only subconsciously. When they invite friends over for dinner, they agonise over the night because deep down they feel if their friends don't like the food or the décor or conversation, they will consequently think less of them as a cook, host or even as a person. When they text a friend and fail to receive a reply, they fear they have offended them and may have caused a rupture in the friendship. These things *could* happen – although it is highly unlikely that they will – and those of us who are comfortable with uncertainty will be content to wait and see. People who aren't might find the discomfort of not knowing the outcome of their actions almost unbearable.

Many situations can produce discomfort because of their uncertain outcomes. Not knowing if the bus will be on time, not knowing whether the restaurant where you are meeting your friends will have enough vegetarian options on the menu, not knowing if your office manager will laugh at your joke – these are all situations of uncertainty. Most people would not worry too much about them: they'll just tell the joke and see what happens or turn up on time at the bus stop and comfortably wait until the bus shows, or be confident they will find something they like on the menu.

But for some, not knowing exactly what will happen produces significant discomfort. They might choose not to tell the joke, or take their car rather than risk being late, or check the menu online, or even insist they always choose the restaurant when gathering with friends to ensure they get the exact meal they want.

Let's look at your degree of comfort with uncertainty. Consider the following statements:

- Surprises upset me.
- I always prefer to know what the future has in store.
- I feel unable to act when I don't know what is going to happen.
- I worry my plans will be ruined when I don't know what will happen.
- I should be able to prepare for everything ahead of time and prefer to do so.

If you agree with more than two of these, you probably don't cope well when you're uncertain about what is going to happen.

Research findings on people's level of comfort with uncertainty are fascinating. We know that people who are comfortable with uncertainty are resilient. They are also less likely to experience mental illness of any kind. But people who feel they can't cope with uncertainty are more likely to have other problems. Evidence shows us that the more intensely a person dislikes surprises and uncertainty, the more chance they have of experiencing anxiety or depression. These people are also more likely to have other simultaneous emotional difficulties, such as anxiety together with depression, or even anxiety, depression and an eating disorder.

Discomfort with uncertainty also influences people's behaviour: when they encounter an emotional problem, they are more likely than most to react impulsively. Although they tend to describe themselves as 'intense worriers', they seem to weigh up the pros and cons of their resulting actions less carefully than those who don't worry as much.

Why do psychologists think this happens? It seems that people who have discomfort with uncertainty want to immediately escape the uneasiness of sitting with the problem. Unfortunately, this can make them more prone to unhelpful behaviours. When their manager asks to see them the next day, they may buy and down a bottle of vodka the night before, even if they don't know what their manager wants to talk to them about. Or they might go shopping on an already tight budget to take their mind off their fears.

These reactions are all temporary and ultimately unhelpful ways to feel better.

Doing something to immediately take away their discomfort often ends up causing bigger problems than the one they feared. Someone who doubts whether the person they have just started dating wants to take the connection further might ask where the relationship is going as early as the third date. The teen who is unsure whom they will talk to next at a party might go home rather than stick around and see what happens. The child worrying whether they will do well in an audition may prefer to cancel it rather than face the situation. They will feel temporarily relieved by being more in control of the situation but, ultimately, they lose the opportunity to take part in the musical, even as a member of the chorus, as well as the chance to see that they can cope when their preferred outcome doesn't materialise.

The good news is that even people who possess one or more of these traits – anxiety sensitivity, behavioural inhibition or discomfort with uncertainty – can learn how to overcome them.

*If we recognise the cause of our discomfort,
we gain the opportunity to overcome our anxious feelings.*

When adults and children are taught to increase their willingness to encounter uncomfortable physical symptoms and move beyond their initial apprehension to face uncertainty without avoidance, they are less likely to become anxious and do unhelpful (or even harmful) things to escape their unpleasant feelings.

Anxiety and your child

Let's summarise what we've learnt about anxiety in this chapter and how it relates to your child.

Your child's occasional fears or worry are nothing to be concerned about. Children need these feelings to be able to identify dangerous situations and experience the bodily reactions which provide them with the resources to deal with or get out of those situations. Even though fear is normal, and often helpful, some children are born with a tendency to worry and may be extra sensitive to the changes in their body when they pick up on potential danger.

They might also tend to hold back in unfamiliar situations and be shy with new people. Some children are particularly uncomfortable when faced with a situation in which they can't predict what will happen. Often these children will avoid these situations or do everything in their power to escape them, such as refusing to take part in them. This is an indicator that their anxiety has moved from a typical fear to a powerful motivator that, if regularly acted upon, will significantly detract from the quality of their life.

The factors we've described in this chapter are important in understanding why your child might experience anxiety. There are other important factors to discuss that have combined to create what we describe as a perfect storm of conditions to produce anxiety. The gusts of change in parenting beliefs and squalls of technology and social media can easily gather to whip up your child's occasional fears into a tempest of self-doubt, worry, friendship dramas, body image issues, behavioural problems, screen addiction, and loss of resilience and grit. We'll get to all of these, but let's start with the big-time changes in parenting.

CHAPTER 2

Parenting, schooling and anxiety

Our approach to parenting has changed dramatically over recent generations. Most changes have been for the better – children are allowed to be seen and heard now – but through their efforts to give their child a wonderful life, some parents unintentionally make them vulnerable to anxiety.

Parents have always had a significant influence on their children, particularly on how they view their world and respond to it. Typically, the unique combination of a parent's (or carer's) personality, a child's personality and the circumstances the child faces produce their approach to life, both as a child and as an adult.

For example, your confident, outgoing parent or parents may have paid scant attention to the minor fears or hesitations you expressed as a child. Their lack of acknowledgement of your worries might have made you feel unheard and even fearful at times, but it may also have encouraged you to be brave when you needed an extra incentive to take on a challenge.

Or perhaps you had a nervous parent who worried about life and often talked to you about their concerns for your safety. In this case, you might have taken on similar fears and become anxious yourself. Then again, you might have vowed never to be like them and started skydiving as soon as you could.

Your family's circumstances might also have encouraged you to become fearful or brave. If your parents got into a spot of financial difficulty, you may have become concerned about financial security, careful in your investments and focused on saving more than spending. Or the experience might have made you stronger and more capable if it forced you to get part-time work at a young age, showed you not to expect a charmed existence, and helped you become more confident of your skills to get through tricky episodes in life. Negotiating that challenging period might even have made you braver and more willing to risk your money or time on new ventures than if you had not learnt to cope with lean times. You might be unafraid of change and approach new challenges with confidence, unhampered by a desire to hold onto what you have.

But our approach to life is not always a simple equation of a parent's personality + a child's personality + family circumstances = a child's or adult's approach to life. While genes have an effect – anxious parents can pass on their temperament to their children – it doesn't always work that way. Each child in a family can react differently to similar circumstances. Even siblings with relatively comparable personalities can have completely different approaches to life. A classic combination often seen is that one sibling is nervous and one is happy-go-lucky. Although it's subconscious, it is as if one sibling decides they need to be chilled for the other panicky one, or one decides that the other is too brave and they need to do the worrying for both.

Most importantly, people aren't necessarily stuck with a particular approach to life. If you really want to, you can change your beliefs and actions through deliberate self-led modifications or therapy to become the person you want to be.

This is not to deny that parents alone can have an important and ongoing influence on their children's tendency to be fearful or worried. This is particularly true in contemporary parenting.

Parenting today

Every parenting generation is different from the last one, and some change in approach between each successive generation is not new. Having said that, the rapid transformation of the 20th and 21st centuries, including changing economies, increased technology, smaller families, shifting careers and workplace structures, less gendered roles for women and men, and more education and information about children's wellbeing have combined to result in very different beliefs about the best ways to raise children than those held by previous generations.

This shift is easily seen in the goals parents have for their children. Many of today's parents strive to give their children an upbringing filled with success and happiness. This doesn't mean that parents of past generations wanted their children to have a life of failure and misery, but the current generation of parents is more focused on trying to give their children a super wonderful childhood.

Underlying this is a misunderstanding of wellbeing, particularly a misinterpretation of the relationship between self-esteem and accomplishment. As detailed so well by Professor Martin Seligman in his book, *The Optimistic Child*, research has always found that people who feel good tend to be doing well in life. Seligman explains how the link between these two became mixed up back in the 1970s. Of course, it's hard to feel good about yourself unless you are broadly doing well in life and coping with the challenges it presents. But psychologists, teachers and others in caring professions started to think it was the feeling good part that chiefly determined how well one would do in life.

Because of this erroneous belief, parents, teachers and other carers began to feel it was their responsibility to make children feel happy all the time to build their self-esteem and maximise their potential. They believed this approach would increase a child's confidence, and a constant delivery of assurance would then secure the child's future success and happiness. This idea quickly took hold and has stuck around since, even though the interpretation of the causal link between feeling good and doing well was mistaken.

Making children feel good about themselves, in and of itself, is not a terrible thing to do, and you wouldn't deliberately encourage a child to feel bad to give them a great future. But many parents now go to extreme lengths to give their children magnificent and easy lives. This can cause problems because their children often end up with a poorer chance of future satisfaction. Children raised in this way also have a greater chance of developing anxiety. How does this happen?

Parents who devote a lot of time and effort to ensure their children's contentment and success face a hard task, made tougher by the normal ups and downs of life. Even though they have the picnic basket packed and everyone ready to go, the rain waylays their plans and temporarily disappoints their child. And despite the basketball clinics, the nutritious meals and the enthusiastic cheering from the sidelines, their child's height may mean their desired professional basketball career will never eventuate.

Most people lead busy lives these days, and you can understand why some parents might rely on short cuts to produce what they see as essential constant joy in their children, particularly when real life steps in to temporarily frustrate or disappoint them. These parents might constantly praise their child to make them feel better, or immediately give them everything they ask for to ensure they do not feel neglected or inadequate compared to their peers. Their child might be made the absolute centre of parental attention to ensure their self-esteem isn't temporarily challenged when they are momentarily ignored. To save their child from any disappointment, some parents might allow them to win every family Monopoly game or only have the family play the sports in which their child shines.

If a child has a disappointing experience, some parents these days provide treats – 'You didn't get on the A team? Let's get you an ice-cream to help you feel better!' – or reassurance – 'You were by far the best on the day, that coach is a fool!' – or step in to resolve the situation by contacting the coach and badgering them into letting the child be on the team to immediately restore their happiness. If their child has a minor friendship quarrel at school, some parents email the teacher or go straight to the principal to demand they sort out the issue without delay. If a child initially struggles to master a new toy, some parents step in straight away and show them the right way to handle it, so that they don't experience any frustration.

These parental actions are perfectly understandable. Sometimes parents feel they don't have the time to listen and talk through experiences which fall short of their child's expectations to help them think through disappointment to the point of starting to accept it and feel better. Heading to the cookie jar can be the easiest and fastest way to turn their child's frown upside down. And standing their ground and dealing with their tween's anger at not getting cool new jeans to wear to a birthday party is a time-consuming and draining task. You can appreciate why it is easier to go online or head to the department store rather than deal with the tantrum that ensues when their child hears, 'No, wear the jeans you already have.'

Time pressure and ease are not the only factors influencing parents' efforts to give their child a constantly happy and successful life. A focus on Freudian-style analysis of childhood (précis: blame childhood and your parents for everything) and a misunderstanding of how current events influence the future have given rise to the mistaken idea that even a slightly difficult or sad event in childhood can establish a pattern that will continue to play out in our lives. To reduce the potential domino effect of one minor but upsetting childhood event inevitably leading to further disappointments, some parents work to immediately alter the outcome to be one of success, or the child's reaction to be one of happiness.

Parents' emotions are often involved as well. An event their child faces can trigger their own past worries or disappointments. The sting of friendship difficulties in their childhood or the pressure of wanting the child to have the same success the parent had in their school years can cause some parents to step in too strongly and too early when their child has any friendship or academic challenge. These parents may catastrophise: 'If Keila doesn't go to Jade's birthday party, she might not have any close friends by the end of primary school – I'd better call her mum to get her invited.' Or 'If Liam gets a poor result on this Science project, he won't get a merit award and he'll lose his confidence – I'll give him a hand just to be sure it's okay.'

To protect their child from facing challenges and to allay their own fears, some parents take preventative steps, such as overhelping them with schoolwork to ensure they do well, even when the child is in their late high-school years. Some even anticipate potential difficulty for their child and engineer the coming situation themselves to prevent it, such as contacting the school to ensure their child is placed in a class or camp group with their best friend, so they are not faced with the need to make new connections.

Don't underestimate the power of an uncertain outcome to lead some parents to worry unnecessarily and step in to save the situation. A child who can't immediately master a particular skill, such as stacking blocks or executing a new tennis shot, might show temporary frustration, anger or sadness after their first few unsuccessful attempts. A parent can think in that moment, 'This disappointment could crush their confidence.' This thought might provoke them to step in and save their child from such feelings of temporary failure by stacking the blocks for their child, or by praising their mediocre tennis skill excessively. Alternatively, they might give them a different toy to play with, or suggest their child changes their after-school sport to an activity they can master more readily than tennis. These actions are understandable, but if done every time the child encounters difficulty, they won't learn to cope with momentary frustration.

This is more than temporary scaffolding erected to support a child while they gradually develop their skill. We are talking here about continuing parental involvement which can extend beyond childhood. Some parents now try to take an active part in their child's tertiary studies, calling university lecturers to enquire about their young adult's results or request an extension on one of their assignments. We have heard of parents attempting to be actively involved in their teen or young adult's work life, calling supervisors to complain about the inconvenient shifts on their roster or asking why their adult child missed out on a promotion. The most extreme story we know of involves a parent turning up to a job interview in lieu of their child who was 'busy that day'.

This type of parenting is often referred to as *helicopter parenting* – where parents hover over their children to ensure that they don't come to any harm, in a manner that is developmentally inappropriate. The term was first coined for parents who still fuss over their child when they are in university. *Lawnmower parenting* is a similar term applied to parents who mow all difficulty, even the most minor trickiness, out of the way so their child experiences nothing but constant success and happiness.

Our preferred term is *overparenting* because, really, it is simply overdoing good parenting behaviours. Making sure your toddler is not playing with a knife is a good parenting action for their safety, but forbidding your 15-year-old to take public transport in a safe area because you worry about their security is overdoing it. Likewise, while setting up routines and gentle reminders about homework in the early school years are caring parenting actions, reminding a young adult to do their university assignments would be taking things too far.

> *Overdoing parental care,*
> *while no doubt kind and well intentioned,*
> *is usually not helpful to children.*

Such actions are an over-reaction to a child's temporary frustration or disappointment. Immediately making things better for the child can also have an insidious result: overparenting stops the child from learning to face life's typical trickiness. By overcoming their own challenges and slowly building their skill set, children develop their comfort to face challenges and improve their sense of personal mastery and self-esteem. While lovingly intended, overparenting is more than unhelpful: it can significantly increase a child's risk of developing anxiety.

When parents overhelp their children

When parents give their children instant good feelings through praise or providing immediate solutions to their difficulties, they also give them a sense of short-term success or contentment. However, this benefit can be accompanied by a whole bunch of long-term problems.

Sure, a parent can try to give their child a consistently perfect life, erase all of their challenges, and instantly turn their moments of disappointment into nicer feelings. But this risks the child expecting that joy and contentment will be their everyday reality. Unfortunately, real life will always step in. Without practice in coping with tricky days or uncomfortable feelings, children raised this way won't cope as well as children whose parents have allowed them to face age-appropriate challenges and taught them how to deal with some difficulty.

Over-protected children react with more intensity to unexpected difficult times. When they lack experience in coping, they become more fearful of potentially tricky situations in their future, making them hesitant to try anything challenging and keen to avoid activities where their success is not guaranteed.

Children who experience nothing but happy outcomes are likely to be fearful of tricky situations and potentially difficult days. A child who has been brought up this way is at risk of becoming anxious or developing increasing anxiety as they grow up.

We don't think all parents of anxious children behave in the ways we are about to describe. And we certainly don't hold parents responsible for all children's anxiety. But we do think some parents feel pushed to adopt the problematic approaches we are about to discuss by societal expectations and the attitudes and behaviour of other parents.

We also acknowledge the overarching influence of technology on everything we set out in this chapter. Our constant use of technology – particularly our ever-present phones – has changed the norms of connection between parent and child. This has intensified many of the problems we discuss here.

Children become reliant on constant reassurance

When parents constantly praise their child, they encourage them to become dependent on positive feedback and regular reassurance.

> *A child who is accustomed to praise begins to expect it, regardless of their efforts or outcomes.*

Some children who rely on their regular hit of reassurance start to do tasks more for the appreciation they receive from others than their own sense of accomplishment. All kids do this to a certain degree, but some get truly hooked on reassurance. They might consistently ask for encouraging feedback when they are young – 'Look at me helping, Mummy ... now, look at me again! I'm a good girl, aren't I?' A little of this is not problematic, but if they are still seeking and gaining this level of validation in the upper primary years, they may be becoming 'praise junkies'. Our hunch is that this over-reliance on affirmation can lead children to habitually post selfies on social media to get the reassurance of 'likes' or seek instant confirmation through endless texts to friends once they have access to a phone or social media. These children might feel they are nothing without being regularly told by other people they are something special.

If a child is uncomfortable with feelings of uncertainty – 'Was my English oral presentation okay?' – then the praise or attention of another person will give them a brief sense of relief. These days this relief is easily accessible through the instant connection provided by phones.

Let's consider Shani as an example. She has been invited to audition for her city's youth orchestra on a Saturday when her parents are working. Shani is understandably nervous, and her parents wish her luck as she leaves to get the bus to the audition. Her nerves are such that she sneaks a phone call to her mum on the way to talk about her fears. Her mother reassures her that she will do well and there is nothing to worry about.

While waiting for her turn, Shani spots a talented classmate also waiting to audition. But rather than talk to her, Shani texts her mother with an update. Her mother replies with a shocked-face emoji but reassures her that she will be okay.

Five minutes later, Shani performs her piece for the panel. As she is leaving the building, she calls her mother to tell her all about the performance and what she did well and not so well. Her mother listens intently to Shani's account and commends her.

Imagine that scenario in the days before mobile phones. Shani would have had to sit in a state of anticipation during the bus trip and before her audition, without phoning or texting her mother. After her performance, she would have had to continue to wait until her parents got home that evening to tell them about it.

Many parents will read that scenario and think, 'Thank goodness for the phone!' and we agree. But only in part. We think there is only one phone interaction in that scenario that is truly beneficial, and the other two are not. Can you guess which? We'll wait while you decide.

Okay. We think the phone call after the audition is the useful one. Wanting to call someone after a big event is understandable and debriefing by talking through what happened is helpful. After doing something significant like Shani's audition, you want to connect and share your news, and the phone is great for that.

But we are not fans of the text and the earlier phone call. The phone call made on the bus to get reassurance about what will happen does not give Shani practice in coping with difficult feelings in the lead up to an event. This practice is essential for her to develop self-regulation so that she doesn't need to call someone every time she feels uncomfortable.

Shani's text telling her mother about the classmate also attending the audition seems minor. But choosing to communicate with her parent instead of taking a moment to chat with her peer is a missed opportunity. Indeed, one of the biggest problems of allowing phones at school is that many children choose to communicate with their parents as opposed to getting to know their peers, who could offer comfort and support when needed. If Shani had elected to talk to her classmate rather than text her parent, she may have gained a boost of confidence from finding out they were both nervous.

When children constantly lean on their parents for support, they don't develop the self-reliance they need for life beyond their childhood years, which won't always offer instant hits of connection, praise and approval. Most workplaces don't schedule hourly praise opportunities or encourage staff to regularly text a friend or family member to get their required hits of love or affection. As a result, young adults making their way in the world can feel inadequate and disheartened when they don't receive the level of praise and reassurance that they came to rely on from their parents. If they continue to seek regular reassurance and affirmation elsewhere, they risk not developing their personal judgement and are likely to remain overly dependent on others, more focused on what their co-workers or friends think of their performance than their own sense of accomplishment.

When they don't receive the approval they want, children who have become reliant on the affirmation of others are particularly affected because their sense of wellbeing can be dependent on receiving this approval. As they become older, they might catastrophise when no one gives them immediate reassurance that their oral presentation was fantastic, or their latest Instagram selfie fails to generate sufficient likes. Their moods are likely to seesaw throughout the day in line with the number of red hearts and thumbs-up that appear on their screens.

Understandably, a child who is reliant on reassurance will feel unappreciated and less capable when they don't receive it. We know that parents of anxious children tend to reassure their child more than others. Ironically, the more these children are reassured, the more they will become dependent on it.

Children don't learn to cope with constructive criticism

When children become used to receiving exclusively positive feedback, they don't learn to cope with constructive criticism or any response that doesn't flatter them. When a parent or teacher gives feedback which will help a child improve, these children can take it too much to heart. Then, to make themselves feel better and remove any uncomfortable sense of self-doubt, they often focus their thoughts on the person delivering the news more than their own performance.

This can be particularly so for children who are anxious about excelling academically. These children can personalise any constructive criticism – 'My English teacher doesn't like me' or 'My English teacher is mean' as opposed to 'My English teacher didn't like some parts of my presentation'. They can also catastrophise the feedback given by an assessor. A relatively good mark, such as an A minus, might have them believe their presentation was mediocre (while simultaneously believing that the teacher doesn't like them as much as the student who got an A plus).

Some children never learn to cope with all types of feedback. We have worked with university students who react with tears or anger when shown ways to improve in their work, regardless of how considerately and constructively the feedback is given to them. Ironically, they have less chance of improvement when they view any feedback other than fulsome praise as unwarranted, mean or invalid. These students also tend to be less creative in their work because they are more focused on approval and perfect marks than their personal mastery or innovation.

Their parents may have exacerbated this tendency. When faced with a child who didn't do so well in an assessment or selection trial, some parents try to make their child feel immediately better about their ability – 'That's crazy you didn't get on the team – you are so much more skilled that the other children. I knew that coach didn't know what they were doing!' Even when they are in the team, their parent may not allow them to feel the sting of a missed goal or an ill-timed tackle by blaming someone else. We see this all the time when parents on the sidelines scream at the referees when they give unfavourable decisions or snarl at the coach when their child has to sit on the bench. Most of these parents do this in a misguided attempt to support their child, and it will usually make the child feel better for a time. But it will ultimately bring out the worst in them.

Seeing any shortcoming as someone else's fault can encourage a victim mentality which is not helpful for a child to improve their performance over time.

Children who never see themselves at fault and blame others for every disappointment also fail to learn that things won't always go their way. This will make them overdependent on daily success, unlikely to take personal responsibility for their mistakes, and less accepting when things turn out better for others. It also risks them overthinking minor failure as major failure – the perfect environment for anxiety to take hold.

Children become pressured by too much praise

Praise from parents can encourage a child to put in their best effort. But it shouldn't always be laid on too thickly. We understand that when your child comes home with an A for their assignment, you want to shout it to the rooftops and take the whole family for ice-cream, but over-the-top praise for every one of their achievements can lead your child to believe that you expect an A level of accomplishment for everything they do. Children raised this way start to worry way ahead of time about their final high-school results or be overly concerned about upcoming tests or oral presentations because they think they need to do things perfectly for you.

Unfortunately, regardless of how often you remind your child how much you love them and all you expect is for them to try their best, anxious children tend to misinterpret your enthusiasm for their past achievements as high expectations of their future performance. You can see why some children start worrying about their end-of-year result long before they need to.

Children don't learn to cope with not being the centre of attention

To feel important and loved is a cornerstone of self-assurance: a person who knows they are valued and loved by their family typically has more confidence than others going out into the world. But continual and excessive attention is unhelpful. If a child is used to having an 'audience', particularly an extremely receptive one, they tend to always seek spectators. It can make it difficult for them to feel comfortable with their own company or dissatisfied when they are not the centre of attention.

We sometimes see this in children who are anxious about separating from their parents. When we delve deeper, we often find that these children have become accustomed to (and reassured by) their parents' enthralled attention and are less used to amusing themselves by playing independently. Such children may react strongly when separated from the people who constantly cheerlead for them. For some younger children of kindy age, the parent might have taken the role of the child's main companion. This can lessen the need for the child to seek similar-aged friends or develop their social skills.

As they become older, these children may feel less relaxed in their own company and less capable in groups where conversational give and take is expected, than those who have not grown used to a personal cheer squad. They can easily become anxious in such situations and may prefer to stay home on a Saturday night rather than be one of many contributors to a conversation among peers. They may also experience social anxiety about saying the 'right' things or being 'perfectly' attired and be overly dependent on other people expressing their appreciation of their contributions and attire.

Children become used to getting their own way

When a child becomes used to their family always going along with their wishes – always giving them the last piece of cake or letting them choose the takeaway meal – they will not be prepared to be in the company of other children who have their own opinions and wishes.

These somewhat cossetted children might see others as being 'mean' to them when they don't do everything they tell them to, or they might reject the company of children who don't comply with their every wish. This can make them hesitant in social situations where complete agreement among peers is not guaranteed. They might be bossy with their friends, and this may make them unpopular. Consequently, they may prefer to spend time with younger children, who they can more easily boss around.

At multi-family gatherings, they may elect to stay with the adults as opposed to same-aged peers because adults are more likely to give them attention so they feel super special, while their peers expect them to be one of many. Their parent might explain their reluctance to participate as the result of anxiety, but their child's fear might be more about dislike of not being in charge and in control of the game.

They might also be fearful of the outcomes of games – such as not being the winner of the egg-and-spoon race – or decline to participate in group games when the outcome is unknown. If an anxious child is used to triumphing in every context, they might not cope well when other children are the victors. They might fear or try to avoid situations where they risk coming last or even second, because they don't think they can cope with not being the best. Indeed, if they are used to winning through their parents' efforts, it is likely they will be anxious about their performance and want to be in control of the result as opposed to accepting whatever happens.

Children become over-reliant on assistance

Parents who always smooth the way for their children inadvertently encourage their reliance on other people's help and lead them to expect that others will take on the role of making them feel better when required. When parents always step in and improve situations for their child, the child will start to constantly rely on others to help them or develop a sense of entitlement that others will always make things better for them and help them to solve problems. They often expect their parent to buy everything they ask for and become teary or angry when they don't get all the material goods they demand.

The more you help your child, the more helpless they become.

Over-helping children leaves them at risk of *learned helplessness* – a person's belief that they can't effect change in their life and must rely on others. It is a trait strongly associated with depression because helpless people become dependent on others and lack the autonomy to set the direction of their life to achieve what they desire. This increases the likelihood of anxiety: when someone predicts they can't cope without a lot of assistance, they are likely to fear future events. This is particularly true if a person has a vivid imagination about what *could* happen.

If a child is already behaviourally inhibited, over-protection will make them feel even more nervous. That's because their parents' constant hovering and saving them from challenge suggests they need fortification against normal life. Sometimes just the offer of helping them, such as walking into a new school with them on their first day of high school, will suggest to an already anxious child that the event has potential danger and that they need to be accompanied.

Imagine if you were about to go for a job interview and your friend offered to help you with choosing your outfit. If you were not anxious, you would think they were nice to offer. But if you were somewhat anxious, your mind might personalise it – 'they think I don't have good dress sense and I get it wrong' – or you might catastrophise their offer – 'my friend thinks I need help – I am not capable and there is no way I will get the job'. Ironically, your friend's offer of help may lead you to feel less confident on the day. Now think of the number of times a parent might offer help to their child before they ask for it. What message might they be sending, particularly if their child is already something of a worrier?

Parents who help too readily and too much also risk hampering their child's skill development. The more a parent or teacher helps a child or teen, perhaps by overediting their assignments or even supplying the words to use, the better the child is likely to do. At first this may not seem to be a problem, but it becomes problematic when the excessive help stops.

Over-helped children can develop a sense of accomplishment without developing the requisite skills.

If your child becomes used to regularly receiving good marks because of excessive assistance, they are unlikely to do as well when they start doing the work on their own, particularly if the help gained them a result beyond their natural ability. Being unused to anything but good marks can lead a child or teen to develop a fear of not doing well because they haven't learnt to cope with occasionally less than stellar results.

We often find clinically that children whose parents overhelp them with homework get extremely worried about exams because they know they won't get the help they receive at home. Sometimes this looks like perfectionism – a fear of not being perfect – but there can be an egotistical element in their belief that they are capable of being perfect. This is understandable if other people's excessive help has delivered them almost perfect results in the past.

Schooling and anxiety

A child's journey through school has become a source of stress for many families. Pressure for parents can start when they first begin to contemplate which school they will choose for their child. Children may feel pressure when preparing for selective school admission tests or when their parents question the value of their investment in independent or faith-based schooling or the long daily drive to and from a selective school. Various forms of pressure can be felt throughout the school years, culminating in the tension felt by entire families about a child's final university entrance results. Consequently, the experience of attending school risks exacerbating anxiety in students, their parents and sometimes even their teachers.

The pressures of schooling

Several factors contribute to the likelihood of a child's anxiety increasing during their schooling. Each can fall on the other like a domino, building a child's vulnerability to anxiety.

Pressure on parents to choose the 'right' school

In some neighbourhoods across Australia, people ask parents which school they have their child's name down for from the moment the child is born. The interest in choice of school conveys the view that there is a *right* choice out there. Unfortunately, the pressure to make the right choice sometimes doesn't let up: when children are in primary school, parents are asked which high school they have chosen for them. Websites like *My School* and regular opinion columns about leader boards for NAPLAN and ATAR results, together with some particularly evocative advertising from schools keen to increase enrolments, continue to apply this pressure.

The focus on parents' choice of school and its associated financial commitment in turn create a level of meticulous attention to a child's daily experience of school. This plays out in several ways. Many parents regularly review their choice of school to confirm whether it remains correct. Rather than finding out what happened each day in a casual conversation with their child, the discussion becomes troubled by expectations and doubts.

This is understandable. Imagine you were put in a position where you had to choose your partner's employment. (It's a strange notion but work with us here.) And imagine, when making that choice, you were inundated with questions from friends and family about which career you had decided for them. You are also confronted daily with countless news articles about the importance of work in creating a person's wellbeing, and numerous advertisements from companies, each saying they are the one that will do the right thing by your partner and ensure their future success. Feeling the pressure yet?

Imagine you eventually make your choice – accounting it is! – and picture your partner coming home from their first day on the job. Would you casually enquire how their first day went, or would there be an edge to your questions (*did you make the right choice*)? And do you think you would feel satisfied with a few casual details from them? Or would you want to examine every single element of their day to be sure your choice was and remains correct for them in every way? Then, amp that fear up to 11 if you believe your choice of their workplace will determine their happiness and wellbeing for the rest of their life. And that it is totally on you to check that the choice remains 'right'. Every. Single. Day.

Pressure on children to be happy and successful at school

Many students experience even more pressure than parents because they are expected to deliver the outcome their parents have hoped or planned for them, thereby validating their parents' choices along the way. This pressure is often maintained, not through parental demands, but through questions.

Remember, parents are worried about whether they have made the correct choice of school. Their concerns will be exacerbated if they have stretched themselves financially to pay fees and associated costs. To help validate their choice, they increase their enquiries about every aspect of their child's school day. Of course, they are interested in their child's experience, but they are also keen to make sure they are not disadvantaged by any temporary difficulty they may suffer. Consequently, conversation in the morning involves checking whether anything potentially challenging is coming up that day, while afternoon and evening conversations focus on looking for difficulties the child may have encountered and trying to resolve them.

It's all with good intentions, but there's no wonder when children start to view the typical challenges of learning new skills as overwhelming. The parental grilling might also accidentally direct them to primarily focus on any difficult or disappointing elements of their day. This can make an average day seem worse when the conversational focus gets stuck on a minor disagreement with a friend at lunchtime.

Most importantly, students can lose touch with the joys of challenge and the slow but ultimately rewarding steps toward mastery. No one learns how to read or write, debate, swim or develop any new skill without some level of overwhelm, self-doubt, failure and feeling like they're taking steps forward and backward in turn. You don't develop new friendships without comparable experiences of doubt; you don't become a good rower or chess player or Shakespearean actor without a similar journey. In fact, to feel pride in developing a skill, it needs to be occasionally challenging. Instant success feels hollow and unearned; it fails to provide the long-term sustenance of taking the sometimes-rocky road toward genuine accomplishment.

*If occasional disappointments or failures are emphasised,
rather than simply empathised with,
school will seem a much harder place than it should be.*

Moreover, a child will not be inclined to try anything new if the only goal is to be the best at the task or not to have any hiccups along the way. Their school experience should teach children to be comfortable to accept both their weaknesses and strengths, as well as to expect both good days and bad days.

Pressure on schools to be the 'right' school
Many schools are similarly under pressure from parents and students to get everything perfectly right every day. We are not talking here about daily

school experiences that gradually build a broad education for students on a range of topics and life skills. It's much more than that.

A school getting it 'right' means different things to different parents. Some will think that a school needs to extend the students' abilities through more challenging work. It is understandable that parents want to see their child doing things they themselves weren't given the opportunity to do, such as outstanding extra-curricular activities, expansion of skills through use of technology (students delivering PowerPoint presentations in Year Two, for example) and essay topics and tasks that reflect university-level thinking. Sometimes parents want value for the money they have paid on school fees or the effort they have invested in getting the child into the school; they believe the school should make sure their child always receives high marks or is consistently selected for leadership positions. And sometimes expectations arise from the competitive focus of some parents' friendship groups around which school sets the most advanced homework tasks (read: is the most academically challenging school), has the best overseas music or art study trips (read: is the most culturally advanced school) or has the most meaningful volunteering assignments to third world countries (read: is the most community-minded school).

These expectations make sense. In a neoliberal world where life is often viewed in competitive terms, some parents want their child to excel in everything they do at school so they can be sure the child is getting ahead in the 'race' of life. Consequently, parents can feel the school needs to get the swimming carnival, Book Week, speech night and all other typical school activities 'right' for their child's accomplishment to be seen as 'on track'. This puts pressure on schools to ensure that every child feels sufficiently successful, which may lead to a growing number of awards being handed out at speech nights and after sports matches. Even events like Book Week have become performative, which in turn increases pressure on parents and students to turn up in a 'winning' costume for the parade. (Many of you will have joined in the universal sigh of relief from parents the world over following the conclusion of Book Week.)

For some parents, a school getting it 'right' means it must create a similar environment to the one they have created in their home, where students are sure to experience a succession of blue-sky days unclouded by temporary failure or disappointment.

Teachers face this pressure daily. It could be an angry call from a parent demanding that their child receives an A for their Science project, that the coach puts them on the rugby firsts team, that the Prep teacher uses their lunchtime to ensure the child plays their preferred game with their friends, or that the Drama or Music teacher gives the child the lead in the musical. There are even times when these requests are accompanied by a threat to withdraw the child from the school if the parent's expectation isn't met. These phone calls are not acceptable – particularly if they are aggressive in tone – but they reflect the strength of the parent's impulse to protect their child from disappointment. Recall the pressure on parents to ensure their child's consistent success at school. Recall the pressure on students and their consequent desire or perceived obligation to shine. These calls are an extension of those pressures.

A child's school experience is always a collaboration between students, teachers and parents which should focus on ensuring the child gets the best out of their education. Parents often want their child to be sufficiently challenged and extended in school activities, but they can also be fearful of their child experiencing challenge that takes them out of their comfort zone. It can become quite the tightwire act for schools to get the balance right between challenge and overwhelm for every child and every parent.

In a tense environment such as this, you can see why some teachers might be easier with the marks they give, more willing to mark multiple drafts, more accommodating or reassuring to students, less likely to give a consequence such as a detention for poor behaviour, or more willing to add a few more awards on speech night so every child wins a prize.

But these actions provide only short-term gains for students. If they aren't given opportunities to practise coping with occasional difficulties and detours in their school life, they risk being overwhelmed, anxious and incapable of facing real life and all its challenges in their post-school years. Research suggests that over-catering to students in some schools may adversely affect their university preparedness.

The 'predictability' of schooling

A child's experience of school has become somewhat predictable in recent years. Today many teachers prefer to let parents know about everything that happens in their child's school day, from the first sign of a friendship fight to the first time they fail to do their homework. Parents have extensive access now to what is happening in children's schooling through web portals listing the assignments that are due and providing regular communications about daily school activities and what students are studying. There are even web-based applications that allow parents to view their child's schoolwork in real time.

It seems that schools do this to give a sense of added value and control (and perhaps reassurance) to parents rather than to benefit their students. This level of information ultimately serves to create a feeling of predictability for parents and kudos for schools which offer these means of communication.

> *While parents and students might want a sense of predictability and control in schooling, the ways schools provide this are not always genuinely helpful.*

Consider the example of schools and organisations that provide a predicted final school result to students based on their expected results and historical data. We understand that schools are encouraged to do this to help guide students toward compatible career choices and provide an additional sense of control over their future career. But the predicted outcome is not necessarily accurate or helpful to students who will nevertheless learn that life does not always turn out the way we expect it to.

The idea that students should simply do their best and believe they will cope no matter what happens has been replaced by a false perception that their final school results can be known in advance. We think this idea makes it more difficult for students to learn how to deal with things out of their control and less capable of striding forward confidently when the ultimate outcome of their efforts is not perfectly clear.

We believe the focus on communicating every aspect of schooling and attempting to predict likely educational outcomes undermines children's and parents' self-reliance and coping skills, leaving them less capable of managing when things are difficult or don't go as predicted. For example, every year an article or two on news sites conveys the sense of outrage experienced by students and parents when questions in the final exam for a particular subject are contrary to expectations. That people think they should be able to predict exactly what is in an exam shows how false ideas of certainty can result from too much scaffolding, structuring and reassurance. We believe this has come at the cost of allowing people to learn to sit with uncertainty and wait to see what happens.

*Much of the scaffolding and reassurance
intended to help students become more confident
can leave them less prepared and less capable to face the future.*

Getting parenting and schooling 'right' is a difficult task made even harder today by the recent change in what people see as loving and caring parental and educational care. We think it's time to pause and consider whether the prevailing view is truly in children's best interests.

Perhaps you see yourself in some of what you've read in this chapter and now wonder whether the degree of protection and care you give your child could contribute to making them anxious. Or perhaps you feel guilty on occasions when you don't match the level of effort you see other parents put in to ensure their child's consistent success. Maybe your child tells you how Billie's parents cut her sandwiches into bunny ears, how Tristan's parents buy him McDonald's every time he scores a goal, and how Emmie's parents are taking her to Hawaii for Christmas, among other guilt-inducing snippets from their friends' lives. We know that feeling guilty about the extent to which we can provide the good things of life to our children is not unique to this generation, but we think parents today feel guilty and pressured more than their predecessors because of higher expectations placed on their 'performance'.

Don't worry – all is not lost! If this chapter in any way echoes your situation, or your child's experience at school, this book will help you. We look specifically at how to do that in Part B, but right now our attention is drawn to the sound of a howling wind threatening to disrupt everything in its path. It's the Technology Tornado and we examine it in the next chapter.

CHAPTER 3

Technology and anxiety

What a time to be alive! We carry our music, books, photos and correspondence in our pocket, we contact distant loved ones with a simple verbal command, and we can get directions to go anywhere in the world from wherever we stand. But our use of technology has become something of a Pandora's box: we expected it to bring benefits, but it has delivered troubles as well – particularly anxiety.

Technology has helped us become better educated in the 21st century than we have ever been, and we have access to knowledge about the whole world at our fingertips. We can consult a virtual library of history, ideas, works of art and obscure eighties music videos whenever we wish to satisfy our curiosity or win that trivia game, all via our phones.

Technology also gives us the potential for better connection. We can form online friendships and reach new support groups. If we choose, we can share our personal stories with our virtual community or the world at large. By understanding others better, we have an opportunity to create a more tolerant and inclusive society. We can also maintain old friendships more easily: with a tap on our phone, we can link up with that travel pal we met 20 years ago in the line to the Guggenheim.

But the technology story isn't all good; in fact, it can have a negative effect on our lives. While we appreciate the benefits of having more opportunities to connect, socialise, be entertained and play games, technology – particularly in the form of our smart phones – provides these opportunities *constantly*. A device the size of our hand comes with us everywhere and continually lures us with promises of endless connection and entertainment. This siren's call persists even in circumstances where it should not be involved at all – during work meetings, when we're spending time with loved ones, or in private moments when we should be relaxing and not checking work emails.

Indeed, nearly every benefit of technology comes with a cost, particularly for children. This won't be groundbreaking news to anyone: most of us are aware of the dangers of screen addiction. But if we are so aware of the pitfalls, why are so many of us still staring at a screen in the early hours of the morning and allowing our sense of wellbeing to be dictated by our latest social media interaction? Why are children (and let's face it, adults too) so easily addicted?

In this chapter, we discuss how the neanderthal part of our brain meets basic human needs to intersect with the seductive black mirror. This process tends to leave us bug-eyed, prone to anxious thoughts and potentially on the way to an obsession that is not good for us at all.

How we became addicted to our phones

A great way to understand the addictive nature of the phone is to see it as a virtual intravenous device of feel-good chemicals, particularly oxytocin and dopamine. Exactly how each is involved and what each one does have not yet been conclusively shown: as with a lot of neuroscience, we await further research. But we understand these chemicals are involved in some way when we use our phones. We'll go with some basic explanations of what happens with each one to save you the effort of enrolling in a neurochemical course (you're busy – we get that).

Oxytocin is a hormone involved in attachment. Research shows us that it is released during social bonding activity, such as sex, breastfeeding and protecting one's family. We used to think that touch was an essential part of oxytocin production, but research now shows that simply speaking on the phone with a loved one can provide a similar hit of oxytocin as a hug with that person. It's easy to see how using our phone to regularly call the people we love allows us to get that boost, particularly when times are tricky or we feel insecure.

Dopamine gives us another kind of high. This neurotransmitter thrives on uncertainty. It kicks in when we seek a reward that we aren't 100% sure we will get – when we try something slightly risky or where the outcome is unknown – such as placing a bet or throwing a scrunched-up paper into a bin in the corner. Our phones are a great source of dopamine hits because we use them to send out uncertain bids all the time – the text message to an acquaintance you haven't seen for months, the random post on social media, or the email to a group of work colleagues to organise a catch-up. These all create the same uncertain signal, which triggers our brains to expect and crave a dopamine injection into our system.

The feel-good cycle is complete when our bids are successful – the ball of paper lands in the bin, the acquaintance responds warmly, the Facebook post generates likes and enthusiastic comments. The hit of dopamine we receive gives us relief and reassurance.

The problem is that these effects are short lived. The dip we experience when our dopamine hit wears off leaves us feeling empty and unfulfilled. Much of our typical phone activity – games, Instagram and mindless scrolling – deliver a succession of dopamine hits which are maddeningly temporary.

The main problem with the feel-good chemicals we get from some uses of our phone is that they don't stick around.

To achieve lasting satisfaction, we need the involvement of another chemical: serotonin. Neuroscientists have identified that serotonin is generated when we expend effort in our activities. When we invest real effort into achieving an outcome, we gain a sustained feeling of satisfaction and reward. When we master a challenging new guitar piece after weeks of diligent practice or listen attentively while our friend tells us about her day over a coffee, we get a longer-lasting increase in serotonin in return. Rewards involving little effort, like receiving a thumbs-up emoji to a text, scoring a minor point in a video game or laughing at a cat video, do not deliver lasting satisfaction because they don't involve the same release of serotonin.

> *Easy gains are fleeting and only leave us hungry for more.*

Such is the process of addiction. It is easy to see how problems arise when people get hooked on their phones, pursuing easy rewards that can take them away from genuinely nourishing things in life like quality time with friends and family, relaxation or sleep. The lure of the phone can even lead teens to stare at it as a source of connection even while they are at a party or meeting up with others. If they looked up and engaged with their friends instead of constantly checking their phone, they would gain a far more satisfying and sustaining form of social connection.

Even though scientists don't yet fully understand the precise mechanisms involved, they know that our phones and other tech devices provide a shortcut to the temporary effects offered by dopamine. This is why so many of us turn to our devices for a regular supply, messaging back and forth with the friends we saw an hour ago, playing yet another round of Candy Crush or checking Instagram . . . again.

How technology helps fulfill our human goals

Most humans have similar goals they want to achieve daily. Once we have nailed the fundamentals of survival – food, shelter, water – we move on to higher levels of needs. These are the second tier and above of Maslow's hierarchy, which include love and belonging, esteem and self-actualisation.

The most basic of these higher needs are the desire to be liked and to feel important to other people. We also need to develop a good sense of our identity and feel that we have a level of personal mastery over our environment, including our ability to provide sufficient care for the people we love. At our different ages and stages, these needs shift, each becoming more or less important according to what is going on in our lives and where we are developmentally.

The good news is that our devices can provide a sense of accomplishment in all these areas. The bad news is that these same devices can also dole out a huge sense of failure or emptiness, intensifying the doubts and fears that often prompt us to turn to them to begin with. This has direct bearing on our tendency to feel anxious about social connections or unfulfilled following disappointing interactions on our phone or tablet. And when we increasingly use our devices in the pursuit of our social goals, we risk curtailing our accomplishment in other equal or more important goals, which can heighten our sense of self-doubt and intensify fears of personal inadequacy. Let's examine how this happens.

Our need to feel liked and loved

We like to feel we are an important member of a social group – be it our family, friendship group, community group or workplace. We enjoy being told we have an interesting point of view or that we are good company, nice or fun to be around because these are clear indicators of our social worth and our likelihood of being appreciated by those around us.

The people who are most important to us tend to be the people from whom we most want approval. Younger children tend to view their parents and family as the most important people in their lives. They often say to their parents, 'Watch me!' or ask, 'Didn't I do a good job?' to seek their attention and approval.

When children start to reach their peak individuation years – around mid-to-late primary school – many cease to look for their parents' approval and start to look to their peers for validation instead. To do this, they must be in the company of their friends. A generation or two ago, the only way to do this outside school was by visiting each other or using the landline phone. Some readers may remember being on the phone for hours while bonding with their bestie over their love for Rob Lowe, Brad Pitt or Cameron Diaz, or their mutual dislike of the school uniform policy. On your family's one household phone, you discussed nearly every thought you had. That you did this almost every day indicates how important this bonding is in these years.

Let's compare the days of ye olde landline to the current era of the smart phone. Our households no longer share one phone across five family members. In many families, each person has their own device that provides a steady stream of constant communication with their immediate and extended peer group. No one must wait their turn to phone a friend. And each device offers many lines of connection via social media apps, YouTube and TikTok videos, all practically accessible at once.

> *These days, our primitive need to be validated can always be met by our phones.*

Tweens and teens have limitless opportunities to connect with their peers and gain an important sense of community. They also have endless prospects to fine-tune their social skills now they don't have to wait until the family phone is free or for the school lunch break to connect with others. It's easy to understand why a tween or teen's phone is practically glued to their hand. It provides a steady sense of being loved and accepted by others – and it's a way to get a basic human need fulfilled.

The bad news is that a single laughing emoji from their best friend doesn't cut it as sufficient validation for many children and teens these days. And the more a person seeks communication and validation solely through technology, the more addictive it can become and the more their anxiety will grow if it's not available to them. If they go into the cinema or into class time and can't access their phone, these children can feel distracted and unsettled. For some children, receiving no response to a text or social media post can set off a chain reaction of fears about themselves and their social success.

And it's not only our children, is it? Who hasn't regularly checked to see if they have an email in their inbox or a LinkedIn notification even during dinner with friends? That we still seek an extra hit of feeling loved or needed while in the company of friends shows how dependent we can be on multiple sources of goal fulfilment – all at the same time. It also shows how some of us can't tolerate a feeling of not being up to date with everything that is happening to the friends who are not with us at the time. The ability to check in with all our friends whenever we like via social media drives some of us to keep doing this over and over again.

Phone addiction is completely understandable when you view it in terms of fulfilling a basic human need of connection. We don't have to go to the bother of getting dressed and going out to check if we are still accepted by our circle of friends and work colleagues or up to date with their latest news. We can ascertain our value to others simply by texting or posting on social media to receive approval for every choice we make: the food we eat, the article we agree with, the time we start our gym workout, the good wishes we send to our friend on their first day back at work!

Social media is especially addictive because most people who use it understand it's a game of reassurance and willingly play along. Colleagues and family, particularly the super nice ones, know to validate others by liking and commenting positively because they love them and want them to feel good. This reassurance prompts people to post even more.

But it can go haywire. Every now and then the validation received will not be enough. When we post our latest escapade, no one might respond or fewer people might comment than is typical. This will feel particularly uncomfortable for those used to the highs of social approval. In fact, the more we depend on such cyber support, the more we are affected. An absence of overt approval leads us to doubt our value to others and the value of the life we live. The result is the same when the approval we receive is somewhat lukewarm – a thumbs-up emoji rather than a love heart or comment. 😕

It's worse in the tween and teen years when self-doubt and the need to be endorsed by our peer group are at their highest.

> *We have a generation of children who have the technology*
> *to constantly seek validation or connection*
> *by putting themselves out there at the developmental age*
> *when they most seek this contact.*

They often do this not by texting their close friends, but via a chat app to their entire friendship group, or to the whole world in general. (Did someone say TikTok?) It's easy to understand why some become hooked on seeking this connection and approval.

But the more they are hooked, the more they risk feeling miserable when peer validation does not roll in. So many teens feel sad or even devastated when they don't get the approval of likes, when others tell them awful things, or when they are trolled by a stranger looking for opportunities to have a negative impact on just about anyone. The conventions of each medium – texting, Instagram stories and posts, TikTok, Snapchat – can be difficult to comprehend for those who are still developing their social skills. Some easily become left behind in their quest to form connection with others in the ever-evolving spaces of social media. This can make them anxious if they feel they are not accepted well by peers in a very public forum.

There are other pitfalls when we use a device to achieve a sense of belonging. While we probably wished our best friends lived next door when we were growing up, unfortunately for tweens and teens, their friends are virtually in their pocket all the time. So that niggly difficulty with their peer at school can be played out further on WhatsApp that evening, with both parties gathering their troops and raising the emotional stakes in a group exchange. Worse, social media can allow a taunting chorus of the mean gang from school into their home or bedroom to magnify their fears of not being popular enough. A child can quickly be drawn into obsessing about any slight social difficulty once its gravity has been multiplied by a thousand on social media. This has the power to dramatically reduce their sense of belonging and increase their anxiety about their social capabilities and success.

Our use of technology can also lead us to question our social desirability and set off fears of inadequacy in other ways. The ease with which children and teens can check their peers' movements can prompt them to become hyperaware of any activity to which they haven't been invited, potentially leading to feelings of exclusion and isolation.

The devices that can deliver so much comfort can also provide an equal degree of discomfort about our social desirability and belonging. It's also easy to see how quickly we can become captive to a vicious cycle of worrying and seeking reassurance: feel bored, check phone, feel fear, check phone, feel bored and fearful, check phone, feel bored and despondent, check phone, and on it goes.

Our need for a sense of identity

We all need to form a cohesive sense of who we are. This gives us a feeling of belonging and also encourages us to develop our own interests. These might be similar to those of our peers, such as when everyone loves rugby or Billie Eilish, but they might also be more particular to the individual, such as a person's preference for dressing in an American rockabilly style or wanting to perfect their skills in sourdough baking. If you seek to be a well-informed person, you may choose to read widely and keep yourself up to date on politics and world events. If you want to be thought of as quirky and interesting, you might read manga and watch anime, and attend fan conventions dressed as your favourite characters. If you have a good sense of humour, you might watch a lot of comedy performers and fine-tune your mimicry and joke-telling skills.

The goal to form a cohesive and individual sense of self dramatically intensifies in the tween and teen years. In this period of individuation, a child seeks to become their own person, separate from their family. These are the years when they no longer want their parents to choose their clothes, they develop specific tastes in music and films, and form their own opinions and seek to debate their parents on ideas they used to agree on. By deliberate adjustment, tweens and teens create a sense of personal change that strengthens their image of who they are and confirms to them that they are on the path toward becoming adults with their own thoughts and personalities. This reflects their growing maturity, which encourages them to appreciate different ideas and desire experiences separate to those of their parents.

Devices help children and teens in this search for their emerging identity. They can find new interests and create new groups easily via the internet, for example by following their favourite music artist on social media and connecting with others with the same preference. This confirms for them that they have their own musical tastes and also establishes camaraderie with other fans. It satisfies two goals – a feeling of belonging and a sense of identity.

This is also the time when a child develops a sense of themselves as a sexual person and as a possible romantic or intimate partner. During the tween and teen years they become comfortable with their changing body, develop amorous interests, and experience physical attraction to others.

This encourages them to self-assess their desirability to potential love interests. Imagine a teen who looks in the mirror and feels unsure whether their changing body is normal and acceptable, and if they are attractive. It is understandable (but not necessarily helpful) for them to take a photo of themself looking as appealing as possible and post it on social media or text it to a friend to whom they are attracted. They are seeking immediate validation via likes and encouraging comments. This action may be even more tempting if they have seen their peers receive approval for posting similar content. However, editing photos, crafting clever comments and checking for responses can become an excessively time-consuming task which sets up unrealistic standards of personal attractiveness and wittiness for them.

When tweens and teens form their sense of identity in online forums, there are potential downsides and consequences. By seeking new acquaintances on the internet, they could be exposed to nefarious predators and people who take advantage of a child's or teen's genuine attempts to form connections in their search for who they are. Children seeking information about how they fit in are also at risk of encountering deliberate misinformation.

They are also constantly exposed to glamorous or handsome photos of their friends and favourite influencers in orchestrated and carefully filtered shots. When they assess how much they deviate from the often-faked norms of the virtual world, they can easily develop a warped sense of what is normal in the actual world. This can lead them to assume there are defects in their appearance which can prompt them to think they are not attractive enough. They may develop anxiety around their perceived flaws.

Seeking approval via seductive shots sent to romantic interests can set up a domino reaction of needing reassurance, seeking it, getting it, feeling great temporarily and then seeking reassurance again. And when tweens and teens try to establish their personal sense of attractiveness and desirability through sending and posting photos, there are clear risks from other people's predatory behaviour.

When a teen sends a seductive shot to a particular person they are interested in, the recipient might also be looking to shore up their own sense of validation and worth. They may send back a request for a more explicitly suggestive photo, thinking, 'If they really like me, they will send me another sexy shot.'

It's important to remember that in every step of this interaction, either party's actions risk invalidation via negative feedback coming from the person they send their photo to, or the app they place it on. Putting themselves out there and anticipating others' responses creates an expectation of dopamine release: the tween or teen expects a positive reward but if it doesn't come, they experience a dopamine dip instead and feel worse than before. For a teen prone to anxiety, this can prompt fearful thoughts like 'What if one of my close friends responds coldly or not at all?' This cycle is reinforced by a surge in dopamine if the sender receives a positive emoji, encouraging them to post again.

To be clear: we don't approve or disapprove of these behaviours, although we acknowledge the danger of explicit photos being available forever. Given the normal human impulse for a child to seek validation while forming their emerging identity and sexuality, the natural boost from feelings of connection, and the opportunities technology provides to experience this, it's understandable why teens – or adults – can be tempted to post these kinds of photos. But doing this can open up a new source of anxiety and reduce a person's ability to develop robust self-confidence.

Our need to provide and care for loved ones

Our sense of social success and acceptability is also enhanced by our sense of belonging to a group. Contributing and caring for members of our group is a significant way to strengthen our place within it. For tweens and teens, this usually means being available and responsive to peers, which can come at a cost to their responsiveness to their family. The prospect of lingering over Sunday roast with the family when an online gaming marathon with friends beckons is likely to lead to a teen's early departure from the table, simple sandwich in hand. For parents, on the other hand, caring and providing for the family remain prerequisites for the role. They can't opt in and out of this responsibility.

Parents work hard to provide and care for their children by doing all they can to give them a great start in life. They create the financial security to put a roof over their child's head, food on their plate, and textbooks in their schoolbag. And they want to ensure their child's life is as successful, happy and carefree as it can be.

To provide for their family financially, parents need to perform paid work and most occupations today can't be done without leaving home. The disruption of COVID had the welcome side effect of freeing many of us from long train rides or fighting traffic and finding a parking spot. The subsequent normalisation of working from home has helped many parents combine their working lives with the ability to be physically present for school pick up and drop off.

But the 24/7 nature of work today means many of us feel compelled to use our phone, laptop or tablet to connect with our workplaces beyond official (and sometimes reasonable) working hours because this degree of responsiveness tends to be valued by employers, clients and colleagues. We may also be able to shift the times we devote to family and work responsibilities to be more convenient for our family schedule. Working out of hours can also provide some professional payoff, reassuring us about our value in the workplace and allowing us to feel that we are doing a good job both in our work and caring for our loved ones.

But the instant communication provided by our ever-present mobile phones and devices does not always ultimately benefit children or parents. Let's look at an example where technology both helps and hinders.

Imagine you are a parent whose child is attending high school for the first time. You have arranged to pick your child up from the gate, but when you get there, you realise there are four gates at the school. You park your car, watch the students leaving and begin to wonder, 'Is this the right gate? Did my child understand which gate I meant?' You become concerned.

'Are they on their way, or are they at one of the other gates and getting upset because I'm not there?'

There was no quick solution to this dilemma 30 years ago. You would have had to wait until you saw your child. But today, you can simply use your phone to call your child on their phone. Easy-peasy. No uncertainty or worry about what will happen and no cause for concern for parent or child.

But easy solutions like this can come at a cost. When a parent reacts to their own uneasiness by seeking an immediate answer via a call or text, they can inadvertently feed their child's anxiety. The parent's phone message at the school gate quickly fixes a problem, but also removes an opportunity for the child to learn to solve the dilemma of not finding their parent at the gate as expected. If this type of instant solution happens regularly, the child remains dependent on the parent and does not learn to see themself as a capable and resourceful problem solver. That same child might eventually experience more anxiety because they are not used to thinking for themself or enduring the discomfort of uncertainty.

Overusing their phone can also adversely affect a parent's ability to spend quality time with their child, which detracts from their caring role. Research has shown that merely having our phone with us leads us to focus less on what is happening in the moment and reduces our engagement with the people around us.

> *Having our phone in our hand, or on the table, encourages our companions to perceive us as less invested in our interaction with them.*

Having our phone with us can also encourage us to view our companions as uninteresting in comparison to the distraction offered by our device. When we turn our attention to our phone, we miss out on the emotional nourishment we get from being in the company of others. After a while, spending time with family and friends may not feel as satisfying for us (or for them) and will do nothing to allay any fears we may have about our social competence. The presence of our phone may even increase our social anxiety because it means we are not truly practising and developing confidence in our social skills.

Technoference is a term coined to describe the everyday interruptions in personal interactions brought about by technology. But when it comes to parent–child interactions, using phones does more than simply interrupt. When parents engage with their phone, they miss their children making conversational bids like asking a question or smiling at them. Research has shown that when parents look at their phone at the dinner table, they have 20% fewer verbal interactions and 39% fewer non-verbal interactions with their young children.

Children's behaviour is also affected when parents focus on their devices. If a parent allows technology to dominate family life, their child tends to be less capable of focusing on tasks and managing their emotions. Studies of parents who overuse their phone show that their children are at greater risk of depression, anxiety and behavioural problems. This is probably because the attention given to the phone disrupts the parent–child connection and chips away at the emotional rewards and attachment benefits gained from time spent together. Additionally, children may turn to attention-seeking behaviours like shouting or running around in a café to get their parent to notice them. If left unchecked, this can lead to other behavioural problems. Older children may simply zone out watching YouTube videos on their own device, reflecting their parent's use of their phone in family moments.

Our need for a sense of mastery and control

Many people feel more in control of situations when they have their phone in their pocket. Imagine you are driving to a work meeting in an unfamiliar location. Are you taking the best route? There's an easy solution. Check the maps app on your phone and it will tell you in moments if there is a better way. Will you need a jacket in the afternoon? Check a weather app to see the temperature forecast for 4 pm. Using our phones certainly helps us deal with practical problems by minimising the uncertainty associated with these kinds of questions.

Thanks to your phone, you get to your destination early, the first to arrive at the meeting. You look around the room, take a seat at the empty table and immediately reach for your phone again to scroll the feed in a news app or Instagram. Because there's nothing happening yet and that's boring, right? After a short time, several others turn up for the meeting. But they are not familiar to you – which teams do they even work in? You smile briefly, give them a nod and a perfunctory 'hi' before returning your attention to your phone in lieu of engaging them in small talk.

But now your phone is not so helpful: using it to help you arrive at the meeting ahead of time was beneficial to you, but using it to distract yourself from boredom and avoid interacting with people you don't know before the meeting begins is not. This seems like the perfect solution at the time because you remain in your comfort zone, but you relinquish your opportunity to socialise by avoiding any discomfort and awkwardness you might feel if you initiate conversation. You've retained your sense of control at the cost of making new connections. Doing this occasionally is not a problem – everybody does it. But if it becomes your default solution whenever you find yourself in slightly uncomfortable circumstances, you're opting for a quick fix which won't help you become adept at handling the feelings of unrest and discomfort we all occasionally experience. The more we turn to our devices to alleviate doubt, boredom and worry, the more we become dependent on them to seek immediate relief from these tricky and uncomfortable feelings and even avoid them altogether.

> *Our phones provide easy ways for us*
> *to disengage from anxiety-provoking situations.*

It feels like staying in control, but avoiding interaction means people lose opportunities for face-to-face connections that produce a 'real life' reward through connecting with others in person.

The more we turn to our phones or technology to manage our anxiety in circumstances where we feel we have little control over what will happen, the more we may seek to avoid these situations because we have limited practice at facing them. If we choose the phone every time, our comfort and ability with casual conversation continues to decline and our social skills decrease to the point where we become uncomfortable with the real world beyond the small screen. This does nothing for our capacity to calmly face and endure similarly daunting situations in future.

Technology plays a significant role in our lives. But we need to use our phones and other devices with caution. While their magic can solve our day-to-day practical problems almost instantly, we need to make sure we are not relinquishing our independence, confidence and social skills to the distractions and illusory connections afforded by our screens.

For all technology's benefits, it can also directly influence the likelihood a child will develop long-term anxiety. Technology doesn't develop children's independent resourcefulness to solve their worries; instead it provides a way to hide when a child needs to overcome their social fears and learn to positively engage with others. Devices can easily take children away from the very things that will become the cornerstone of their wellbeing – real relationships and personal connections – into a manufactured world of easy dopamine hits that dissipate almost as soon as they arrive.

So how will you technology-proof your child so they reap the benefits of their screens while minimising the drawbacks? And how will you conquer your over-reliance on your phone and learn to trust that your child doesn't need a text or phone call from you whenever you are apart?

We answer those questions in Part B. First it's time to look at a major source of joy in our lives that can also cause us to become anxious in equal measure – friendships.

CHAPTER 4

Friendships and anxiety

Friendships enrich our lives beyond measure, but problems with friends are some of the most vexatious that school-aged children face. That's why making and keeping friends can be a major source of anxiety for many children.

A fundamental part of being human is the need to feel that we belong. We feel secure when we know we have people we can rely on. Feeling accepted by a group brings us great comfort and allows us to develop our sense of self-esteem. The groups to which we belong form essential aspects of our identity.

There's good reason for this. Back in the good old cave-dwelling days, groups needed their members to form strong bonds and a sense of permanent unity. If groups were too fluid, members wouldn't see them as safe, because they couldn't count on the strength in numbers required to face large predators or another marauding tribe. These days, groups operate best when they are more fluid because we don't have the same need to defend ourselves from sabre-toothed tigers or marauders from neighbouring suburbs. While it's good to feel we have each other's backs, we are happier and healthier now when we feel free to choose the people we spend our time with. Today most adults gain validation from being part of a number of groups: our family, our work colleagues, our over 40s soccer team, our old university friends, the gang we meet every afternoon at the dog park, or the school's parents and friends association members.

Children don't usually have access to a similarly large range of groups to get their sense of belonging. They tend to be heavily reliant on their family and their school peers as these are the groups they have access to. But there comes a point when the importance of the family unit begins to recede for children. In mid to late primary school, when children start individuating, they begin to seek validation more from peers than their parents, and this urge becomes stronger in the high-school years. During this time, children are also developing their social skills.

At the stage when children value peer friendships most, they are often least skilled in managing them.

Although these are the years when many children put most of their energy into fitting in with their peers, this is when the challenging dynamics of groups and individual friendships are most difficult for them to manage. Is it any wonder that what is often their main source of belonging and validation – school friendships – can become so fraught? Many upper primary and secondary school children become anxious about their place in the world and their value to a peer group precisely when the tricky politics of the playground, shuffling alliances, nascent social skills and immaturity are all in the mix.

In this chapter, we flesh out the dynamics of school groups and friendships for you to understand what's at play.

The dynamics of children's friendships

It's tempting to simply suggest that the solution to all friendship concerns is to tell everyone they should just be kind, but it's much more complex than that.

The structure of friendship groups

People enjoy hanging out in their friendship groups, whether it be in 'their' place in the playground or at their favourite café after their Sunday morning bike ride. Individual friendships are often formed within these groups. At your workplace, everyone in your team will feel some sense of social connection, but no doubt you have some people you are closer to than others. If you are lucky, you have a few people you call friends at work. Large work groups often function like the intersecting circles in a Venn diagram, where there are some separate catch-ups among several individuals, a mixture of overlapping lunch plans involving different sets of people and, every now and then, Friday night drinks which include almost everyone.

Much like adult work groups, most school friendship groups also contain individual friendships. When you walk through school playgrounds or quads at lunch, you are likely to see a few large groups hanging out or playing with each other. While many will maintain this group contact out of school hours through sharing likes and comments on their preferred social media app, smaller groups of two, three or four friends will also connect without the rest of the group.

Ideally these friendships sit comfortably within the larger group and do not detract from everyone getting along harmoniously, with nothing beyond minor disagreements disrupting the agreeable atmosphere. In reality, this does not always happen because people have different motivations when socialising, centred around their desire for intimacy and popularity.

The goal of intimacy within peer friendships

Some children seek to form friendships primarily as a means of developing intimacy of a platonic nature. To do this they become close to others via disclosure, often of minor details, like chatting about what they did on the weekend or what they thought of a Netflix show. Or they could make more major disclosures, such as revealing who they have a crush on, what their heartfelt wishes are, the changes taking place in their body (their first period or facial hair), or their concern that their parents are fighting much more than they used to.

> *Closer bonds are formed when people choose to reveal private information to others.*

When you give someone a more complete picture of you through disclosing private details and they accept you, warts and all, you gain a sense of being likeable and worthy of acceptance. Without this, you can think there are parts of you that are shameful. This is important when children are not particularly open with their parents, yet they have so many changes happening in their bodies and their feelings. When something happens in their lives that is significant to them – asking someone to be their partner at the formal or choosing their outfit to wear on the night – they feel the need for someone to confide their thoughts and fears to, particularly someone who is encountering similar circumstances and doubts at the same time. When their friends also confide in them, they gain a sense of the normalcy of their experience which can be deeply reassuring.

Disclosure between friends also adds a layer of loyalty to a friendship. When both parties have shared deeper aspects of themselves, their bond is strengthened and the desire to remain close friends who trust each other and guard each other's secrets is reinforced.

Of course, disclosure can come at a cost. There are children and teens who try to form intimacy with others too soon. They might blurt out personal details too early in the friendship, which risks the other person or people using that information in a cruel way. This often happens with anxious children who tell other children their fears as a means of inviting them into their life. They might share what their therapist told them about their anxiety or share their worries about their mum losing her job. If they divulge this kind of information too early as a means of creating connection, the recipient may not be kind with what they have been told.

The likelihood of this happening becomes greater when the person they tell has a goal that's different to developing intimacy. If their confidant's friendship goal is to be popular and one of the cool kids, they may decide to use the shared information to advance this aim.

The goal of popularity within peer friendships

Most children want to be liked and accepted by others. But for some, the desire to be extremely popular and rise to a prominent position within their social hierarchy is more appealing than closeness with others. Rather than look to form typical friendships of familiarity and intimacy, these children deliberately interact with others in a way that cements their personal social standing. This is not simply wanting to be well liked and accepted – it's deliberately pursuing dominance.

Why do they do this? The value of seeking popularity to reach the top of a hierarchy is associated with higher social rewards, such as being in the cool group, and being viewed as successful – sometimes even revered and feared – by peers. Status is an important factor at play here. Intuitively, kids gravitate to children who are admired by others. From an early age, children are aware of people's rank and prefer dominant peers over subservient ones. Friendship with the popular people gives them some reflected social capital. You can understand why children would want to be the kid everyone wants to have as a friend.

Maintaining extremely high status among others is not easy; the most popular children must work incessantly to hold their position. Some may use relational aggression, which is hostility designed to inflict actual or threatened damage to a relationship. These children or teens might deliberately try to exclude others or say nasty things about them to either reject who they are (their personality traits or physical qualities), betray their confidence or spread falsehoods about them – 'Amanda told me Susan's clothes are all second hand and smelly'.

Relational aggression is distasteful, but it has advantages for the person using it. It can reduce someone's popularity so that a potential close contender loses status in the group. If Noah suspects Elijah is becoming too popular, Noah might deliberately spread lies about him to knock him down a peg and eliminate him as a competitor for the position of group leader. Other options would be to give Elijah the silent treatment or find things to say that are sure to embarrass him, whether he is there or not.

People who deploy this tactic also tend to be good at using manipulation to gain a strong influence over the group. Some children display this behaviour early by obviously favouring one parent over another – 'I want Daddy to sit next to me,' or 'Only Mummy can hold my hand.' It can be a way for a child to exert their sense of control in the family by anointing one parent as their preferred one . . . at least until they change their mind.

Manipulation often works to give children a place of authority in social groups beyond the family. In our experience, children who do this are often very skilful at hiding their less kind qualities from adults, so it comes as some surprise when teachers find out that a popular and seemingly well-liked child or teen has become that way through inciting fear and destabilising others.

Some children are also competent at using aggression while gaining the respect of others at school. It's not always the obviously mean and feared children who act this way – some less confident children worry that they are disliked. This encourages them to use relational aggression to assuage their social status fears and shore up their popularity.

How do children become this way? The innate drive to compete for superiority is a characteristic of evolution; we believe some children see their parents model such behaviour and try to emulate it to receive similar status. Perhaps a child sees one parent gain a higher position than the other through constant belittling or mind games, and the child chooses to behave similarly in their own peer groups.

Rather than become critical of these children or teens, we need to understand what might prompt them to behave this way. We should feel empathy for children with a parent who is relationally aggressive, as this hostile approach may also be used against the child. In our clinical experience, homes where any sort of hostility is present are generally not pleasant places to be. It is perhaps no surprise if children from such homes look to gain a sense of personal agency and control in their relationships elsewhere to attain what they lack in their family.

We don't blame parents as the sole cause of children's relational aggression; there are many other ways a child can see this approach to relationships being played out. They might see power plays in older siblings, other family members, peers or the wider community. They might even see their favourite celebrities gain a sense of dominance on social media platforms via deliberate targeting of other personalities.

Children might also find themselves in an environment which is deliberately competitive. If they are at a camp for squad selection with children from other schools, you can see why some might deploy a few mind games to get an edge over others.

The lure of charismatic–aggressive children

While some groups have one king pin, some relationally aggressive people choose to connect with others with similar personalities. Large groups often accommodate several relationally aggressive members. These are often the very well-liked kids in the most popular groups at school (Think of the Plastics in *Mean Girls*, or the Heathers in *Heathers* or even the Pink Ladies in *Grease*.)

There is an admission price to be part of this crowd. Sure, members get to be considered popular, but they sign up to a group where people don't necessarily play fair, and some criticism of others is expected of them.

Their position in this crowd will always be tenuous, given the constant jostling of status likely to take place. For some, maintaining their place in the hierarchy will be daily hard work.

Despite this cost, less popular children will often want to be members of this charismatic yet aggressive group. This is often the case with an anxious child who believes that if they become accepted by the popular kids, they'll gain the social status associated with that group and their fears will be relieved. Some kids who aren't anxious, but simply less popular, might yearn to be friends with the 'gold-star' gang and see this as the chance to gain huge social standing in one move.

These children are often unwittingly entering a dangerous game. The popular kids are usually more mature with interests more in tune with those of older children. There can be up to 16 months' difference between one child and another in the same year level, so some will be more mature and gravitate toward each other, rejecting the less mature peers. It is unlikely that the interloping child (so to speak) has similar interests or experience, so they enter at a disadvantage, with the group possibly speaking almost another language. The 'cool crowd' are also more likely to be skilled in manipulation and using mores within the group that outsiders would not understand, nor be practised in. This means that the child attempting to join in doesn't even pick up on the subtleties of the relational aggression taking place at their expense.

> *Many 'cool' groups are happy for outsiders*
> *to attempt to move in because by being mean to them,*
> *they can use these people to further assert their dominance.*

Those trying to get into the cool group can be lured in and then deliberately cast aside in a show of power as a message to others. It is like a new manager deliberately firing someone to show strength to the other employees and encourage them to toe the line out of fear they will meet the same fate. It's not great management, nor kind, but it displays power to good effect.

How groups change

Children's friendship groups work best as somewhat cohesive units, but this doesn't mean they remain static. Often this is because children change and so do their interests. A child who chooses to be a member of a lunchtime handball group because of their love of the game will eventually get to an age where it is no longer their cup of tea. When they retire the tennis ball, they are likely to change their lunchtime hangout group to reflect what they now enjoy. Likewise, if the interests of the majority of the group change, the one or two who retain the old preferences will start to feel uncomfortable because of shifts in activities or conversations.

This often emerges in middle to upper primary; before then, different personalities in groups aren't so important. Younger children often simply parallel play – they do the same simple things, side by side. As their dispositions form, they are likely to choose to be with others whose preferences reflect their own changing interests in music, tv shows, sports or curiosity about romantic relationships.

When children reach their tweens, there is more jostling to determine who fits with whom. By the second half of high school, most adolescents have found a group where they feel comfortable with like-minded others. But even in these groups, frenemy situations emerge, and these can lead to relational aggression and unhappiness.

Imagine a work situation where a close friend gets the promotion you were hoping for. You may feel disgruntled, and without you realising it, this can affect your ability to be a good friend. Hopefully this feeling will pass, but sometimes it creates a permanent rift. Children and teens can also become disgruntled when their friend gets an opportunity they themselves have been denied. This can make friendships suffer briefly. We've seen this when school prefects are announced. While a prefect's friends are generally pleased for them, some members of their friendship group can become cool toward them, because they wanted the role but didn't get it and so feel a tinge of envy. While this can be overcome, prefects often also start to be friends with each other, because they are doing more together and don't have as much time to hang out with the old gang. This is what happens with friendships when your circumstances change, as in when you partner, have children, move to a different city, or take on a different career.

Groups don't only splinter because of developing personalities or differences in accomplishment, lifestyle or responsibilities. There can be in-group jostling, which can mean that one or two members who were accepted in the past could now be frozen out. This is more likely to happen in groups or among members of groups known for relational aggression. Often the targeting is brought on by envy and jealousy, both of which influence and are influenced by the nature of a person's most cherished goals and their fears of not reaching them.

In-group jostling is often magnified on social media and in group chats, where any friendship problems are easily made worse. Children with heightened social sensitivity are vulnerable here because these platforms are likely to be significant for them. Any cruel jibes they detect can play on their minds and echo harmfully through the night or weekend.

Another challenge posed when groups change is that membership is often viewed as a binding attachment and members should therefore remain loyal and stay in the group. Perceived disloyalty can result in rejection for the child who wishes to support a friend who is being targeted or excluded. Alternatively, they may themselves become the target of gossip or other relationally aggressive tactics. For children still developing their social skills, this becomes a tricky situation to navigate. They must weigh up whether to stay loyal to their friend, go against a powerful member or members of the group and risk marginalisation themselves, or keep quiet and remain in the group. It is a conundrum they will have great difficulty navigating, particularly if they are anxious and likely to worry more about such complexities.

When groups splinter, the most resilient children are those who have a wide range of friends and access to several groups inside and outside school. Children who are broadly aligned with a range of groups can choose to hang out with a different crowd if they find themselves on the receiving end of in-group jostling or targeting. However, setting up these connections can be difficult, given the imperative to remain loyal and stay within the group.

How parents become involved in children's friendship groups

The dynamics of friendship groups often extend beyond the group members. Now that parents often take a strong interest in their child's school experiences, many extend that interest to their child's successes and heartbreaks in the playground. They can provide valuable help when problems arise by giving wise counsel and encouraging their child to adopt inclusive and caring approaches that solve minor friendship upsets.

But there is a difference between being appropriately involved and over-involved, or even contributing negatively to the bad blood in friendship upsets. We've seen this taken to extremes, including one memorable school situation where parents escalated their children's arguments to the point where two families took out restraining orders against each other.

Parents can also have intimacy or popularity goals for their child's friendships. While many will simply want a few loyal friends for their child, there may be some parents in any year level who have designs for their child to be popular and who will attempt to engineer this through their parent friendship groups. A classic strategy is to become friends with the well-liked or high-status parents, so that their child is invited to playdates with the in-crowd parents' popular children.

These parents can use similar tactics to the relationally aggressive child and try to exclude other parents and other children. Some stand at school gates and gossip about students or parents at the school. They might deliberately exclude another parent or parents from a morning tea catch-up or school committee. Or they might play subtle factional games to develop a popular in-crowd. Another plan can be to use children's parties and sleepovers as campaigns to form a well-liked group for their child to be part of. With sufficient diligence and strategising, they may even be able to have their child become the king or queen of that group.

Of course, not many parents behave this way – and, thankfully, your school may have none of these. But it's true that sometimes children are deliberately encouraged by a parent to become popular by almost any means, partly because the parents themselves want to be popular, perhaps because they are socially anxious themselves. They might be reliving their own tricky school years through their child which leads them to feel concerned about the child's social success. It's not unusual for them to inadvertently transfer their social fears to their child.

Over-enthusiastic parental involvement can have an impact on the wellbeing of other parents and students. One of the most heartbreaking situations Judith experienced was at a primary school a few years ago. At the end of Judith's talk, one parent approached her and, through tears, asked if in future Judith could ask parents at the school to be kinder to each other. It appeared that this parent had become a side player to a small cohort who saw their child's schooling as a calculated exercise of power and faction building, and her family was suffering as a result.

Some friendship problems are not easily solved. Sometimes, you can find yourself in an environment where the people – to quote the wise words of

Austin Powers – just aren't your bag. Many of you will have experienced workplaces where you couldn't seem to find friends to hang out with despite your best efforts to fit in and create bonds. There will be times when your child might have similar difficulty in finding a group where they feel they fit in.

> *Don't expect your child to find*
> *a group of kind and like-minded friends*
> *in every situation they encounter.*

This may be because their interests are momentarily quirky or unusual for their age, or they may temporarily struggle to find their friendship group because they are going through an awkward stage. Or perhaps they attend a school where most of the other students are more sporty or more inclined toward the arts than they are. If your child attends a smaller school, they will have a more limited peer group in which to find others with similar interests. If there are a number of relationally aggressive children in your child's year level, this could make forming friendships tricky for them.

We understand that for some parents, particularly those somewhat anxious about their child's social skills, friendship challenges can be heartbreaking and difficult. But don't allow your own fears to unnecessarily amplify your child's worry. Parents can help children move through these times by listening, coaching them to find other activities in breaks, and helping them to find a support network outside school.

Everyone hopes their child will easily make friends who will become great sources of connection and care in their lives. But, as this chapter has shown, friendships rarely run so smoothly. Sometimes they become more fraught when children are sensitive. We discuss this trait and its nuances next.

CHAPTER 5

Sensitive children and anxiety

'Sensitive' is a word often used for children who are more emotional than others, but it actually describes a range of behaviours. We believe it's important that you determine which type of 'sensitive' you see in your child to know what's best to do next.

Many parents think carefully about their parenting choices and choose to tailor their approach according to each child. When a parent decides their child is sporty, they are likely to plan their time together differently than they do with their quieter, more book-loving child.

'Labelling' children by their qualities is an understandable cognitive shortcut that helps parents negotiate their demanding lives. You ask the responsible child to turn off the oven when the timer goes off to ensure it gets done, or the athletic one to run to the shop, or the wordsmith to write the message in Grandpa's birthday card. This classification system can also make it easier when siblings are fighting – you know which one is likely to be the instigator and which one is usually the victim – leaving less Judge Judying for you to do.

But the model is not always accurate. And one label we find to be particularly inexact is the 'sensitive child' label.

'Sensitive' is a word we hear often as clinical psychologists, typically in regard to children more affected than their peers by change or events not going the way they would prefer. They often become highly emotional when faced with unpredictable or uncertain outcomes and seek their parents' presence for comfort or their intervention to change the situation, so they feel more at ease.

In our experience, 'sensitive' describes more than one type of child. In fact, we see the label applied to three clear types of personalities.

The timid child

The first is the shy sensitive child who we describe as the *timid child*: the classic 'fearful' child who lacks confidence and expresses doubt about their abilities. They often run back to their parents rather than toward an unfamiliar activity. Timid children tend to seek reassurance when faced with something new and often need to be coaxed into trying activities outside their comfort zone. They might also prefer to keep their parents nearby in these situations. Even when at high school, they often ask their parents to do things for them that they find challenging, such as insist the parent ask the waiter for a glass of water.

Once the label of 'sensitive' is applied to timid children, many parents allow them to avoid new and uncomfortable situations. With the best of intentions, they set up a cycle of over-protecting their child, who does not get the opportunity to face challenge and learn from it, and so becomes even less capable of facing the next task. These parents, despite their good intent, make their child's shyness worse.

What to do if you have a timid child

A timid child needs to learn to face what they fear, slowly and in an empathetic environment. This is a better approach than letting them avoid their concerns on account of their sensitivity. It enables them to become stronger, not weaker.

We show you how to do this in Part B, but keep in mind that it will require you to let go of some of your preconceptions about your child. You will need to look for opportunities to praise them for qualities you may have thought they lacked and give them chances to develop new skills. Send your 'sensitive' child on errands rather than their 'confident' sibling and then congratulate them on their independence.

Remember, they won't acquire skills if you don't give them the space and opportunity to develop them. It's up to you to make sure they get as many confidence-building chances as you give to the child you have decided is more buoyant.

> *Become genuinely curious, rather than predictive,*
> *about what your timid child will do.*

This will take some effort on your part, because you will have to remind yourself not to expect your child to play to a set type. They will become open to being more capable than they imagined, because you will be more open as well.

The director

The *director* likes to be in charge of their environment. They often appear to lack confidence when faced with activities they don't want to do or situations in which they won't feel in control. Their reluctance is actually more about what they feel like doing or believe they can take charge of, than what they think they can handle. When someone wants them to do something they don't want to do, the director usually reacts differently to the timid child. Shy children will seek support or retreat into themselves; directors tend to get angry and loud when things aren't going the way they prefer. You don't have to coax directors to let you know their feelings: you know. You really know.

A director's sensitivity is typically based on the belief they can't cope unless things are done their way. They have a way of expressing reluctance which sounds like they're anxious but is more to do with their expectation that they need to direct the action. And parents tend to prefer to detect anxiety in their child rather than wilfulness. 'Sensitive' or 'anxious' are kinder labels for the child's behaviours; 'wilfulness' feels critical of the child.

Many parents see a director's traits as indicative of anxiety when the child uses phrases like 'I want Daddy to put me to bed!' and their outbursts have an uneasy, sensitive edge. These parents can think the child is genuinely apprehensive about their mother putting them to bed, or truly worried about not having the first shower. To make family life easier and avoid aggravating what they see as the child's fears and sensitivity, parents find themselves giving in and doing what the child wants. But for the child, the concern is not a fear of the activity being overwhelming; it is much more to do with not prescribing the terms of the action and therefore not being in charge.

Over time, the more often children are allowed to take charge, the stronger they believe that getting their way is the only situation they can cope with. As a result, their enraged behaviour becomes worse when their wishes are refused. At this stage, parents of directors often seek help from psychologists for their child's anxiety which has begun to threaten household harmony. These children can be as young as four years old.

This can be a problem. If a child with director tendencies has therapy for their 'anxiety' and their parents are involved minimally or not at all, therapy can further increase the director's control over the family. The child receives the attention of seeing a psychologist, the family walks around them on eggshells, and by being deemed as having 'special issues' that require 'special allowances', the child subtly gains more control.

Of course, the child might have some genuine anxieties. But their true fears around not being in charge will not be addressed in therapy without the insight of the parents. Motivation is also a big contributor here. A child who has the chance to be in control of the way things are done every day is not likely to actively seek opportunities to have less control. Often, without parental involvement and knowledge of what is truly happening in the family, therapy changes nothing, and a child's domineering behaviours can become worse.

It's good news if children are part-time directors only when they are at home. Some are fully capable of going with the flow at school and following the instructions of their teacher. Some can even be perfect angels at school when they focus their determination on being well behaved and creating a reputation for being mature and responsible. This disparity is often evident in the morning routine. The child refuses to get up when the parent tells them to, carries on when their toast is not made with the bread they like, and screams when the socks they prefer to wear are in the wash or their parent does not do their hair perfectly. But once they finally get in the car, they become extremely worried about being late to school and their teacher being cross with them. They express this by getting angry with their parent for driving too slowly – 'That light was orange! What are you stopping for?' This is characteristic of the classic part-time director who follows the rules at school perfectly but insists on setting the rules at home.

If you have a part-time director, take heart. It means they can follow rules: you just need to establish yourself as the person in charge in your home, just as their teachers have established their authority at school.

What to do if you have a director

You have to be a detective to find out whether your child's behaviours are due to the wilfulness of a director or an expression of genuine fears. Determine if they are simply disputing the terms of engagement in your home and continually seeking to alter them. An argument about which parent puts them to bed and reads them their bedtime book is a director's move. Demanding the first or last shower, and changing their request regularly, is the work of a director arguing their preferences, not an expression of timidity. Insisting you cut the sandwich diagonally is another director's move if they are happy to eat the sandwich only if you present it exactly to their specification. But if they are nervous about an ingredient in the sandwich or ask you to cut it up into very small pieces because they are afraid of choking, they are likely to be genuinely anxious and not just randomly dictating how they would prefer the situation to be.

It can help to ask them what it is about their fear that they don't want to face. If they don't want the first shower because it means they have to walk upstairs by themself in an old, shadowy house, their fear is due more to timidity than a director's concern about not being in control. Just remember that sometimes children are very good at making up an anxious-sounding reason – so be something of a detective here. For example, do they walk up the stairs happily when there's something they want up there?

If your child's sensitive traits are mainly signs of wilfulness, the ease of turning the situation around depends on how long your child has been under the impression that they are chair of the board in your household. The longer this has been so, the harder it will be to change their beliefs and have them fit in with everyone in your family.

To get your child's expectations and behaviour back on track, you need to take charge. This is easier when you remember that you are the sensible adult and the best person to decide what happens in your home. Establishing this in their mind takes more than occasionally announcing your status to them.

If you need to tell your child you are in charge, you probably aren't.

It is a bad sign if you need to persuade your child that what you say goes. Your actions, more than your words, will convince them to believe this.

Putting yourself in charge again involves regaining their respect for you. Children with director tendencies typically lack basic respect for others and think their own needs are much more important than everyone else's. This makes them unpopular in the playground and likely to bully others and be domineering in peer groups. These children also often lack self-regulation skills because they always prefer to go with what they want to do rather than what they need to do. Their resilience is often deficient, as they do not learn how to cope when they are not in charge. They will not reach their potential if they keep going the way they are. You can turn this situation around by taking decisive action. We show you how to do this in Part B.

The timid director

You might be thinking to yourself, 'Hmm . . . sometimes my child is timid, but they can be a director occasionally too.' Congratulations, you might have a *timid director*!

Timid directors are a combination of the first two types of sensitive child who show different traits at different times. One moment they seek cuddles and care, the next they are Godzillas, storming around, telling everyone what to do and whose air they can breathe, and erupting because their slice of pizza has fewer olives than their sibling's.

Children often use a combination of timid and director traits to get their way. They ask their parent for a Freddo Frog at the supermarket and when the parent says no, they throw themselves to the floor, kick their legs and yell in a proper mega tantrum. If their parent stands their ground (go parent!), the child takes a different tack, becomes needy, and tearily asks for reassurance and hugs. And sometimes the parent is so pleased the child has stopped the tantrum, they yield and the child gets the hug and the chocolate, because it almost looks as if they have complied with the parent's initial response.

Let's put our detective hats on again. The child has actually given a performance of super sweet and sensitive behaviour to get their way – an act of emotional manipulation because their initial anger did not work. Smart move, but not great for their compliance and respect for your authority.

Another classic timid director manoeuvre is the charming note. Maybe they want to go to the park in the afternoon, but you are busy and can't take them. They scream and yell until eventually you send them to their room to calm down. After ten minutes, they emerge with a note for you – 'Dear Mummy and Daddy, I love you very much and I am very sorry. You are the best Mummy and Daddy in the world' – with a few love hearts, kisses and glitter thrown in. You are so relieved the whole episode is over, you give them a lengthy hug and offer a brief trip to the park as additional consolation. Congratulations, you have been played. They've simply kept trying alternate director and timid traits until they have achieved what they want. Older children use a similar technique when they suddenly become charming and attentive to your feelings – asking how the preparation for your work presentation is coming along or commenting on how much they think your new haircut suits you – which is their way of buttering you up before they ask you to buy them a new pair of jeans (despite you saying no to the same request the previous week).

One of the difficulties in dealing with timid director behaviours is that parents tend to primarily notice the shy traits in their child and consequently attribute any wilful behaviour to anxiety. The child's increasing rudeness or aggression is not picked up until they are older. This is problematic because the timid director's timidity tends to recede over time, and the director takes over in the individuation years from mid primary and above. The whole family can end up on tenterhooks, trying to appease the Alfred Hitchcock they now live with. It is far better to push back against their difficult behaviours before they become entrenched.

What to do if you have a timid director

The solution for both types of sensitivity in your child lies in slowly encouraging them to face circumstances they aren't comfortable with – developing their confidence to do unfamiliar things and cope with situations where they need to follow rather than lead. The more they do, the more they believe they are capable of doing, and the more varied and rewarding their life will become. They'll also be better company for their family and friends: when they no longer feel they need to lead or direct everything that happens, they will be able to better fit in with their peers and participate in their activities.

Your priority must be their wilfulness, but you also need to address their timidity. The solutions for wilfulness we suggest in chapter 10 will serve to reduce the unruly and defiant elements of your child's behaviour without harming the timid side of their nature. When your child expresses hesitation about doing something they need to do, the steps we outline in chapter 13 on helping your child deal with day-to-day challenges will enable them to slowly face their fears.

When your child is rude to you or disobedient, be consistent in the way you respond with consequences (also detailed in chapter 10). Don't play amateur psychologist by asking yourself why they are being rude or uncompliant. While a certain level of defiance is understandable when children are tired or wanting to assert their independence, to excuse it every time is not helpful. Be sensible about when you ask your child to do things – request that they do chores on Saturday morning rather than late Saturday afternoon after being at their friend's party. But don't make a habit of excusing them from normal expectations.

Because parents are generally kind and think the best of their children, many attribute all of their tricky behaviours to anxiety or sensitivity. This is well intentioned, but it can bring out the worst in children. Remember wilfulness is not a terrible trait – harnessed well it can build leadership and responsibility. But if you allow your child too much personal agency due to their sensitivity before they are ready or mature enough to handle it, they will not be able to fit in with others and thrive at school or work, where they need to comply with the rules and expectations of their teachers or managers. No one gets to be permanently in charge and always do what they want to do; everyone needs to accept that, including your child.

Now that we have looked closely at the nuances of sensitivity and anxiety, we will examine two powerful emotions that commonly influence our relationships with others and our likelihood of developing anxiety. You may even have experienced them yourself. We're talking about fear of missing out (FoMO) and envy.

CHAPTER 6

Envy, FoMO and anxiety

We humans are not good at resting on our laurels. We tend to compare our laurels with others', hoping our future will be as bright and 'laurelful' as theirs. This is not always helpful. Sometimes it can be downright anxiety provoking.

It's a rare person who doesn't compare themself with others. This impulse seems to be part of human nature. We need to know where we sit in our social structure to help us survive and thrive. Back in neanderthal days, it would have been particularly useful to know your relative strengths and weaknesses. This knowledge would help you decide whether you should stand and fight the sabre-toothed tiger or let someone more skilled take care of it while you run away. Today it might be knowing you are best to arrange the sunflowers brought by your visitor and leave your partner to pour the drinks, or that Kate is the best one to put together the flatpack furniture at the office while you do a coffee run.

When we make career choices, it helps to know our relative strengths and weaknesses compared to the rest of the world. This allows us to understand that our comparative lack of skill in managing crises means the role of air traffic controller is best left to those who are better at staying calm.

Comparison is in our nature, and it is often useful. But it does not necessarily help us; occasionally it makes us anxious and depressed.

Comparing ourselves with others

The process of comparison with others typically goes in one of two ways. It is a *downward comparison* when we compare ourselves with someone who is not as accomplished as we are. This makes us feel better about ourselves – who we are and what we have done – because it confirms that we are doing well relative to the other person.

Imagine you have just begun studying for a postgrad degree and you are feeling slightly nervous about how prepared you are for the course. While waiting for the first lecture to begin, you start up a conversation with the student sitting next to you. As you chat, you discover they don't have as much professional experience in the field as you do. You might feel more confident now because, in your mind, you have determined that you are likely to achieve higher marks than they are.

But sometimes comparison goes the other way. It becomes an *upward comparison* when we realise that we don't come out on top. You might find out that you are the least experienced student attending that lecture. Or, when visiting a friend's house, you might suddenly see your own house as small and slightly shabby. At your child's gymnastics class, you might realise that your child is the least coordinated in the group, or the least capable of following the coach's instructions. How does it feel when we come out on the downside of the comparison? We often end up feeling envious or that we are missing out on something others are enjoying. And neither of these feels good at all.

Envy

Envy has a bad name. Among the seven deadly sins, it's known as the green-eyed monster. We think of envy as a distasteful reaction when we consider it alongside the more positive response of taking pleasure in other people's happy news and successes.

Sure, we can feel good about other people's wins. Imagine your colleague is promoted to head of their department. You could delight in their achievement and be generous with your praise. Or you could feel so envious that you make your excuses to avoid the special morning tea to celebrate their success.

The way your reaction goes depends on your situation relative to theirs. If your colleague achieves something you don't give two hoots about for yourself – they're in IT, which you don't enjoy, let alone want to manage – you feel no envy when they are appointed Chief Operations Manager of Information Technology and Communications.

But if their success is something you once hoped to achieve but gave up on in the face of your life's other responsibilities or challenges, you might feel slightly envious when your colleague's achievements remind you of your lost goal. 'I planned to do that IT course, but when I was so busy with the baby I decided not to, and the opportunity never came up again.'

And what happens if your colleague achieves a goal you actively desire right now? Your peer, whose qualifications and experience are similar to yours, has just been appointed to the role you both applied for. You would not be the only one to feel downright envious in this scenario.

Or perhaps you don't. Overall, your colleague's life may have drawbacks that yours does not. They've got the job, but their parent is suffering with Alzheimer's, or they are coming to terms with their own diagnosis of a chronic health condition. Such heart-wrenching circumstances are likely to prevent you from feeling envious of them.

Not feeling envious – not even the slightest tinge – can be a hard task. Upward comparison gives rise to uncomfortable feelings for most people. It makes us doubt ourselves and our value compared with others, which leads to anxiety about whether we will ever meet our life goals. It can also bring us feelings of shame and resentment.

Although we think of envy as a negative emotion, it's more nuanced than that. Psychologists believe there are two types of envy – *malicious* and *benign*. People feel malicious envy when they have resentful thoughts about someone they consider to be doing better than they are. They may not want to engage in any way with the colleague who got the sales award and hefty bonus or the classmate who pipped them to become dux of the year. They may even gain some satisfaction when they hear that something unfortunate has happened to the object of their envy (the friend who is picked for the second XI cricket team instead of the first as expected) or they discover something about them that lessens the gap between the two (the sudden realisation that your always-well-dressed co-worker has a coffee stain on their shirt today). This is schadenfreude, a German word meaning pleasure in others' misfortunes; most of us have felt it at some point, though we may be reluctant to admit it.

Benign envy is a better use of our efforts. People feel benign envy when they use an upward comparison as an impetus to focus their thoughts positively. It may encourage them to identify their own path to achieving success, perhaps with an adjusted goal of their own choosing.

Imagine two friends, Ali and Syed, who are in the same Year 9 Science class. When their exams are handed back, Ali receives an A and Syed a B minus. Ali looks up, smiling (of course!) but Syed frowns and hunches his shoulders. High marks are an important goal for him; he dreams of becoming an engineer. He wanted to get an A! If his envious feelings are benign, he might catch up with Ali after class and ask him how he prepared for the exam and if they can study together before the next one. He's hopeful that this way he'll get an A too – just like Ali.

But if Syed feels that he will never close the gap between them, and he feels malicious envy, he might say something cruel to Ali in the playground later that day or choose to hang out with another classmate who didn't get an A. Benign envy inspires him to take action to catch up to his friend; malicious envy does not.

Perception of similarity also contributes to our feelings of envy. We tend to feel more envious toward people we know well and to whom we feel alike. This is why it's easy to feel envious of our siblings – we typically feel close to them and have a shared background. It's also common for us to feel envious of people we work with or grew up with because we are more likely to compare and contrast ourselves to them and our perception of their success or failure.

How we feel about ourselves is also significant. Research shows that people with stable high self-esteem report lower levels of malicious envy than those whose self-esteem fluctuates. Syed has not been feeling good about himself lately because of his father's displeasure over his recent poor report card. His less than buoyant self-esteem could encourage him to harbour resentment toward Ali rather than focus on ways to improve his marks. When we're not at our best, we are more prone to make envy a roadblock in our friendships or allow it to further chip away at our wellbeing.

Other research findings further complicate the picture of self-esteem and envy. Some have shown that individuals with *high* self-esteem are likely to continue to think well of themselves when faced with someone ostensibly doing better than them, but also to think and act negatively toward them (aka malicious envy) whereas those with low self-esteem are more likely to simply accept the difference. This indicates that parents who focus on maximising their child's self-esteem may risk encouraging them to be mean to their high-achieving peers.

Anxiety increases the likelihood of someone feeling envious. Socially anxious people often perceive the world as hierarchical and competitive, and others as dominant and superior to themselves. This leads them to engage in more frequent upward social comparisons. Social anxiety leaves us vulnerable to feeling envious of new acquaintances when we discover aspects of their lives that our own lives lack, like having a university degree or travelling overseas. As soon as someone starts a story with, 'When I was at university . . .' or 'When we were in Paris . . .', we feel less confident about our part in the exchange and sometimes even ashamed that we have no equivalent experience.

FoMO

FoMO – Fear of Missing Out – is our fear that we are being excluded from the shared experiences of others. It's no surprise that FoMO and anxiety interact – 'fear' is the first word of the acronym, after all. Popular notions of FoMO associate it with glamorous opening nights and cocktail parties, or dinners with friends at the hottest new restaurants. By contrast, JoMO (Joy of Missing Out), describes the feeling you get when you choose not to go to Friday night drinks so you can experience the joy of an evening spent at home watching Netflix and eating pizza on the couch in your pyjamas. Sometimes missing out sounds like pure pleasure.

Psychologists view FoMO in a much broader way. We see it as the experience a person has when they feel they are missing out on belonging. It relates to our fundamental fear of being excluded from the rewarding experiences that members of a group we want to be part of are enjoying together. FoMO is often about losing our sense of belonging through day-to-day activities, like seeing a group of work friends heading out for coffee without asking us, or hearing that we weren't invited to a relative's wedding when our sibling was. It might be finding out that a group of families from your child's school had a barbeque last weekend, but your family wasn't involved, or that your child wasn't invited to a classmate's birthday party.

> *While the desire to belong stays with us throughout our lives,
> fear of not belonging can sometimes be stronger
> in certain stages of life.*

Adolescents are particularly hard hit by FoMO; this is the stage when friendship and connecting with others usually start to become critically important. Research has found that 50% of adolescents will experience FoMO.

Envy, FoMO and social media

Social media has the power to turbocharge our experience of both envy and FoMO. Danielle's research team recently published a study that shows 11% of adolescents feel more anxious on social media because of intense FoMO. It's easy to see why: social media is the master manipulator of FoMO and envy. It encourages people to share (and show off) aspects of their lives, so it stands to reason that most people choose to put their best foot forward and present the most glowing version of themselves in the 'shop window' of their social media posts. They post the most flattering photo of themself sitting in the front row of the new must-see stage show, together with a selfie taken when they meet the stars of the production in the lobby. Or they upload a deliberately staged and filtered selfie, fit and smiling before a background of jaw-droppingly beautiful mountain scenery on their European skiing holiday. When we see these bragging posts in our feeds, we are prompted to compare ourselves and our lives to these images – and come out wanting.

Social media doesn't simply focus on individuals winning at life. It presents people with their friends, winning at life together. People love posting images of themselves having a whale of a time in the company of others, 'proving' they are popular members of happy groups. They are less likely to post photos and updates when they are alone at home with unwashed hair, watching mindless television and eating leftovers in a stained old t-shirt and sweatpants.

Posting your best self is understandable and satisfying to a degree. But constantly viewing other people's best selves is not always rewarding. People who spend hours on end aimlessly scrolling glamorous and boastful images of others with their friends experience reduced wellbeing as a result. Adolescent girls who are heavy social media users are more likely to be at increased risk of self-harm, depression and lower levels of self-esteem; after using apps like Instagram or Snapchat, one study shows around two in ten girls will feel worse about themselves. Their dissatisfaction will be about their friendships, body image, social status and popularity.

We know that envy has a huge influence on the likelihood of a person feeling depressed after scrolling through their social media feed. And the more you are affected by envy, the more likely that images of people having fun and enjoying each others' company will affect your mood.

Scrolling through apps like Facebook and Instagram can also produce fears about life accomplishments and fitting in beyond the social sphere. Think back to Syed who didn't do as well as his friend Ali in the science exam. As Syed scrolls through his Facebook feed after school, he sees a post about a group of students from his year who have been nominated to participate in a state science competition. He stares at the image on his screen; there is Ali, together with the other children who no doubt all got As in their exams, smiling proudly. The more Syed looks at the photo, the more miserable he feels.

Adolescents experience FoMO when they follow influencers who market lifestyle and wellbeing products to vast audiences as much as they do following their friends, both actual and virtual. The higher their FoMO, the more these alluring posts can lead them to feel worse about themselves and anxious about realising their own hopes in life. The real 'influence' of these social media stars and celebrities may ultimately lie in their effect on the wellbeing of their followers, and it might not be good news.

The trouble is that social media can start a feedback loop that spirals the user further and further down a rabbit hole of increasingly low self-esteem. One study shows that adolescents who are depressed use social media more than their less depressed peers. They also tend to compare themselves more with others and seek feedback more often to try to form a connection, which can make them feel worse if it does not eventuate. Adolescent boys have been shown to do this even more than girls.

Using technology and social media to show yourself and your life to others and strengthen a feeling of belonging can work for some people, particularly those with strong social skills to begin with. But, particularly for vulnerable teens, using social media can increase anxiety when mindless scrolling takes what can be an innocuous, mildly distracting activity into the realm of bad feelings and even distress.

What is the solution? If parents simply say to their child, 'Stop comparing yourself to others' or 'Just stop looking at Instagram and you will feel better' will that work? We are dealing here with an intersection of primitive urges with immature and sensitive minds. Handling the emotional repercussions of envy and FoMO is often beyond our children's capacity when their efforts to establish their self-worth and connect with others are played out publicly on social media platforms.

Don't despair. We discuss ways to help your child manage these feelings in Part B. Now we look at two other major contributors to the likelihood that your child will experience anxiety or anxiety-like symptoms: your child's confidence and level of self-belief.

CHAPTER 7

Self-regard and anxiety

It's a fine line. You want your child to be confident and motivated, but not so much that they start to become boastful or consumed by a need to do everything 'perfectly'. This chapter is all about negotiating that fine line.

These days the 'self' prefix is important to us. We want our children to have self-esteem and self-determination. But we don't want them to become self-aggrandising or so self-deprecating that it affects their self-belief. We want our children's thoughts about themselves to be just right, so they walk out confidently into the world without fears or unrealistic expectations holding them back. This chapter looks at the traits that influence whether they achieve that Goldilocks sweet spot or not.

Self-consciousness

Imagine you are heading out to a party where you will see people you know well and some you know only distantly. It's a Sunday afternoon barbeque so you put on a casual dress or shirt and a pair of comfortable, well-worn

Converse sneakers. Once you get there, you see that nearly everyone else is better dressed than you – some in linen or silk, some in expensive-looking loafers or colourful summer wedges. Immediately you feel ill at ease.

You mingle and make polite conversation, but you can't stop thinking that the person you are talking to – heck, even people across the room – are noticing your comparatively scruffy outfit. And you can't help but focus on your belief that they are all thinking you are underdressed.

Or imagine you arrive at the same party in a more polished outfit. You clock that everyone else is dressed similarly (that's a win!) and you settle into casual conversation with people. But when speaking to a group on the deck, you make a comment that sounded funny in your mind but falls flat when you say it. The conversation continues, but you ruminate on what you just said. Even the next day, you are still reflecting on your foolishness, and that people are likely to think badly of you.

Or picture that it's a lovely day and you head to the beach. You see a busy beachside coffee cart, order a flat white and get out your phone to pay. You tap it against the eftpos reader and start to walk away. But you go only a few steps before you hear the barista say firmly, 'That payment didn't go through. You'll need to do it again!' Your heart sinks as you think they will automatically assume you were trying not to pay. You slink back, complete the payment and skulk away. Time stands still until your name is called, and you grab your coffee and exit quickly. On your way your mind keeps saying, 'They think I tried to cheat them.' You vow never to go back, convinced they will forever think of you as a would-be coffee thief.

These scenarios are all experiences of anxiety and fear about what others think of you. Of course, they would feel awful. But . . .

These situations might also bring you some faint comfort. Each one puts you front and centre of everyone else's thoughts. In the scenario where you feel underdressed, you believe that everyone is focused on you and thinking about your outfit more than connecting with their friends. In the situation where your comment falls flat, you are convinced that not only do others notice what you think is an off comment, but they will also continue to dwell on your faux pas. Even though it is one of many comments people make in conversation through the afternoon, you think your contribution will stick in people's minds from that point on. And in the interaction at the coffee cart, you remain convinced that of the hundreds of customers the barista sees that day, your face stands out and is now indelibly printed in their mind.

While all these scenarios feel upsetting to you, they are also absorbing because you see yourself as the object of everyone else's attention, and that is rather self-indulgent.

Of course, it would be better if people kept thinking of you for good reasons. It would be wonderful if they couldn't help but focus on and continue to recall your perfectly put-together outfit, or that your comment was the most hilarious observation they heard all afternoon, or how you reacted so generously in that moment you went back to pay for your coffee. But whatever the reason, if you think people were still thinking about you in the minutes, hours or days after an event, it borders on egotism, doesn't it? What's the difference between a person thinking that it's their shining presence or their clumsy mistakes that make people continue to think about them? We argue they are different points on the same spectrum.

The scenarios reflect an inadvertent preoccupation with what you are doing and how others react to you at all times. To a certain degree, this is how we naturally observe the world. If we were making movies of our days, we would always be the lead actor. Other people's movies would not be similarly focused on us. But if you think of yourself as the star in every situation, you will never develop a sense of your real place in the world as being one of many. A person whose sole focus is on *me* and *my reaction* to every situation fails to see the big picture where they aren't the centre of everything and everyone else's thoughts. And because you think you stand out, you will likely be far more worried about what you do when all eyes are on you. And if you have any degree of anxiety and you think that everyone is looking at you, your anxious feelings will increase significantly.

There may be good reason for people to continue to think about themselves and dwell on their mistakes. An adult may think this way because of their past experiences. Perhaps their parents were extremely critical and punitive, and this has made them self-conscious. Perhaps their formative friendship years were marred by a group of mean children who poked fun at everything they did, so they have become aware of every faux pas they may make, however minor. Perhaps they work in a cutthroat environment where they feel they are constantly being judged, so have become concerned about their every action and how it is perceived by others. Or perhaps they became very used to the spotlight when they were young. Maybe their parents lavished so much attention on them that they continue to think all eyes are upon them, making judgments, be they positive or negative.

Regardless of the cause, self-consciousness is likely stopping them from relaxing in moments that should be enjoyable and free from any sense of needing to perform or conform to expectations, as well as the anxiety that often accompanies self-focus.

Narcissism

People need to feel broadly good about themselves to wake up and face the day with confidence. But self-regard tips into unhealthy territory when it becomes so high that it adversely affects family, work or social relationships. When people feel this way, we call it narcissism.

It seems every second article shared on social media these days claims someone's ex-partner/family member/manager is a narcissist. Or offers faux psychological advice, such as '10 signs your co-worker is a narcissist'. As with many psychological terms nowadays, the narcissist label is widely overused and misunderstood.

Let's be clear about the difference between healthy self-esteem and narcissism. Healthy self-esteem is based on internal beliefs about oneself that slowly develop as people mature.

> *People with healthy self-esteem don't evaluate their worth based on what others think of them.*
> *Nor is their internal sense of value dictated by what has happened in the last five minutes.*

This kind of self-esteem is not dependent on other people's overt approval or regular 'wins', like being picked first for the swimming team or triumphing in family Monopoly games. Healthy self-esteem does not slide up and down; it remains firm despite momentary criticism, disappointment or minor personal blunders.

Narcissism is more than high self-esteem. It is the chronic pursuit of self-affirmation primarily provided by other people. It is making one's own worth highly dependent on other people's obvious approval or winning at everything. A narcissist cannot manage occasional off days when they are not successful. Coming third in a casual barefoot bowling game would be untenable for them. They are unable to accept any less than favourable feedback, such as being given brief constructive criticism on their lifting technique by the instructor in their weights class. They struggle to cope when other people are in the spotlight and would prefer to avoid participating in events like a celebration for a friend's promotion. In their mind, these occasions make them publicly 'less' than others, and they do not tolerate feelings of not being successful or sought after.

Narcissism has two forms. The first, *grandiose narcissism*, is the most well known. It's characterised by attention seeking, arrogance and entitlement. Grandiose narcissists often label themselves with superlatives – the best, the smartest, the most successful – and can think of themselves as geniuses. Even though their belief is not substantiated by reality or results, they continue to think of themselves this way. Many will often manipulate people into believing in their superiority by using self-promotion and excessive charm to entice others to fawn over them.

The other form, *vulnerable narcissism*, is less well known. Vulnerable narcissists have extremely high self-doubt about their performance and are exceedingly sensitive to situations where they believe their failings will be exposed. They often appear shy, insecure and lacking in social skills.

Many will read that definition and think it sounds like anxiety. But these narcissists *actually expect* to do very well and desire extremely positive feedback. When it does not come, their confidence plummets.

A person with healthy self-belief might enter an art competition and be a little nervous about putting their work on show. But they would not avoid it: they know their self-esteem is sufficient for them to be content with any outcome, whether they come first, second or even last. Their sense of achievement might be more dependent on enjoying the experience of creating the art or facing the challenge of submitting their work for appraisal, than how they are judged by others. The satisfaction of their accomplishments is likely to be reward enough for them, and their self-esteem will stay healthy whether they win or not. When asked about the outcome by friends, they would not be ashamed of being unplaced in the competition because they don't think it would disrupt their social standing.

A grandiose narcissist might submit expecting to win. If, despite their predictions, they do not do well, it will be crushing for them, but their ego will come to their rescue with some quick cognitive distortions. To feel better about themself, they might believe that the judges weren't clever enough to see the prodigious talent of their entry. They might let everyone know this opinion as if it were fact, to ensure that other people continue to think of them as extraordinary.

A vulnerable narcissist would be terrified of entering anything where they risked the result not being the win they think they should receive. So they avoid any sort of competition, and catastrophise the potential experience as being unbearable.

What is interesting about vulnerable narcissists is that when they express such trepidation, often with tears and fears, many of the people around them will step in and reassure them. This is particularly true if the narcissist is a child and the competition is something they can't avoid, such as needing to submit a piece for assessment in Year 9 Art. In this instance, they might express great hesitation and fear about the work. Friends and family will tell them winning is not everything, and that they are sure that they will do well.

But in the mind of a vulnerable narcissist, 'doing well' is not enough. Winning is the only acceptable result. And while they might appear noticeably upset and fearful about entering their work for assessment, there is an underlying vanity and conceit in their need to triumph, similar to that of the grandiose narcissist but expressed in pitiable ways. With such high expectations of their performance, you can see why they might not want to submit at all or try to obtain parental permission to avoid it, so they can dodge the potential humiliation of not being awarded the top mark.

Children with vulnerable narcissism often lean heavily on their parents to help them as another strategy to ensure success. However, because of their secret expectations to excel, these children can also be highly critical of a parent's assistance if they see their parent's attempts are unlikely to get them to the standard they think they deserve. This might involve yelling and storming off as the parent attempts to meet their child's expectations. Or there may be a lot of parental cheering required for the child to even start to put paint to paper.

Many parents believe this scenario is caused by their child's anxiety. This makes sense because the child is likely to be catastrophising the outcome, using highly emotional statements such as, 'I'm going to look like a loser!' The child has expressed great fear of starting the art assignment, and the parent has judged this reaction on the face of it, believing their child's low self-esteem and fear of not being good enough have caused their angst. But the nuance that is missed in this situation is that the child does not believe they are hopeless: they secretly think they are great and are afraid they now risk being judged as 'not great'.

Unfortunately, the subtlety of the true underlying causes here means not many parents will pick up the real problem. A complicating factor is that their beloved child is crying, and parents are less likely to think critically of their offspring in that emotional moment. And if the child is being inappropriately critical of their attempts to help, a parent is likely to blame this poor behaviour on the child's anxiety, rather than the possibility that it reflects some arrogance and vanity in their child. As often happens, love and empathy give us blinkers on the bigger picture.

Why do people become grandiosely or vulnerably narcissistic? The cliché is the abandoned child, unloved by their parents and overcompensating in adulthood with extreme self-love. Recently, however, other parenting approaches have been associated with young adults becoming narcissistic. One is indulgent parenting, when parents give their children abundant affection but don't have sufficient behavioural boundaries for them. Another is when parents consistently demand that their child perform to the parents' high standards, rather than to the child's internally developed standards. This can cause the child to become used to looking to other people's judgements rather than their own for their personal sense of worth. This leads to overdependence on others' glowing evaluations to sustain their elevated self-view.

Some psychologists believe recent changes in parenting may have given rise to an increase in narcissism, be it grandiose or vulnerable. American research particularly shows the trend. Dr Jean Twenge, an expert in the field, found that college students in the 2000s were significantly more narcissistic than students from the 80s and 90s, and that there has been a particularly steep increase in more recent years. She has noted that research in as early as 2009 showed that two out of three students agreed that their generation was more narcissistic than their predecessors.

We live in an age when we have raised generations of children to think that they are very, very important. That's not terrible – and certainly better than raising them to think they are completely unimportant. But we believe there is a drawback to this. We often tell children how central they are to everything the family does and everything they are a part of, either explicitly or through our constant consideration and attention. We tell our child how much their singing stands out in their choir group, we call out praise or commentary only to them on the sports field, and the photos we take of the book week parade are close-ups of our child only, excluding the rest of the class. These actions are expressions of love, but they also encourage the child to believe that their participation in any activity is conspicuous, and that any missteps or blunders they make will be as noteworthy as their successes.

Likewise, when we repeatedly tell a child they are remarkably clever / talented / good looking – in short, amazing – we inadvertently set them up to expect to *be* amazing. All the time. Such praise can lead them to expect to continuously perform at an extremely high standard. When they do not deliver the superlative performance they expect of themself, they often react with sensitivity. Their expectations are not limited to their own performance; they may also include the amount of praise others are required to provide for them to feel sufficiently reassured.

> *Children accustomed to constant attention and appreciation become almost like praise junkies, dependent on their regular hits of applause.*

These days children 'perform' much more in their schooling than they ever did. There is so much more deliberately manufactured acclaim and recognition now, and endless evaluative commentary. Student-of-the-week awards sometimes start in day care. We have sat in school auditoriums where there were almost more students on stage receiving principal's awards than in the audience. We have witnessed secondary students receive their end-of-year certificates as if the scholastic year were a race, with students deliberately placed in order from lowest achieving to highest.

A child's expectation of applause and regular celebration is not unreasonable today, particularly when praise is often so effusive. And it is understandable for children to think their day-to-day lives are being publicly scrutinised when judgement is offered so frequently. This will give children awful crashes of mood if the main source of their self-esteem in the past – accomplishment and acclaim – is withdrawn from their lives.

The understanding of the bell curve – that some children are better at certain things than others, some are worse, and the majority are average – has been replaced by a belief or expectation that every child can get an A in everything. Many parents mistakenly believe that confidence is only gained through good results, rather than understanding that a child can build confidence from all kinds of results as long as they have tried their best and learned from their mistakes.

Today, a cognitive assessment is almost seen as de rigueur for a child to end up getting that A they 'deserve' or need, regardless of their underlying ability. Teachers mark so many drafts of essays that the idea that students can and should produce a 'perfect' essay has taken hold. And children understandably think everyone can get an A if they put in the work required when this is what their parents have told them. Consequently, some children believe they deserve outstanding results and are not keen to disappoint their own or their parents' expectations. Professor Carol Dweck has shown that when a child is praised for their intelligence, they often start to attempt less difficult schoolwork, because doing only work they find easy will allow them to keep their perfect record. Praising their efforts rather than their results encourages them to keep trying a range of tasks to continue to prove they are hard workers.

Use of social media – essentially a vehicle of self-presentation and performance – is also likely to have contributed to the recent increase in high personal expectations and narcissism. Many parents may inadvertently reinforce the performative nature of a child's daily life starting with the first Instagram post of the elaborate gender reveal through to the constant flow of updates for their child's every outing, sports match and school occasion – even what they wear on non-uniform days.

The idea that children can believe they are constantly performing their lives for others is understandable in the social media age.

Research has shown a link between narcissism and social platform use, particularly in the number of selfies taken by adolescents and the number of friends they have on social media. It's not yet known whether social media use influences narcissism or vice versa. But we can't help but think that constantly perfecting one's selfies mirrors the mythological Narcissus's obsession with himself as he stares at his reflection in the lake.

Perfectionism

Like narcissism, perfectionism is a rather overused term today which has started to lose its precise psychological meaning.

Perfectionism is the expectation or desire to be flawless – in other words, to never make mistakes. Psychologists are divided on whether perfectionism can be healthy in any way, or whether it is always harmful. Many believe there is an adaptive form of perfectionism where we hold high standards for ourselves, yet cope when we make human errors and fail to deliver the level of performance we would have liked. This is considered positive because it helps us work hard but doesn't cripple us with fears about not being perfect, nor leave us with excessive personal recriminations for making errors.

Maladaptive perfectionism – the 'bad' sort – is accompanied by acute internal distress. It is characterised by constant excessive self-expectations that go above what a person can perform. The failure to accomplish these expectations leads to extreme personal disappointment. People who place unrelenting pressure on themselves will ultimately experience poor wellbeing, anxiety and depression.

Psychologists have identified three types of perfectionism. People who are *self-oriented perfectionists* are internally motivated to never make mistakes. They are usually highly self-critical of their failure to live up to their self-imposed personal standards. *Other-oriented perfectionists* hold extremely high expectations of other people and are very critical when those others fail to live up to them. *Socially prescribed perfectionists* believe that others expect them to be perfect. These types are not mutually exclusive: it's possible for a person to experience a combination of all three.

Perfectionism in children and young adults appears to be on the rise. American, Canadian and British research shows that levels of perfectionism in college students – particularly socially prescribed perfectionism – are currently well above the typical levels of 25 years ago. Australian research shows that in 2015, as many as three in ten students had maladaptive perfectionism.

Researchers don't know exactly why this is happening, but many suspect this increase is linked to the way many people now view their personal worth as a reflection of their achievements (at school, university or work) instead of their values and skills. The neoliberal notion that the 'perfect' life is available to anyone who tries hard enough has become popular today. When a person is seen to be successful through obvious means – their school results, salary, size of house – this is regarded as a reflection of their effort, social standing and importance, which in turn is taken as a sign that the person is winning the 'race' of life and therefore worthy of admiration.

This way of thinking has shifted the prevailing view of education. The process of learning and developing skills is now less valued than the achievement of good results. Top marks are seen as evidence of success, and a belief has arisen that all children can and should be at the top of the class – which is clearly not achievable. Understandably, many parents view themselves as ultimately responsible for their children's successes and failures. They may feel compelled to employ every effort to have their child excel in academic studies, extra-curricular activities and popularity to start them on a sure path to success or otherwise risk leaving them catastrophically behind everyone else.

When coming first or getting 100% are the only markers of 'good enough', you can understand why perfectionism is on the rise. When parents fear their child is not keeping up in the race to succeed, they tend to intervene to correct the situation. As a result, the child may take on the parents' fear of 'mistakes' and can become preoccupied with making potential errors they think will be unacceptable.

The pressure of ensuring students achieve high marks also puts stress on educational institutions. Concerned parents keen to identify potential areas for improvement in their child's academic performance can expect teachers to give regular elaborate feedback. This can result in minor issues becoming needlessly magnified in response to parental urging to identify areas of improvement for their child to work on. Pressure can also emerge from students themselves: some take to frequently emailing their teachers to check they are always exactly on the right track in each assessment piece they attempt.

The intent here is altruistic. Everyone is trying to make sure students do well, but the combination of these actions can set up a feedback loop that puts the child on edge about being perfect rather than allowing them to simply do their best in an unpressured environment.

Ironically, a child's performance can suffer from too much intervention by parents and teachers. When adults intercede too frequently, the child does not develop their skills sufficiently and their fears about completing their work unaided can be justified. Indeed, we suspect that the more a parent is perfectionistic about their parenting performance, the more they act on their own fears and step in to over-help their child. (Just quietly, we suspect perfectionistic teachers may also tend to over-assist their students for the same reason.)

Of course, it may be that a parent's perfectionism acts as a role model for their child, or that their excessively high standards cause a child to become fearful of their parent's reaction and more likely to work extremely hard to avoid provoking the parent's anger or disappointment. But we also suspect that a child's perfectionism might cause a parent to become more alert to and worried whether the child is reaching the high standards they feel they need to achieve, so there may be something of a chicken-and-egg situation happening as well.

Narcissism, perfectionism and anxiety

Many readers will see similarities between anxiety and what we have described as narcissism and perfectionism. Although we know they are linked, at this stage there is no definitive model that clearly outlines the causes, consequences and connections between narcissism, perfectionism and anxiety. Research shows that when we talk about one of these traits, we might also mean another.

Clinically, we have observed children who have been thought to be anxious can be filled with self-doubt, yet also show traits of self-aggrandisement. These children can be difficult company in moments of success or defeat; playing card games with them tends to be exhausting, whether they win or lose. When they win the game, they like to parade their glory and insist everyone takes notice; when they don't win, they may insist others provide comfort and consolation. This victor/victim approach may be complicated by anxiety, narcissism, perfectionism and intense self-focus.

We certainly don't think all cases of anxiety are connected to narcissism or perfectionism. But it's important to point out that sometimes narcissism and perfectionism can look a lot like anxiety, and sometimes narcissism and perfectionism in children contribute to anxious behaviours.

Treatment

To treat people with heightened self-consciousness and fear of making mistakes that others will notice, psychologists guide clients to deliberately make what they see as 'mistakes' to reduce their expectations of themselves and realise that many of the blunders they fear making are not actually serious and simply don't matter. This way they learn that they can calmly live through the experience of making a so-called error. This helps them discover that people around them don't necessarily notice, or if they do, that the moment typically comes and goes quickly without incident.

This part of treatment sometimes involves something of a blow to the ego for the client, particularly if vulnerable narcissistic tendencies are at play. To accept that we are imperfect human beings who are actually quite unimportant – as we all are – is incredibly freeing but can cause discomfort. Unless people are willing to consider a certain level of insignificance for themselves in the big scheme of things, they are likely to cling to the belief that their presence and mistakes are always noted by others. This view will continue to detract from their enjoyment of life but has the flip side of subtly allowing them to feel more important and central to other people's considerations (positive and negative). While problematic, this approach to life can feel familiar and comfortable, which can sometimes be more attractive than making the effort to challenge its validity.

We know the approaches we set out in this book will help, regardless of the cause of your child's anxiety. If you have concerns about contributing factors or whether narcissistic or perfectionist tendencies are relevant to your child's worries, we recommend you obtain a formal, tailored diagnosis from a clinical psychologist to determine the exact nature of your child's distress and the clinician's recommended treatment.

We are almost at Part B, but before we get to solutions, we want to discuss the subtle benefits anxiety can bring. 'Benefits?' we hear you say. 'How on earth could any incarnation of anxiety have benefits?' Read on and we will show you what we mean.

CHAPTER 8

The subtle benefits of anxiety

There's no question that anxiety can detract from our enjoyment of life and reduce our potential. But you may be surprised to learn that it can bring some comforts as well as disadvantages. And these underlying benefits risk reducing our ability or readiness to do the hard work of overcoming anxiety.

Few things in life are purely good or bad. Most happy outcomes carry some costs, and most troubles have a silver lining if we look hard enough. This holds true for the ways our minds work. If we look deeper, traits we often think of as negative usually have some positives as well. Psychologists call these benefits *secondary gains*.

Secondary gains form part of the experience of many health conditions. A person who has broken their leg endures pain and inconvenience, but they may also be relieved of home and work responsibilities, plus receive special attention from their family and friends. A person who wants to overcome anorexia may also be fearful of relinquishing the sense of personal control the eating disorder has given them through the exercise of extreme self-restraint. Someone in couple therapy might be keen to develop a better relationship with their partner but reluctant to work toward this if it involves acknowledging their contribution to the couple's problems.

One of the impediments to change is the thought of change itself. Many people find it easier to keep living their lives exactly as they are, even if the way things are isn't so great. Many feel anxious when they think about the process of change even though its purpose is to improve their lives. The comfort of maintaining the status quo is a secondary gain.

> *To quote W H Auden:*
> *'We would rather be ruined than changed.'*

Secondary gains are often deep rooted and picked up only through close examination and extensive reflection. Consider the example of Sarah, who feels she needs to spend most of her weekends catching up on emails and finishing projects, although her workplace doesn't require this level of commitment. Sarah's secondary gain – feeling constantly busy and needed – offsets the discomfort of acknowledging her loneliness away from work and the effort it would take to re-establish her social life. She would rather keep going the way she is than start the hard work of reconnecting with her old friends and making new ones, so she resists overcoming her unhealthy work habits even though they leave her feeling isolated and miserable.

Secondary gains from anxiety

Recognising and understanding the beliefs and behaviours that deliver anxiety's secondary gains are important steps toward overcoming them. Let's examine some of the unexpected silver linings of the dark cloud of anxiety.

Preparedness through catastrophising

Anxious people tend to anticipate difficulties and catastrophise. When your partner is running late on Friday evening, your mind runs the gamut of possible scenarios: they are enjoying an after-work drink and have forgotten your dinner reservation, you will be late and your table will have been given to someone else, you will be charged a no-show fee, you will be banned from your favourite restaurant . . . Now you feel stressed, of course. But there is a payoff for you when anxiety prompts you to imagine this range of negative outcomes.

Let's look back to your dating days to understand the impulse to catastrophise. Imagine your romantic interest of a couple of months texts you and asks you to meet them for lunch tomorrow. 'That's odd,' you think. 'We've never gone out to lunch before. Why the formality?' This brings on a host of uncomfortable guesses about what is going to happen during the meal. You predict the worst possible scenario: 'Oh no, they're going to dump me.' You mull over all the silly things you have said and done in the last few weeks. You become convinced that the relationship is about to be over, and you'll be abruptly single again.

You feel so uneasy, you call a friend – perhaps a few friends – to talk through your fears and examine every piece of evidence with them. They try to calm and reassure you: they are sure it will be okay – it's obvious your partner is besotted with you. When you insist that you *just know* they are going to break up with you, your single friends try to make you feel better by painting a vivid picture of the wonderful times you will have together as singletons again.

You feel reassured after some uplifting phone calls and messages, but once this brief respite is over, you resume your state of nervous dread. The next day, you fearfully turn up to meet your partner. Amazingly, lunch goes without incident. Indeed, over the course of the meal, your partner tells you that a colleague said the restaurant had a great lunch menu and they thought it would be good to try it together.

Relief! All your fears evaporate, and you go from feeling nail bitingly anxious to on top of the world. So why put yourself through all that worry? Why imagine worst-case outcomes worthy of a worry-wart Nostradamus?

For many people, catastrophising has some underlying advantages. Worst-case conjecture can allow us to feel we know what is going to happen. As we said in chapter 1, uncertainty is uncomfortable for many people. Anticipating the worst-case scenario is a way for us to feel prepared for its associated letdown. It lets us think we will not be unduly surprised or taken aback when it happens.

If the worst case did happen, and your partner let you know they wanted to end the relationship, you would undoubtedly feel awful. But . . . there is a teeny, tiny part of you that would also feel relieved that you had prepared for it. You would feel that you knew this would happen and that you anticipated it exactly by thinking about it continually. Being 'right' allows you to feel in control and gives you a sense that you are able to see what is going to transpire.

Even when you share the bad news with your friend, you'll be able to claim predictive skill through your tears: 'I knew they were going to dump me.' Now you feel confident of accurately forecasting any peaks of drama and disaster looming ahead. It's a blessed feeling of future surety – a false one – but a powerful one.

A sense of control from satisfying schemas

For some people, their prediction of doom seems inevitable because it fits with the particular view they have of themselves, their interactions with the world and their understanding of how best to protect themselves in those interactions.

Psychologists call these belief systems *schemas*. They are unique patterns of thought that give rise to strong feelings, mostly based on people's past experiences, which can entrench them in unhelpful behaviour. For example, a person whose parents were cold and unloving might come to view themself as unlovable or unworthy of love. It's not a positive feeling, but over time, a schema like this becomes predictive and provides a way for them to shortcut their experiences and feel they know how to protect themself against what they expect will inevitably transpire. Seeing a co-worker who fails to acknowledge them fits in perfectly to their schema of being unlovable, rather than what it might have been, which is that the co-worker didn't see them or was simply preoccupied with their thoughts.

If a person subconsciously predicts that they will be ignored and then is actually ignored, the experience can be oddly comfortable for them. That's because their accurate prediction gives them a misguided sense of mastery in their life. They might choose to avoid certain experiences because they feel they know what will happen, such as not asking a potential friend for coffee, because they foresee rejection.

Of course, people with fully formed schemas will frequently come across conflicting evidence, but they will often distort this to fit their established view. Even when they weren't dumped by their partner at lunch, they may continue to think, 'Well, not today . . . but it will happen . . . and maybe soon.'

It is possible to turn this thinking around, but it's tough work. In treatment we find many clients want to hold on to the reassurance of feeling prepared or correct about their self-beliefs and ability to foretell bad things on the horizon. We can teach techniques to overcome this so people don't feel they are always only one step away from disaster, but some are reluctant to let go of the comfort provided by the secondary gains of a sense of control and predictability.

Conversational attention and reassurance

Think back to our imaginary scenario when your partner asked you to lunch. As part of your preparations for the inevitable, you called a friend to discuss your worst fears. That's not unusual. When we face situations we are worried about, we almost always want to talk to someone about it.

Some of us, particularly children and teens, develop a conversational approach that regularly includes the segment 'things I am concerned about today that I want you to listen to or help me with'. Depending on their age, children might seek this solace from their parents or their friends repeatedly.

There's nothing wrong with seeking a parent's or a friend's support in worrying times. In fact, there are more potential problems when we bottle up our fears. Some people don't talk enough about their goals and concerns in life to trusted loved ones. Verbalising can help us gain perspective on priorities and doubts and adjust our efforts accordingly.

On the other hand, some people can begin to seek this support compulsively and form a habit of leaning heavily on others in conversations where they mainly talk about their anxieties and imagined outcomes.

A person can easily receive a lot of conversational attention by regularly talking through their fears.

In addition to attention, these people often receive copious amounts of reassurance from the person or people they speak with. You might have a friend who regularly leans heavily on you by calling with every worrying thought that has entered their head. Those conversations can easily become one-sided and all about them, as you feel you need to reassure them how good they are at their job and that they won't get fired, or that you are sure they will impress in their work presentation.

The trouble is that these people connect with others mostly over their problems. We have worked with families whose entire conversation on the drive to school is focused on everything the child is worried about that day. We have overheard young adults walking around campus on phone calls with their parents talking through every problem they have encountered or anticipate.

In this pattern, a child or adult learns that their anxieties and catastrophised futures get them a lot of attention. Of course, their fears are upsetting, but there is a special kind of comfort when those fears give rise to special time with their parent, friend or partner.

This is more than being a so-called drama queen – and no, we aren't fans of the popular term being so gendered, particularly when we see drama kings too. It's more than talking up wild possibilities to get attention. When someone's fears get too much airplay, they can feel encouraged to rehash their worries to maintain the level of conversational attention and reassurance they desire. Some friendship conversations can become so stuck on the worry topic that you or your friend almost go searching for concerns to discuss. Some parent–child chats might habitually involve the parent deliberately taking the child through the activities of their upcoming day so they may talk through anything they are nervous about in advance.

Benefits don't only occur in the lead-up to worrying events. Recall the scenario where your partner breaks up with you and you call your friend to tell them. The support they give you in response is affirming and wanting it is understandable on your part. But let's delve further into how this works. You get two for the price of one: the conversational attention for what you think might happen, as well as the conversational attention when it does happen.

What if the scenario doesn't play out as you fear, and your partner doesn't break up with you? Often that results in a further conversation with your friend. They are supportive of you when you're concerned, and they also listen to you express your relief when you know how the situation works out – lunch is evidence of your partner's love for you. 'How wonderful is that? They truly care about me!'

Of course, there's nothing wrong with having this type of interaction every now and then. You're distressed and a friend or family member steps in to comfort you. Both action and reaction are completely understandable. The friend would want to support you if the news were bad, and they would want to be happy for you if it were good.

But if this type of exchange happens regularly, it will be helpful for you to change the frequency of indulging in this behaviour by limiting the number of calls you make to friends or family with your concerns and making the conversations you do have more positive. This will allow you to get the support you want but not at the expense of your coping ability or your friends' patience.

Your child's secondary gains from anxiety

Our clinical experience has shown that there are some particular secondary gains for children who experience anxiety.

Immediate soothing

As soon as some parents notice fear in their child, they do pretty much everything in their power to help them overcome that feeling or take it away.

When a parent realises their child is anxious about something, many will comfort the child with physical affection and conversational attention. They might continue this by becoming more involved in the child's daily activities to help them feel stronger, such as holding their hand as they walk into school. Some parents might even offer this support when away from their child – putting loving notes in their lunchbox or checking in with them via text message during the school day.

Parents might reassure the child that they will do well in their upcoming challenge and tell them that nothing will go wrong. This will temporarily make the child feel better; however, it is false reassurance since the parent doesn't actually know they will do well. Some parents might try more realistic advice – telling their child they will cope whatever might happen – but this may not be sufficient for a child who wants to *know* they will do well, and so parents may suggest that the outcome the child wants is the outcome they will likely get.

If a parent attends the feared event, they might act in an especially caring way, continually praising the child to pump up their confidence during the activity. They might shout out words of encouragement from the sidelines during the child's swimming lesson to make sure they are self-assured enough to proceed. Or insist on speaking regularly on the phone to them, in a manner that takes them away from the fun group activities involved in the Year 6 trip to Canberra.

Often, when the child is overly concerned about schoolwork, a parent will offer assistance to help them do well. This might involve writing much of their speech for the debating competition or doing most of the work for their science project. This soothes the child immediately because they think they will do better with their parent's help, particularly when they still truly value their parent's opinions and think they are more often right than wrong. (That very short period in their life!)

Parents might also give their child extra support after day-to-day events. Given the child's fears, the parent might show heightened interest in their child's daily experiences and ask them lots of questions on the way home – more questions than they ask the child's more confident sibling who is also in the car and participated in the same event. There's also a chance that the anxious child might be praised more for the same achievements the robust sibling did quite matter-of-factly.

When parents behave this way, their child might realise that pointing out what they are nervous about gets them much more interest and parental time and effort before, during and following the event. They can learn that expressing any doubt leads to an immediate reward in the form of attention and help.

Avoidance

When faced with their child's anxiety, many parents do more than simply make the child feel better in the moment through reassuring words, affection and assistance. They may try to completely remove their child's concerns. If the child worries about wearing a pair of jeans that aren't cool enough to the school disco, the parent, keen to make them feel more confident, might buy them a whole new outfit to make them feel better. The child may well learn that if they express enough worry about what they have, they can quickly get what they would like to have.

> *Parents of anxious children often seek to reduce*
> *the expectations and demands of normal life*
> *to allay their child's concerns.*

A parent may give permission for their child to avoid doing an activity they fear. Schools tell us that some parents regularly write letters giving reasons as to why their child can't attend the Year 5 camp, or participate in a sports class or the cross-country event, due to unspecified illness, doctor's appointments or family commitments.

And if the child does participate in the activity, parents can still intervene to make sure they avoid the feared outcome that concerns them. They might send an email to ensure their child has specific friends in their cabin because of their expressed fear of not being with their preferred camp group. Or they might agitate for their child to be put in the netball team, even though other children performed better during trials. They might take the extreme measure of stepping in and insisting their child won the swimming race with video 'evidence' they recorded on their phone from the grandstand (yes, schools tell us this actually happens).

Although such interventions represent the care of a loving parent, each action delivers the anxious child a degree of benefit from their expressed worry, sometimes to the extent that their feared outcome is completely removed. In recent years, easily accessed technology has increased the likelihood of these interventions. An anxious child with a phone or laptop can remain in contact with their parent during the school day to delve into feelings, worries, panicky experiences and potential disasters, with the chance that the parent will immediately step in to take away those feelings. This does not benefit the child in the long run.

An essential part of a child's growing up is their willingness to gradually face more demanding challenges.

To eventually become adults, all children must face tougher and tougher activities. But some anxious children get a reprieve, or even a virtual halt, in facing increasingly difficult challenges. They detect that by expressing fear, they might not need to step up to the hard things of life, or they may be able to do less of them due to their parent's help. They pick up that the more they express fear about the upcoming school trip or swimming carnival, the greater the chance their parent will make an excuse so they can stay home instead.

Missing school

The incidence of children refusing to attend school is increasing. As clinical psychologists, we find there are two main ways students can miss or refuse to attend school.

The first is by pleading to stay home in the morning or the night before school. Children might tell their parent about school fears, separation anxiety, or sadness or overwhelm. Alternatively, they might have physical symptoms of panic, such as 'funny tummy' or feeling lightheaded – normal responses to temporary discomfort. These symptoms may be catastrophised by the child as indicators of illness.

Children or teens may request a 'mental health day', to overcome school stress like assignment or friendship challenges, anticipation of missing their parent, panic symptoms, boredom or difficulty focusing in class. A child might believe they can't cope with the upcoming school day. Parents, concerned about their child's wellbeing, might agree.

A few days or weeks later, the child may present a carbon copy of the request that got the desired result the first time. The parent now has difficulty in responding differently to insist their child go to school.

Children may use aggression, tantrums or highly emotional statements (like threatening self-harm) about what they will do if their parent insists that they have to attend school. Parents will have difficulty refusing, particularly if they lack confidence or skill to manage such situations. Also, in families where parenting approaches are heavily child centred, children may be more dominant than parents in the home and have more say in what they do.

The other means children take to try to miss school is to make use of their phone or email, if either are accessible. Many parents tell us they frequently receive emotional messages from their child asking to be picked up midway through the school day. These can occur after an argument with a friend, when the child feels excluded from a group, or when panic symptoms arise out of the blue or because of an unexpected difficulty. The child interprets the unpleasant feelings prompted by these experiences as signs of illness. Of course, these could indicate genuine illness, but for some children, symptoms simply represent the temporary discomfort of facing momentary challenge. Some may even describe panic symptoms as a result of finding their schoolwork boring, so their parent will allow them to go home. The child's sense of discomfort may be amplified if they are unused to the feeling of slight boredom or ennui.

Of course, children don't text their parents, 'I'm bored, I need you to come and get me right away.' The typical message is something like, 'I don't feel good' or 'I feel sick / worried / dizzy' which sounds more like panic than boredom. Or the child might say, 'I'm really upset. I can't get through this. Please get me at recess.'

We understand why a parent might drop everything and pick the child up, but this is not helpful.

> *When a parent 'rescues' the child, they deny them the opportunity to realise that when they stay the course, a momentary tricky feeling will go away of its own accord.*

Pushing through boredom or panic symptoms usually happens in conjunction with something else that diverts a child's attention, like an interesting class or a conversation with a different peer. Schools are great places for diverting interactions to occur; allowing a child to come home prematurely won't teach them to overcome and outlast temporary feelings.

Unfortunately, once a pattern of school refusal is established, it's difficult to change. Over time, it easily becomes entrenched, and the child misses more and more schooling. This brings them huge secondary gains beyond the relief of not having to face tricky or boring moments in the school day. The main advantage for the child is that the parent is not able to provide a similar experience at home: they cannot provide the same lessons and expectations of effort, or the peer-group situations. Often, a working parent will allow the child to use devices for their schoolwork while they try to get their job done. Parents who hold out and deny screens often have to deal with their child's emotional responses; it is easy to understand why some parents, faced with unrelenting pressure to meet demands at work and home, relent and allow their child to console or occupy themselves with their favourite screen activity. Of course, this simply maintains the problem. Using devices at home becomes the child's easy alternative to tolerating and learning to cope with temporary difficulty, discomfort or boredom at school.

The parent who agrees to their child's request to pick them up from school rewards them initially with conversational attention and then again by allowing them their absorbing screen-based activities at home. Children who spend more time on screens become less able to calm themselves without their devices.

The more a child is offered the chance to be at home, the less they will learn the skills needed to face temporary challenge, which makes future difficulty even more challenging for them. Often the child will dwell on any minor feelings, which can exaggerate their real fears of facing situations they predict will be difficult or attempting activities they may not master straight away. A child who feels ambivalent about going to school may amplify their genuine feelings to demonstrate distress or desperation about the day ahead. And parents, made fearful by their child's extreme emotional response, feel they almost have no option but to keep them at home. This can become a vicious cycle.

We are seeing an epidemic of school refusal right now. We believe this is because parents offer staying home as a viable alternative to attending school. Taking 'mental health days' is becoming normalised, as if children need regular reprieve from attending school beyond weekends and holidays. It's a slippery slope from an isolated occasion to multiple days off; many children slide down it to a point where their family seriously considers schooling at home.

Being in charge

Sometimes a child's fear gives them a position of power in the family. Think of the classic childhood fear of getting into an elevator. This often means one parent goes to the trouble of leaving the rest of the family and walking up sets of stairs with the child who is reluctant to use the lift. But there are benefits for the child. They get some special alone time with their parent and are treated a little more importantly than the other family members who are happy to take the lift.

Anxious children can gain influence over the family schedule in this way. They might be able to say who gets dropped off at their school first, or where they sit in the car. Parents might ask a more robust child to acquiesce with their sensitive sibling's requests or demands to let them press the walk button at pedestrian crossings, sit in the padded booth seat when they go to a café, or hold the dog's lead on their afternoon walk. Often parents do this to keep the peace; an easier-going sibling is likely to accept the other's preference with little fuss.

While siblings of anxious children might appear to receive less attention, they also benefit by learning to go with the flow. Given that life is somewhat unpredictable and doesn't always go our way, this is a useful lesson for them. Sometimes they are also rewarded by their parents telling them how great they are for helping their sister or brother, or how much the parent appreciates their uncomplaining nature. This kind of approval may further develop the child's laidback nature: a looping effect can occur where children feel encouraged over time to exhibit more of the traits for which they are given most attention.

Your child's secondary gains from therapy

If your child is diagnosed with anxiety, treatment with a therapist should assist them to overcome it. However, it's important to be aware that therapy can bring its own set of secondary gains, which can leave children less willing to change. This is particularly true if therapy is more focused on immediate good feelings than long-term good feelings.

Immediate relief

For a child, the act of simply talking over all the things that trouble them and having the therapist reassure them with empathetic or sympathetic statements often feels comforting. It can feel freeing to talk about how nervous they are about their exams, why their rowing schedule is making them too busy, or how losing the weekend argument with their sibling about whose turn it was to take out the bins still rankles, and having the counsellor listen, or even better, side with them. It might also feel good to voice all of the things that have annoyed them about their parents that week or talk through some of their latest friendship tiffs.

This venting feels satisfying, but when put on repeat and used as the primary focus of therapy, it doesn't have any long-term benefit in determining more helpful ways for the child to deal with their anxiety outside the therapy room. What it delivers is secondary gain because the child gets to sit and be listened to . . . endlessly.

'Examining this week's problems' therapy risks a child becoming so comfortable with the therapist and their advice that whenever they encounter anything unsettling or challenging, they are reliant on the therapist for counsel. This potentially stops them from seeking advice from other respected people in their life.

They may also come to value the assurance of discretion and privacy in the therapy room to the degree that they no longer believe in their own ability to find a safe space outside a therapeutic relationship. Therapy can become a weekly or fortnightly review of worries about the past and the future, similar to what someone might say when talking through their week with a friend over a drink on Friday night, although the conversation is limited to recounting their problems with no need to listen to the friend at all.

> *Rehashing this week or fortnight's problems*
> *is not the purpose of therapy. This approach can derail*
> *a child's readiness to overcome their anxiety.*

The child may sense that if they learn to apply proven techniques to overcome their anxiety, they won't need to see their therapist and so risk losing a relationship they have come to rely on. They may prefer to continually see a therapist rather than undertake a challenging treatment process, even though this will leave them feeling much better in the long term without the need for regular therapeutic sessions.

Effective therapy helps children create social networks by encouraging them to join groups, developing their ability to discern who will and who will not make worthwhile friends, and growing their confidence to speak up in a classroom and initiate conversations with a range of people in their lives, including others in their sports team or who walk to the train station after school. Actions like these are often difficult for anxious children; good therapy will help them gradually develop these skills and become socially confident and supported without overly relying on the social support of a therapist.

Therapy can also provide reprieve – when a therapist takes away a concern that has been weighing on a child or causing them distress – as a form of short-term relief. Therapists may provide a psychological reason for why a distressed university student cannot get their assignment in on time and needs to be granted an extension until they are ready to do it. For school students, a psychologist may clinically assess a child's situation and formally ask their school to allow the child to miss school camp or attend only if in a camp group with their preferred friends, or ask a teacher to allow a child to do their oral presentation individually during lunchtime rather than in class.

Sometimes reprieve is essential. For example, if a student has just lost a beloved family member, of course they can't get their assignment done and a therapist's note is warranted. But there is a point where therapist-sanctioned removal of challenge has a secondary gain for the child who gets to delay or avoid a worrisome activity.

Therapy is sometimes initiated to enable reprieve. Some parents take their child to a psychologist to get a diagnosis of an anxiety disorder that they can present to the school. They might see this as a way of enabling the child to not face something challenging for them – fears about doing a school talk, being in class without their best friend or being placed with their less-preferred teacher. Occasionally we have heard that once the diagnosis and letter have been given, parents cease appointments with the therapist.

We do not always think that parents are wrong to make these requests. If the child's wellbeing is compromised due to extreme fear of going to the camp or talking in front of the class, a letter may well be warranted. But that letter must always be accompanied by effective treatment – therapy that ideally enables the child to attend the next school camp or do the next oral presentation to the class.

Without that therapy, some children want to hang on to the benefits of the original diagnosis. If seeing a psychologist gives them the initial advantage of not having to face what they fear, it's easy to see why children or teens might decline the chance to let go of it and resist doing the therapeutic work involved in overcoming their anxiety. Some prefer to stay focused on their problems to keep the reprieves coming, rather than move to solutions.

It is essential for therapy to teach techniques
that allow children and teens to face the typical challenges of life.

The university student needs to learn ways to become more organised, or to not allow their perfectionism to overwhelm them when writing their assignments, or be able to put other minor concerns to the side and do what is required to complete the requirements of their degree. The school student needs to learn techniques to be able to participate in school camp, answer questions in class or cope with constructive criticism. They need to learn they can make new friends, solve minor friendship squabbles, and cope with a firm but fair teacher. These are all life skills they will draw on when they leave school and university and go into the world of work, where other challenges will emerge.

If opting out is presented as an end in itself, the secondary gains of staying the way they are may be so great that developing essential coping skills is the student's less preferred alternative. Because of this risk, therapists should give this type of reprieve sparingly. It is far better to quickly move on to therapeutic techniques, so the child or teen is able to climb out of the hole of their anxiety, face whatever they fear, and live the full life they deserve.

Longer-term relief

Longer-term relief is achieved when a child does the work that will ultimately resolve their anxiety. This can feel uncomfortable in the early days because it involves learning to sit with difficult feelings, challenging long-held beliefs, and slowly facing feared activities and learning they will cope. To do this, a child needs a high level of personal motivation because most of these activities happen outside the treatment room while meeting the demands of home and school.

Some children and teens resist moving toward improvement in this way. They may subtly bring up more and more problems in their week or month to put off the tough stuff and return to immediately feel-good, chat-only therapy. They might also continue to ask the therapist to justify extensions on their assignments and provide excuses for them to avoid challenges they think are beyond them.

Students are usually quick to pick up that a therapist is more about change than chat. Some children leave the therapy room after the therapist starts mentioning 'homework' and tell their parents they no longer 'like' the therapist. We believe this is often because the child sees that the therapist intends to have them confront their concerns when they mistakenly believe they are better to stay stuck in their patterns of avoidance.

Some therapists continue with the immediately feel-good stuff because it provokes less pushback and the child continues to 'like' them and their treatment. But unless there are complicating factors such as attention deficit disorder, autism, trauma, problematic gaming or addiction, which require longer therapy, we think the harder work of facing anxiety triggers should be adopted as soon as possible so that improvement can happen relatively quickly. This will be better for everyone concerned because ultimately the benefits of overcoming anxiety far outweigh the temporary costs of momentary difficulty.

We believe that good anxiety therapy specifies goals and the means for a child to reach those goals in a reasonable time. There are no psychological treatments for straightforward anxiety that cannot be taught in a short period and then implemented. Professor Gavin Andrews, anxiety expert at the School of Psychiatry, University of New South Wales, suggests that if therapy does not produce any improvement in your child in 30 days, you should go back to your general practitioner for a recommendation to see another professional.

It's important to note that improvement is dependent on children and teens doing the homework set by the therapist between appointments to help them face their anxiety triggers. If they don't, therapy is not cost effective and risks further entrenching their own and their family's beliefs that their anxiety is unresolvable and that they need to continually receive psychological help.

We are not suggesting that mental health professionals have nefarious reasons to keep children or adults feeling anxious via ineffective techniques. And we do believe that sometimes treatment takes a little longer because the client needs to address their lack of motivation to change or other complicating factors like unexpected events, addiction or the illness of another family member. But for the majority, treatment should focus on solving concerns, motivating the client to change their approach to life and start producing noticeable improvement for them within four to five sessions.

The irony is that if therapy does not effectively assist a child to overcome their anxiety, more therapy will be needed. The child, overwhelmed by difficult feelings when faced with day-to-day uncertainty or situations where they lack the skills to face their challenges, will request to see their psychologist more often. And their parent, seeing their child cope poorly with everyday challenges, will try to have their child see a mental health professional regularly. But if treatment does not actively work toward long-term relief, more sessions will not be effective.

*Getting out of a therapy room
and into the richness of life
is the purpose of psychological treatment.*

Tertiary gains from anxiety

People close to someone affected by a condition like anxiety can also derive subtle benefits from the situation. The partner of someone who is injured can feel needed, even indispensable, when their help is required. They might enjoy this feeling so much that the extent of their assistance compromises their partner's ability to recover and regain their independence.

Such benefits are known as *tertiary gains* – the benefits someone receives from another person's problem or condition. Secondary gains often mix with tertiary gains to form a mutually 'beneficial' situation for all involved.

Tertiary gains are often thought of as more deliberate than secondary gains and accompanied by self-serving or even mean intentions. People sometimes think of tertiary gain in terms of Munchausen syndrome by proxy, where a parent deliberately makes their child sick to get attention or special considerations.

We are talking here about tertiary gain in a much kinder way. We believe that most people have broadly good intentions when it comes to someone experiencing distress. Their noble goals prompt them to try to help the person who is suffering. And their caring actions are often highly satisfying and applauded by others.

But sometimes those same actions have unintended negative consequences if they don't encourage the receiver to get better. Psychologists call this *pathological altruism* – any action where the intention is good, but the outcome is not helpful or harmful. The partner of a chronic pain patient who makes cups of tea, fluffs pillows and does all the domestic chores for their loved one as an act of kindness removes the need for the partner to do their own tea making, pillow fluffing and share of the chores. As a result, the patient is likely to become more dependent on their partner and see themself as less capable of doing things they might otherwise be able to do, despite their pain. What appears to be mutually rewarding can insidiously impair the person it is meant to help.

By harming the receiver, this behaviour can disadvantage the giver as well. The two could be involved in more positive activity, like going for walks in the park or heading off on that indefinitely postponed holiday to Tasmania. Either would be more satisfying than sitting with fluffed pillows at home, drinking tea. The well-intentioned care seems mutually rewarding but can turn out to be unhelpful all round.

It's not uncommon for people supporting anxious children to experience tertiary gains.

Tertiary gains for parents

One of the most rewarding aspects of parenting is being needed by your child. Sure, this can be the hardest part as well, but when your child needs you and you are able to respond with your presence, affection or assistance, this can produce deep feelings of fulfilment and satisfaction. That's because you love them, you love being in their life, and their needing you keeps the relationship and time together vital for both parties. Indeed, many parents can still recall the sting they felt when their child no longer felt the need to kiss them goodnight, or their heartbreak when their child skipped happily away from them on the first day of school without a backward glance.

As they grow older, children's increasing independence sees them become more comfortable with activities they do on their own or in the company of their peers. But there are situations where parents can retain their indispensable role in their child's life or become needed by them again.

When a child is anxious, they seek their parent's presence often. They feel safe with mum or dad and therefore try to have them around as much as they can and regularly seek their reassurance. They may linger in the car at school drop-off or remain attached to their parent's leg at parties. And as awful as their anxiety is for them, and for their parent to know they feel that way, there are some subtle benefits here for the adults as well.

Their neediness can help some parents feel wanted. A child's anxiety can delay the normal individuation that takes place in the mid- to late-primary years when they start to seek their parents' company less and choose to spend more time with their friends. This is when they typically start to be too cool for school, or roll their eyes at parents' comments, or want to converse with their friends more than with their mum or dad.

Of course, anxiety doesn't completely put off that transition – your anxious child might still do their share of eye rolling and shift their alliance to their friends. But they may also occasionally go back to being more dependent on you, and for many parents that feels reassuring because they feel central to their child's life again.

The degree of benefit the parent receives will depend on how much they like to feel needed. If your child's anxiety causes them to want to spend time with you and seek your counsel, it probably feels positive to you. But if their anxiety means you can't get them out of the car in the morning and makes you late to work every day, there's little benefit in it for you.

> *Most parents experience exasperation*
> *mixed with a tiny degree of satisfaction*
> *when they see they are needed to help manage their child's fears.*

Parents are very quick to point out the tricky side of life with a fearful or sensitive child, but few recognise that there can be some aspects that all parties also enjoy or feel good about to some extent. Unless a parent's tertiary gain is addressed, treatment for the child can become more difficult because when therapy develops the child's independence, the parent can feel less needed by their child.

Tertiary gains for other adults

Just as parents like being needed, so can other adults in a child's life. Imagine you are at a child's birthday party and one child stays with the adults who are preparing the food. This is not unusual: anxious kids often hang out in the kitchen at a party, and many of their parents will explain this is because their child is shy and lacks confidence to go out and play with the group. And that might be true.

But there are also subtle rewards to be found in that kitchen, both for the child and any adults present. The adults are likely to make a fuss of the child – pepper them with conversational questions, offer them the first sausage roll out of the oven, and compliment their sparkly hair clips or their superhero costume. These actions will feel good for the adult, as they are seemingly helping a shy child feel better. Their caring behaviour will also enhance their standing with other adults, who will see them as 'a nice person', and especially to the child's parents, who will appreciate the kindness being shown to their anxious child.

The actions of both child and adult are mutually beneficial, providing secondary gains for the child who scores attention and treats, and tertiary gains for the adult who enhances their social standing as well as their perception of themselves as caring and kind.

Unfortunately, these come at a cost. Staying in the kitchen at parties might feel so much more enjoyable for a child than the trepidation caused by joining in with the other children's activities. It makes sense for them to choose the comfortable option, but this can ultimately hold them back from any desire to head out the kitchen door. The secondary gains for the child and tertiary gains for the caring adults together encourage the situation to recur at the next party.

Tertiary gains for teachers

Teachers are typically in the profession because they care about children and want to help them. Some will be particularly inclined to do an enormous amount of work to support students and want to feel they are assisting them in the best way possible.

Fortuitously, there will also be students who look to their teacher for additional reassurance and approval. These students will appear to need the teacher much more than their confident peers do. They might seek their teacher's attention more regularly or try to charm them by greeting them warmly and hanging around them in class. They might write nice notes – 'Mrs Ryan, you are my favourite teacher' – in a bid to receive additional warmth and special attention. If they are not confident socially, they might seek their teacher's 'friendship' more than that of their peers, and try to chat with the teacher on playground duty, rather than sit with their classmates.

What happens when a teacher who enjoys feeling indispensable meets a student who apparently needs their teacher to be indispensable? Well, Dexter, that's a perfect match. You can understand how some teachers could start to almost prefer the students who over-rely on them and charm them. These students might be more rewarding to teach than their more independent classmates who don't need them so much and don't write fawning notes.

Remember there are always teachers with different personalities and students with different personalities. Most teachers are extremely professional, assess every child's social strengths and weaknesses, and try to ensure their social skills are age-appropriate and fittingly developed. They might gently prompt anxious children to be more robust and encourage overly dominant children to become more capable of listening and less reliant on always getting their way.

But there will be some teachers whose assistance style is more about care and comfort than gentle improvement. These teachers risk helping students too much and may offer to assist anxious students before they even ask for help or give them more reassurance than their peers.

Some teachers might even agree to spend time with socially anxious students at lunchtimes for them to gain a sense of connection, rather than encouraging them to form more appropriate relationships with peers. The problem here is that these children, who have the capacity to make friendships and learn better social skills, may become disinclined to make the effort to mix with their peers because the teacher effectively provides them with easy social interaction in the guise of care. And so the subtle benefits of mutual neediness and dependence continue.

Teachers can also be drawn into regular check-ins with parents regarding a student's wellbeing and progress. Some parents feel that alerting a teacher to their child's anxiety gives them permission to frequently email the teacher to ask for additional information about homework or assignment requirements and reassurance about how their child is managing in class. When the teacher engages with these requests, neither the child nor their parent learns that the student needs to build the skills to listen in class and write down their responsibilities. If they don't step up and do this, they won't learn to cope with the doubts and feelings of uncertainty arising from their lack of attention. Nor will they experience the consequences of their disorganisation by facing the penalty for failing to complete the correct homework because they failed to write down what was required. Parental emails to the child's teacher might stop the consequence for the child and stop the child's growth as well.

Some parents also contact teachers at the slightest hint of a child's friendship difficulties, requesting they 'see if it can be sorted out'. It's understandable for the parent to want their child's quarrel to be resolved, but this approach doesn't teach the child how to cope with the minor ups and downs of friendship.

There's nothing wrong with teachers providing additional reassurance, care and assistance to students when necessary. But in our experience some teachers go over the top in this endeavour because it feels so satisfying for them. Judith, an ex-teacher, refers to these teachers as *treacle teachers* because they emphasise the caring elements of teaching over encouraging children to slowly mature and become more independent in their learning.

We are not saying that students don't need any assistance and should be left to manage entirely on their own. Students need some scaffolding when they are beginning to develop their skill set, particularly those with learning difficulties. But it is critical that much of this scaffolding is gradually dismantled as students become capable of doing more for themselves. If their additional support is not slowly removed, receiving more assistance than they need risks becoming an ongoing secondary gain for the student. Feeling indispensable to their students also risks becoming a tertiary gain for the teacher.

The importance we place on good relationships between teachers and students these days can make it more difficult to relinquish that scaffolding. We know there are teachers who don't engage in out-of-hours email check-ins and who are prepared to tell parents that their child will be able to sort out their own friendship squabbles. But this can come at a cost; sometimes they are viewed as not caring enough and end up as the 'less-preferred' teacher. You only need to glance over social media to see the types of teachers who are most valued there. Those who send home regular notes of praise to students or answer an email from a parent or student any time of day or night are seen as the 'good' ones. And teachers who act like friends to their pupils are often seen as 'more likeable' than those who don't.

*The false dichotomy – nice or not nice –
doesn't do teachers or their students any favours.*

You can see why some teachers feel encouraged to go over the top with their reassurance, particularly if parents request this treatment. Teachers risk being called out on WhatsApp parent groups if they are not willing to mark yet another draft or make themselves permanently available out of school hours to answer emails. Here the underlying reward for teachers might not be about feeling needed and loved by students, but rather not getting criticised by a social media mob for requiring students to step up to age-appropriate challenges and encouraging their parents to let them do this.

Unfortunately, the more help and reassurance anxious children are given by parents and teachers, the more they will think they need them. In the long run, this approach chips away at a child's desire and capability to become more independent. Worse, it will make them less capable than their more independent and resilient peers. No adult does this to them deliberately – it emerges from good intentions that inadvertently produce bad outcomes.

Secondary and tertiary gains in school policies and programs

These days all educational professionals are extremely aware of children's mental health, and they work hard to mitigate the incidence of anxiety, depression or any other wellbeing disorder in students. Their objectives are admirable and often genuinely helpful. But there can be pitfalls with school policies and the content of some school programs designed to prevent mental health problems. At the minimum, some of these initiatives or treatments don't address the very issue they claim to treat. At worst, they exacerbate or create more problems. Many are complicated by secondary or tertiary gains which cloud judgement of their true usefulness.

We describe such programs as Seems Like A Good Idea (SLAGI) Programs. Ostensibly they often seem helpful and anyone delivering these initiatives will feel they are making a genuine difference. But some of these good initiatives risk pathological altruism – the intention is good, but the outcome can be unhelpful or even harmful.

We are aware of a program which involves issuing children with a particular coloured card. At any point during a lesson, if they feel overwhelmed, a child can put this card on their desk and be excused from class for as long as they need. This might be helpful for a child who has experienced a recent traumatic event and is slowly becoming comfortable with being back in a classroom. But what does this program do for other children who have open access to such cards? It allows them to leave a situation that feels in any way challenging for them – be it a class quiz, group project work or a tedious task they want to avoid – and spend time in the bathroom (perhaps on their phone) or in the 'wellbeing room' doing something much more pleasant than Maths. These are tempting immediate feel-good benefits to the child.

Similarly, some schools allow children to leave the class they are in at any time to go and see the school counsellor. This also seems helpful, but it risks a student not learning to cope with temporary agitation, boredom or lack of motivation to do what is asked of them in that class. It also allows them to avoid facing and enduring their fears in the moment and eventually overcoming them. The counselling service can also come to be seen as a 'drop in' preference rather than a planned interaction to improve students' coping skills.

Of course, not all students use the school counsellor's services this way, and many schools put measures in place to prevent this. Most school counsellors also ensure their assistance is directed to helping students develop the skills they need to face temporary challenge, rather than delivering immediate rewards in response to some students' momentary whims.

Wellbeing initiatives that focus primarily on improving students' current mood may overlook the need to include helpful but demanding activities designed to improve their future mood. It's important to maintain a healthy scepticism about classroom techniques taught to adolescents to improve their mental health. Multiple studies have shown minimal changes in wellbeing as a result of participation in school classes which provide information about mental health disorders, teach techniques such as reciting positive affirmations, changing negative thought patterns, scheduling and monitoring daily activities and developing better communication skills. While most initiatives seem sensible, relevant and temporarily reassuring, they do not reliably develop students' long-term skills in feeling confident and prepared to face challenge when delivered in large class settings. And if a school's budget and curriculum time are spent on such initiatives, fewer resources and lessons are available for strategies that will be effective for students in the long term.

Some school programs involve use of mood monitoring apps which ask students to regularly log how they are feeling. Asking students to frequently review their feelings may unintentionally encourage them to dwell on their temporary low moods. By relaying students' emotional state to their teachers, these apps may also inadvertently invite students to report problems to secure an immediate appointment with a preferred teacher or counsellor to get help with what might be momentary feelings or to avoid a task they don't want to do. Because the notification to teachers comes from the app rather than from the students themselves, they can come to passively expect help rather than take the initiative to seek it when they need it.

Until initiatives like these have proven long-term positive effects assessed through evidence comparing wellbeing data from schools that have been randomly assigned to use or not use these programs and apps (a randomised control trial or RCT), schools that take them up risk creating temporary good feelings or illusory solutions without genuinely helping (and even potentially harming) the students who participate.

Some research already demonstrates that some mental health programs aren't necessarily helpful. A large study of mindfulness training in schools in the United Kingdom found that while some students found it useful, the adolescents with specific mental health needs did not benefit from the program. Across the 43 schools that implemented the program, the study found that mindfulness practice among the student body was low, and that the additional attention the program drew to upsetting thoughts, feelings and mental health concerns was not useful and was even detrimental for some students with emerging or pre-existing mental health difficulties. The study also showed that delivering the program was no more helpful than the typical wellbeing care provided by the schools involved. It may be that the mindfulness program assessed needs tweaking. It may be that some programs thought to be helpful don't actually help or that they harm. Until further research is in, the reasons why these programs are not more successful are unknown.

We believe that schools have genuinely good intentions with any program they invest time or money in to improve students' wellbeing. Many parents and community members think highly of schools that include the types of programs or apps we've described, and school leadership teams and teachers might take pride in the belief they are taking steps to stem the tide of mental health problems in young people. We assume that the people who develop and provide wellbeing programs and apps also think their products are doing good and likely derive an emotional reward from this. It is possible that this sense of being helpful could trump clearheaded examination of the objective value of such programs, particularly when egos, businesses and livelihoods are at stake.

Until we have clear evidence of the usefulness of these programs, we question schools investing heavily in them. At the very least, we think schools should require independent evidence that these programs deliver noticeable improvements in students' wellbeing, rather than simply accepting providers' intentions, beliefs or anecdotes that purport to justify the significant investment of time and money involved. We also think that, at a minimum, wellbeing speakers should have the sort of professional registration and expertise that proves they are suitably qualified and up to date with research in the field of advice they are giving, rather than relying on personal anecdote as the primary source of their knowledge.

It's important to remember that thinking we are doing the right thing often clouds our ability to question its value. Research has shown that when we judge someone's intentions as good, we are less likely to question the true effectiveness of what they are doing. At times, even psychologists have been blinded to the true value of interventions because of their altruistic intentions. Everyone can be prone to bias and believe that actions done with good intentions are always helpful.

Meaning well can blind us to the true value of our actions.

Seeking immediate comfort and pleasant, warm feelings can allow us to feel good immediately but may encourage us to become complacent and steer us in the wrong direction.

Now that you have read Part A, if you feel you have made some mistakes in how you have tried to help your fearful child, remember you are likely to be in good company. With the best of intentions, we are all prone to making these errors, particularly when popular views encourage us to over-discuss our feelings and over-assist our children through helping them avoid their fears and difficult but age-appropriate challenges. These well-meant actions have not done our children any favours; they have instead produced more fear in children than ever before.

Are you ready to do the tough stuff and encourage your child to do likewise to overcome their anxiety? Great! We are about to let you know what to do because now, we announce . . . (ta da!) . . . Part B, where we give you a ladder of truly effective steps you and your child can take to help them climb out of the hole of their anxiety.

Part B

CHAPTER 9

Climbing out of the anxiety hole

In this section, we go back to basics and show you how to prevent anxious tendencies arising for your child. We also offer solutions for managing your child's anxious feelings and your own anxiety about your child.

First, we give you the important parenting fundamentals that will set your family up well for both the present and the future. The ideas we present will help prevent your child developing anxiety. Even if they have anxious symptoms right now, our approach shows you how to support your child to overcome their fearful feelings and become more capable and confident. These preventative ideas form the solid base that allows your child to reach their potential, even when they are buffeted by gusts of challenge.

We show you how to introduce screens into your home in ways that give you the best chance of making technology an anxiety-free asset for your child. We also present groundwork you can do as a parent to develop your child's social skills so they are ready for the ups and downs of friendships. You will learn how to help them feel more capable and less prone to being overwhelmed by social situations and the typical dramas of childhood and teen friendships.

Then we move on to more targeted strategies for dealing with your child's worries and concerns. We include steps to take in the lead-up to challenging events like their first day of school, and how to help them manage any nerves or concerns. We discuss ways to deal with any tricky problems and fears your child may experience to have them feeling more capable about their strengths when facing and overcoming challenges.

We also offer you ways to manage your own anxieties so that your tendency to worry doesn't affect your own or your child's wellbeing. This helps you as a parent to strike the right balance between caring for your child and encouraging their sense of accountability and eventual maturity.

We are confident these strategies will help prevent or overcome many anxiety-related concerns in children and teens. But if these methods are not enough, you or your child may wish to see a psychologist or other mental health professional. We look at some of the best ways to get the most out of such assistance, together with some Q and As that come up often in our professional work.

Let's start by discussing the five essential skills you can develop in your child so they are ready to face the ups and downs of life.

CHAPTER 10

Getting your child on the right track

These days many parents prioritise two ambitions when raising their children – making them happy and making them successful. Spoiler alert: there are more valuable goals to aim for.

Every parent wants to 'get it right' with their child, and most parents do all they can to make sure their child thrives. But sometimes, parents' best intentions backfire. That's because actions which help children feel good immediately don't necessarily build the long-term skills that ensure they continue to thrive when out of their parents' care. We believe this can greatly affect children's anxiety levels.

The ideas in this chapter draw on Judith's work helping parents help their children get on the right track to developing true confidence and capability. We'll start with the fundamentals.

Responsiveness and demandingness

When psychologists look at how parents raise their children, they usually focus on two aspects of behaviour – responsiveness and demandingness.

Responsiveness describes parental actions which use warmth and care to respond to a child's emotional needs and show them love. When a child falls over and cries, their parent shows a high level of responsiveness if they embrace them and try to soothe them. When a teen receives a best and fairest award in rugby, their parent shows responsiveness if they hug them excitedly and tell them how proud they should be of their accomplishment. When a parent genuinely asks how their child's school day turned out, they are being responsive and caring toward them.

Demandingness describes parental actions which require a child to step up to age-appropriate expectations via rules and consequences. If a child is reluctant to stop watching TV and set the table for dinner, their parent shows a high level of demandingness if they insist the child turns it off and does their chore. If a child becomes excited when they meet their grandparents at a café, their parent shows demandingness when they ask their child to limit loud, exuberant behaviour which may disturb others dining there.

Being responsive and demanding are equally important in parenting. A parent must be responsive enough for their child to know they feel loved and cared for. Without this, children aren't likely to feel supported and safe. But a child also needs their parent to be equally demanding of their behaviour for them to learn age-appropriate skills. If this does not happen, the child is less likely to become sufficiently mature and capable to cope well in life.

As you will recall from chapter 2, many parents now see their main responsibility to their child is to give them a happy and successful childhood. This involves a well-intentioned attempt to give them a level of self-esteem that will start them off well. Often the belief is that a perfect childhood produces a greater chance of a perfect future life – like a push in the right direction.

Happiness and success are worthy goals. But many parents take well-meaning but unhelpful shortcuts that deliver their child regular joys and triumphs with little effort on the child's part. To do this, some parents become good at the caring side of parenting to the point of overdoing it, while underdoing the demanding side.

There's good reason for this. A parent who demands that their child does the tougher stuff of growing up will no doubt momentarily challenge, annoy or disappoint the child. Insisting that a high school-aged teen finishes their homework independently, or completes their chores before going to a party, or saves some of their birthday money instead of spending it all on frivolities is reasonable. But requests like this can sometimes produce interactions which require the parent to stick to their guns. The child won't like it and will probably let their parent know they aren't happy with them, possibly by accusing them of being mean.

Some parents aren't willing to be the tough guy so much. To avoid potentially unpleasant scenes, they may lower their expectations of the child to keep things comfortable for everyone, perhaps by over-helping the teen with their homework, letting them off doing their chores so they can leave immediately for the party, or letting them spend up on sweets and sweet-smelling stationery paraphernalia to add to the already full drawer at home.

This is understandable but not helpful. Parents who adopt an approach of extreme responsiveness coupled with low expectations of their child do not end up producing the happy, capable young adults they are hoping for. That's because children treated this way do not learn to ignore their temporary feelings to do what they need to do.

*Parents who demand too little of their child
can actually prevent them becoming ready
to do the tough things in life to get the good things in life.*

In fact, when parents do too much to make children happy and successful in the *short term*, children don't develop the skills to help them become happy and successful in the *long term*. Ironically, extremely loving parenting actions fail to encourage the skills that enable a child to become broadly confident going out into the world and coping with whatever comes up. It's short-term gain that risks long-term pain for the child.

The five skills your child absolutely needs

The skills a child needs to eventually be independently ready to face life are critical. They are (ta-dah!) *resilience, self-regulation, resourcefulness, respect* and *responsibility*.

Your child needs to have all five to be prepared for what life will throw at them. There is some overlap between them – sometimes developing skill in one area facilitates building it in another. This is particularly true in areas that are closely linked, like resourcefulness and resilience, respect and responsibility, and self-regulation and responsibility.

When your child successfully develops these foundational skills, they will be less susceptible to anxious traits or diagnosable anxiety because they will have confidence in their ability to cope with what life brings them. They will not think of themself as less capable than their peers or develop fears about their ability to face tricky situations in their life. They won't wish to hide in a hole of anxiety, avoiding any potential challenges; instead they will prefer to stay above ground, where they have the best chance of reaching their potential.

Let's start with the skill which is possibly most important to protect a child against developing anxiety.

Resilience

Resilience is the ability to bounce back from challenge. It can only come from experiencing some sort of struggle and learning how to cope. There is no way to teach your child resilience other than allowing them to semi-regularly face tricky situations.

If you take away all challenge from your child, they won't learn how to manage difficulty. They won't have enough experience of coping with temporary setbacks, and they won't develop the know-how to pick themself up after disappointments. They will likely catastrophise minor difficulty as unbearable.

Lack of resilience also leaves them less willing to face potentially tricky situations. Children who think they won't be able to deal with challenging events tend to shy away from them. This sets up a vicious cycle of avoidance, reduced resilience and further avoidance, which directly leads to anxiety about facing anything they see as potentially difficult.

More importantly, if you remove all challenge from your child, they will not learn to experience life as it truly is – some good days, some so-so days, some tricky days. They will be less confident about what they think they can cope with and may underestimate their skill to get through potential hurdles – something anxious children often do. This is why it is so important for fearful children to regularly face all types of challenges, learn how to cope, and gain confidence from developing their skills.

Resilience and anxiety

Resilience is practically the opposite of anxiety. An anxious child almost always lacks resilience – they don't cope as well as their peers with difficulty and take longer to bounce back from challenge of any sort. This doesn't always reflect the reality of their coping capabilities. In fact, anxious people often inaccurately believe they lack the inner strength to face discomfort. If they expect they won't be able to face future problems, they can try to avoid situations that potentially involve struggle of any kind without even testing their theory.

And that is where the real kicker lies. By not facing difficulty, they never learn that the experience isn't as bad as they predict. They also fail to develop the ability to stay in the moment, remain calm when challenged, and be confident they can cope when things don't go to plan. Their resilience ends up less developed than that of their peers who faced the rain during the camping trip or came last in the egg and spoon race and coped nonetheless. Their peers got the chance to face these setbacks and now don't excessively fear them. But the child who didn't face their challenges hasn't developed similar confidence and capability. The fewer challenges they have faced, the less resilience they have and the more anxiety they are likely to experience.

Here are some signs that indicate your child might lack resilience:

- They attempt to avoid things they are worried they won't do well at, such as trying to get out of tests or athletics carnivals.
- They send you a text when circumstances get slightly tricky and ask you to solve the situation for them, such as asking to be picked up when they are walking home and it starts to drizzle.
- They dramatise by groaning or stamping their feet when they can't master new skills or tasks immediately.
- They overreact to disappointment: they whine, complain, sigh, sulk and generally act like a victim when things don't go exactly as they wish.

Strategies to increase your child's resilience

You need to allow them to face challenge. Don't let your caring actions stop them from stepping up sufficiently. Start small and slowly encourage them to face trickier situations which will allow their skills to improve. You can offer empathy for their plight or feelings, but don't prevent them from facing age-appropriate challenge like typical school events and curriculum demands. Adopt the following strategies.

Allow and trust them to face challenges

For your child to develop the confidence to face challenges and the skills to cope with a level of unpredictability in tasks they attempt, they need to practise. This means you must let them face life events that have an element of difficulty or likelihood of disappointment, and they need to do this fairly regularly.

Their challenges need not be large. Tricky situations can be minor, such as not always getting their way. If they want to press the button for the lift, and their sibling beats them to it, don't apologise. Be rather matter of fact about it. Shrug a little when they protest. Once they've met this challenge, move on to bigger things. Don't buy them another ice-cream when they drop theirs through carelessness, and don't immediately replace the smashed screen on the tablet they have been careless with recently.

Don't allow them to suggest there is overwhelming challenge when there is none. If they say they want their dad to put them to bed after being told that mum will do it, keep the plans as they are rather than always changing to suit their penchants. Be nonchalant about their unreasonable requests and demands or unnecessary, melodramatic tears.

Your child's preferences should not dictate household activity.

Ask yourself, 'Is this a genuine need or just something they would like to happen?' Also, 'If I acquiesce to this, will they start to think they need to have more control than is likely to be possible when they are with others?' Teach them in these moments in your care, so they are more ready for the reality of life when out of your care.

If they arc up and show extreme anger or aggression when they don't get their way, view this as a behavioural problem and give their inappropriate performance a consequence. (More on consequences in the section on respect.)

Your child must also learn to face challenge when out of your presence. This builds their confidence in being independently capable. There are two simple ways of developing their resilience when away from you.

Sleeping at a family member or friend's house allows your child to test out their independence. This normal developmental activity allows children to separate from parents and develop a sense of confidence in themselves. From an early age, children might sleep at a family member's house and later at a friend's place if the parents know the friend and their parents. We encourage parents to permit this as soon as a child shows interest in it. When parents choose to not let their child do this until they are much older, it is often more indicative that the parent is not ready for the child to be away from them and develop independence, rather than the child not being ready. Remember your success as a parent is not having your child remain dependent on you, but instead becoming independently capable. If you don't want them to have a sleepover, at least encourage them to have full days away from you.

The other simple way of developing their resilience (and resourcefulness and responsibility) when away from you is to have them take public transport to and from school when they are of an appropriate age. Support them at first by accompanying them or walking with them to the stop or station. Or consider going with them to a friend's place so they can travel together as an important first step. Then they can progress to getting themself to school on their own when required. The age you start this will depend on the area you live in and the distance to school. Your natural parenting instincts might resist this, but remember you are in the business of slowly growing a capable and independent adult; travelling under their own steam is a significant step in that direction.

Don't go overboard with praise or attention

Praise has its benefits: it encourages children to behave appropriately and helps them feel good about their accomplishments. But it is important to get the balance right between appropriate recognition and making your child dependent on constantly hearing good things about themself. Too much of the latter means they become reliant on regular external approval.

Praise your child's effort rather than their performance, since this is something they can control. Try to avoid laying praise on too thickly as it can easily become pressuring. If you shout to the rooftops about their A in Design, they will likely feel burdened to get the same result next time. Additionally, make sure you are not giving so much praise that your child doesn't value it. If you give lots and lots of praise, it will become insignificant to them. Pull back and make your feedback sparser and more meaningful, so they value the merits you single out.

Don't only give praise to your child. Children should be ready to hear and accept a range of responses. Take care to insert some constructive criticism into your feedback. They need to learn that reactions to what they do can be both admiring and critiquing, and that each can be equally helpful to them.

Let them face frustration

Try to avoid racing in to save them as soon as they experience the frustration of things not working perfectly. If they are stacking blocks and their structures keep falling, resist the urge to step in immediately to solve the problem. You want them to learn to persist. As often as you can, leave them to it without hovering over them to check that all is working well for them. If you do step in, do as little as you can to edge them onto the right track. Don't feel you need to go overboard with praise to keep them working hard, as this is a type of help they could become reliant on.

> *You want your child to understand that rehearsal is essential to success.*

When your child is allowed to circumvent all potential frustration because you or their teacher step in too early to help, they won't learn how to get through initial difficulty. They'll also miss out on the genuine satisfaction of authentic personal accomplishment that comes from trying and failing a few times before they eventually get things right.

Self-regulation

Self-regulation is the ability to forgo current pleasure for future gain. It is the capacity to focus on one's long-term goals and do things that are a little annoying, slightly displeasing or uncomfortable now to get something better in future. This might be turning off the latest TV binge marathon so you can get a decent night's sleep, not going on the expensive weekend away in the vineyards so you can continue to save the deposit for a house, or holding your tongue with your in-laws for the sake of a peaceful family life. It can even be enduring some initial embarrassment on the ice-skating rink or being willing to make a few inevitable mistakes in your first few group guitar classes so you can slowly develop your skill.

Many parental actions these days seem kind in the moment but are not, in the long term, helpful for children's self-regulation. When parents take on the responsibility to always prompt their children to do what they need to do, children fail to develop the skill to manage their own schedule and behaviour. Parents who remind their child to finish their assignments might save the child from the momentary upset of receiving reduced marks or detentions for failing to complete their work on time. But, by avoiding these consequences, the child will fail to develop the self-regulation skills which will help them in their future, when they are away from the walking alarm clock that is their parent. Parents need to resist the urge to constantly prompt their child, particularly today when it is so easy to send text message reminders.

Parents also pause the development of children's self-regulation when they step in to protect them from facing the slight embarrassment that comes with not being good at activities that are new to them. Accomplishing anything worthwhile usually requires hard work over time. Children need to be taught to endure the initial discomfort of not getting something right to gain the hard-won goal. Unfortunately, some parents catastrophise their child's experience of initially not feeling good when they try new things and can easily be persuaded to let their child avoid activities they see as tricky. Anxious children are more likely to decide 'I am hopeless at this' early in their karate class because they can catastrophise their understandable early awkwardness and personalise the improvement feedback given by the coach. They may want to pull out of future classes. If their parent lets them do this, they inadvertently suggest to the child that they can't live through initial discomfort and need to immediately withdraw from activities that make them feel this way.

To develop self-regulation, we need to focus on our long-term goals (to master a new skill like cooking Thai food or playing chess) rather than our short-term feelings (our embarrassment at not knowing how to pronounce the names of the ingredients or cut the vegetables in the correct way, or our impatience and slight boredom at having to learn the rules of play and suffer initial losses). If short-term feelings rather than the ultimate aims are your primary focus, you would probably choose not to come back; you could resolve from now on to buy, rather than cook, Thai food, or play solitaire, where you know the rules and no one else sees you win or lose.

Additionally, when parents step in and ask their child how they feel about an upcoming challenge like their first day at high school, they encourage the child to focus more on their current feelings than the goal of achieving the next important milestone in their life. This is done with good intentions but actually hinders the development of the child's self-regulation skills because the focus is less on achieving their goal and more on their current feelings of apprehension or nervousness, which can make their challenge feel bigger than it needs to be.

Self-regulation and anxiety

At the core of self-regulation is a willingness to endure minor discomfort. This only comes from practice: enduring temporary trickiness or challenge and gaining the longer-term benefit after getting through the initial stage of discomfort. If a person is allowed to avoid those early difficult feelings, they won't learn to tolerate them and they won't go on to accomplish bigger-picture goals.

Children who lack self-regulation are likely to be anxious because apprehensive feelings about upcoming tasks are uncomfortable, and many children do what they can to avoid those feelings.

Signs that your child may have poor self-regulation include the following:

- They need to be reminded to do what they need to do. Repeatedly.
- They cannot manage moods such as anger and sulkiness, and don't easily move on from them. Their mood might have a huge impact on the rest of the home, and they can rapidly escalate their bad moods if not appeased.
- They need 'compensation' for being inconvenienced. If you ask them to help clean up before their grandparents visit, they need a 'sweetener', such as a biscuit or excessive thanks for chipping in. They might also need regular rewards for basic activities, such as expecting hot chips as an incentive to keep going to their learn-to-swim classes.
- They tend to convolutedly blame you for things that are their fault. For example, they say they didn't get their assignment done on time because you won't buy them the latest tablet.
- They have poor impulse control. When they are doing something pleasurable, they find it hard to stop or they refuse to stop when asked, which easily escalates into throwing a tantrum or giving you the silent treatment for a few hours.
- They disperse moods like momentary frustration or annoyance to everyone else. If they have no yoghurt to eat at home, they text you and expect you to pay immediate attention to their complaint. They could insist on an 'apology' for failing to ensure their favourite snack is on offer. They might even expect you to buy yoghurt on your way home.
- They text you regularly to make sure you are aware of the annoying things in their life, such as the boring tasks in their part-time job or

how tired they feel at the 'lame' party they're at where everyone is 'tedious' and the music is 'zzzzzz'.

Strategies to increase your child's self-regulation

To develop their self-regulation, a child needs to learn to accept that their life is not all good times, and that they can't always have easy, immediate success. Parents must slowly teach children to face their responsibilities and the temporary difficulties and tricky feelings that arise in day-to-day life, like momentary boredom, frustration or nerves. This shows children that the worthwhile parts of life come from hard work, and that we need to occasionally face uncomfortable feelings to get hard-won outcomes. This realisation is particularly important for an anxious child who focuses too much on their current feelings and not the beneficial future results of enduring those feelings.

The most difficult aspect for your child is that they have to experience the cost of not regulating their temporary feelings and reactions as a first step. If you protect them from the consequences of their choices, they won't be motivated to improve their skills.

> *Parents must allow children*
> *to face the results of poor self-regulation*
> *and not protect them from learning from their experience.*

If your child is not self-regulated enough to do their homework, they must experience the consequence of their choice and get a detention or poor grade. You must allow them to face this and learn from it or they will remain oblivious to the long-term costs of their inaction. If they are in a cranky mood at school and respond rudely to their teacher or coach, you must allow them to face the cost of their failure to manage their feelings in the moment. This could be a reprimand, a detention or being benched for the game the following weekend.

Similarly, if they don't learn to endure their nerves and are allowed to avoid auditions, they won't get the chance to be on the debating team and acquire further skill and confidence. You can't circumvent the process of learning these lessons: you must step back and allow it to happen. In fact, it is important that they still go to the game if they are benched because of their actions. If they don't go to see their teammates and instead binge-watch a TV series, they won't feel the cost of the reprimand and learn to take responsibility for their actions.

We understand it is hard work to see your child cope with the nerves of an audition, the sting of a detention or benched game, or the brief shame of receiving poor marks when they didn't hand in their assignment on time. But – and we can't stress this enough – this moment will absolutely end up being worth it for them as a learning experience.

If you don't allow them to learn these lessons in their day-to-day challenges, they are likely to fail at something much more important when out of your care. Overprotected children can sail through school with their parents' regular reminders, assistance and protection from disappointment. But their charmed lives come at a cost: their self-regulation will not develop and they could remain disorganised and lack necessary planning skills beyond school. Often this means they end up dropping out of university or fail to do as well as they could in their work or personal lives.

To prevent this happening on your watch, try the following ideas.

Practise co-regulation

Younger children, particularly those under seven years old, don't have the maturity to self-regulate. Managing their feelings in the moment is tricky for them. Continuing to do what mum and dad want them to do (keep walking to kindy) and not what they want to do (keep looking at a green bug) is hard for them.

Parents and caregivers have an essential role in helping their young child develop self-regulation skills through a technique called co-regulation, which involves coaching a child through their tricky experiences to help them slowly learn how to cope.

It's a relatively simple process. When parents see their child dealing with a difficult emotion like frustration, they can help them label the feeling and validate their response. Then they can coach their child to move through the feeling and support them to do what the situation requires. On the walk to kindy, parents might say, 'You want to keep looking at the bug and you feel frustrated that you must keep walking instead. I understand – it's a cool bug. But we need to keep walking so you don't miss out on anything.'

Over the years parents can reduce their co-regulation as children learn to manage their emotional reactions. But parents can still assist. If your teen doesn't want to go to netball training because she's still upset about only making the B team, you can empathise, but also remind her of her responsibilities. 'Your reaction is completely understandable, and I know you worked hard. But you still have a responsibility to your team, and you still love the game. Maybe look at this as an opportunity to improve your skills, so the A team remains a possibility for next year.'

Don't apologise for basic expectations

While you can be empathetic when they have to wake up for school after a late night at their cheer championships, don't go overboard into excessive sympathy or apologies.

Never apologise to your child about what they must do.

It is not a parent's fault that a child has to go to day care or school, or do their homework. When parents apologise for a child needing to fulfil the basic expectations of life, the child develops a 'life is unfair' mentality. This has direct implications on their ability to get on and do what's required of them because they fixate on thoughts like 'why me?'. This makes doing routine tasks difficult for them.

Normalise uncomfortable feelings

Let your child know that while some feelings are uncomfortable, they are normal reactions to the difficult things in life. It is important to coach acceptance and endurance rather than avoidance. When your child says they feel nervous about their exams, empathise and let them know that most people feel the same way. When they say they are finding a subject boring or difficult, tell them study isn't always super interesting, and some topics are harder going than others. We say more on this in chapter 13.

Have them focus on their end goal, not their current mood

You can't expect your child to bound out of bed every morning, full of enthusiasm about getting ready to go to school. Or race to the car super excited about fulfilling their responsibilities at school or in their part-time job. Or stride into their trumpet exam, excited and eager to face the challenge of being evaluated.

But you can keep reminding them of why they do what they do. You can say they need to go to school to get the knowledge that will let them find meaningful work, or that they need to put in the hours at their job to save up for the car they want to buy when they get their licence. Being matter of fact about the temporary feelings that tend to come along with these normal responsibilities helps. Acknowledge their feelings, empathise a little if you wish, but don't dwell too much on their hesitations and be nonchalant about their temporary moods.

Don't set up a mini anxiety club

We understand you want your child to feel better in the moment when they express reluctance or nerves about an upcoming event or fears about making friends. You can empathise, normalise and even say you remember feeling similarly at school. But you should not tell them that you currently have anxiety, or you had anxiety at the same age which wasn't effectively resolved. Such confidences risk your child bonding with you over anxiety and subtly forming a desire to continue that connection with you. This would make them more inclined to express ongoing anxiety, which might allow them to stay in the unofficial connection you created.

If you had anxiety and overcame it successfully then by all means mention it – but only as a way of offering them hope and ideas for overcoming their fears. We don't recommend that you talk about anxiety if it is an ongoing problem for you. Most importantly, you don't want your child feeling that they have to comfort you. That perception of responsibility will be overwhelming for a child and risks creating pressure on them to support you before they are able to.

Demonstrate your own self-regulation

One of the best ways to help your child self-regulate is to model your own skills for them. You can even talk them through the process. 'I am really angry right now that I forgot to take the bins out – but I am taking deep breaths and setting up a reminder on my phone so I'll remember in future.'

It's also essential that parents don't have regular tantrums or lose their temper at the slightest provocation.

> *Let them see it is okay to be in a bad mood,*
> *but it is not okay to take it out on everyone else.*

Set an example here as well. You want to make sure that your home is relatively calm and considerate of others. On that note . . .

Deal with their moods

Generally, if your child's mood is not disturbing anyone else, let them be. But if they start to adversely affect or harm themself, other people or property, step in and give them a consequence for their choice. Remember it is not the mood that makes them do the inappropriate thing, it is their behavioural response. They need to learn to regulate their feelings and not act on their temporary emotions in a manner that impacts others. You can help them at first but slowly they must face the consequences of their choices. We provide more ideas for suitable consequences later in this chapter when we discuss how to develop children's respect.

Resourcefulness

Resourcefulness is a person's ability to alter their response to fit their situation. You see it in people who are able to quickly change plans when the weather changes unexpectedly, rethink their transport options when the scheduled bus doesn't show up on time, or creatively adapt the menu when one extra person shows up for dinner. You may have drawn on your own resourcefulness when you quickly made up a white lie about heavy traffic to save your friend's feelings when you are late for coffee because you dawdled while you were getting ready. (Yes, lying is a form of resourcefulness when it neatly solves a tricky situation like this.)

Resourcefulness ensures a person is always capable because they are ready to adjust their response when needed. They put most of their effort into solving a problem rather than complaining about its unexpectedness or how annoying or unfair the situation is for them. They are the best type of co-workers or travel companions because they are flexible. You can count on them when things get tricky and not need to support them by taking on all the responsibility to solve problems yourself while they continue to complain.

Resourcefulness and anxiety

Most parents have learnt the skill of resourcefulness. They've probably had to re-chart their course to save the situation for their family countless times. When they plan to make jaffles for dinner and at the last minute find the bread has gone mouldy, they cook pasta instead to feed everyone. Or when the usual route to school is blocked off by roadworks, they take the back roads and still manage to get their children to two different schools on time. So you probably have resourcefulness in spades. Teachers too. In fact, anyone who's job is to remedy situations without the option of a white knight galloping in to save them has this skill.

But the extent of your problem-solving experience might mean you are not so helpful for your child. If you are particularly good at sorting situations, you may be likely to look at your child's problems as opportunities to exercise your own special ability. You might also do this for family members or work mates. Others may even turn to you for help or seek your advice when confronting their own challenges.

When a parent deploys their resourcefulness to adjust situations for their anxious child and smooth out the challenges in their life, the child fails to learn how to solve their minor problems. Often parents do this because when they see fear or worry in their child, they will do everything they can to make their child feel better right away. But, despite their good intentions, their children can fail to learn to tolerate temporary experiences of things not going to plan. Such children tend to pout or fall in a heap rather than thinking creatively, adjusting their actions and getting on with it. They may also come to believe that the obvious solution to any difficulty is a phone call to their parent to outsource their problem-solving even in their post-school years.

The more a parent solves their child's problems,
the less a child believes in their own ability to resolve difficulties.

A child with poor resourcefulness tends to focus more on their problem and their emotional reaction to it than how to solve it. Other signs your child may lack resourcefulness include:

- They lack persistence and put more energy into non-verbal grievance indicators like pouting or grimacing than finding solutions.
- They often see themself as a victim or view any difficulty as 'unfair'. Even low-stakes events can cause them to think this way.
- They easily become bored when life is not super entertaining for them. They insist you give them interesting things to do, both indoors and outdoors, rather than use their own creativity via imaginative play.
- They personalise things that aren't personal or deliberate, such as mistakenly being overlooked when pieces of birthday cake are

handed out. They put more effort into suggesting they've been victimised than calmly telling the host they didn't get a slice.
- They text you often with their problems, and either suggest or directly ask you to fix them. When they forget their top hat for Saturday rehearsal (even though you reminded them about it twice), they text you and ask if you will drop it off. When they can't sort out their phone plan, even though they are in their final year of school, they text you a request to fix it for them.

Strategies to increase your child's resourcefulness
Building their resourcefulness is simple: allow them to start solving more of their problems. Don't respond so much to their whines and sighs. Start small with minor challenges, then move on to allow them to solve bigger issues without your help.

Before you start, it is critical for you to understand that helping your child become resourceful is a stronger expression of your love for them than forever solving problems on their behalf.

> *As the person who loves them most, ask yourself not what you've done to make your child happy each day, but what you've done to help them help themself.*

Teaching them resourcefulness is a gift that will keep giving. It will be the skill that keeps them bobbing back up regardless of what happens to them. Don't let your default thinking be that your child can't handle challenge and that their solutions will always be suboptimal to your solutions. Trust that if you give them chances to learn to be resourceful, their solutions will eventually be effective.

We suggest you work through the following strategies to help your child develop their resourcefulness skills.

Don't offer help before they ask
When you offer assistance before they start a task, you suggest they need your help. This can be a major confidence deflater for them, or a subtle encouragement of their dependence. Trust that when they face a challenge they can, and should, do most of the work to resolve it. Also feel confident that if they need your help, they will be resourceful enough to come and ask for it.

Don't encourage whining

Watch out for signs your child is seeking your help via a Nonverbal Grievance (NVG). This is a loud sound, such as a drawn-out sigh or high-pitched whine, or a facial expression like an exaggerated frown or grimace. It can also be a groan, rolled eyes, or melodramatically altered vocal tones.

When they ask what's for dinner, your response might evoke an exaggerated frown if tonight's meal is their least favourite dish. When they arrive home from school, they might walk around sighing or groaning to demonstrate their general world-weariness on account of their slightly boring or dissatisfactory day.

Most times the display is performance. They want someone to show an interest in what could bring on such nonverbal displays of angst. Asking 'what's wrong?' gives them permission to say what it is about their responsibilities or their life that displeases or annoys them.

Parents often inadvertently reward NVGs. Mum or dad sees the disappointed response to the dinner choice and immediately offers an alternative. Or they see the shoulders sag and automatically give their child a hug so they will feel better.

> *When parents always respond to nonverbal grievances, they encourage victim-like behaviour in their child.*

This will not be helpful for them in future because they'll tend to focus on what is wrong in their day and put the onus on others to fix it or do something to make them feel better. This expectation will directly chip away at their resourcefulness.

Whiny kids tend to become whiny teens: slamming their bedroom door, speaking to their parents in an accusatory tone, and regularly finding fault with their less than perfectly stellar life. Life with these teens can be almost unbearable for the whole household.

How do you prevent this? Try to ignore your child's bellyaching from a young age. Keep doing what you are doing without asking your child what is wrong or offering an alternative to whatever it is they are whining about. You'll know it's attention-seeking behaviour if their sounds get louder when ignored. Keep ignoring their sighs and expressions of woe. They need to get on with the responsibilities of life, not try to delay them with grievance theatrics or attempt to get a solution by making weird sounds.

When they whine, tell them you can't understand them. When they stop, increase your attention toward them to reward their improved behaviour. If they have a habit of whinging in the car as you drive them to school, ignore it or tell them you don't know what they are saying. You want them to bring their problems to you in an appropriate way. Children often make whiny noises because what they feel is a form of non-specific ennui, boredom or bother.

If your child takes their attention-seeking display to the point of bad behaviour, address it with a consequence. Avoid asking them to provide justification for poor choices such as why they hit their brother or kicked the cupboard. They'll probably give you some nonsense about their brother simply looking at them or say something completely unrelated, such as they have too many chores. In general, there is really no excuse if they become physically aggressive on account of their minor grievances, and you need to give consistent, unemotional instructions or consequences for such behaviour.

What if they take their whiny tone out of their voice after being asked to speak properly? Perhaps they politely say they don't want stir-fry tonight and would prefer tacos. In this instance, they have followed your instruction, and you should pay attention to their response by showing you heard them and reward their adjustment by praising them. Perhaps also offer them some understanding and hope by suggesting you will prepare tacos next week. Better still, offer to teach your tween or teen how to make tacos and give them the chance to occasionally cook the meal for everyone.

You want your child to know they can complain and be heard if they bring their grumbles to you in an appropriate manner. This will encourage them to be considerately communicative.

Check their resourcefulness before you step in

Imagine that your child regularly forgets their lunch and, since you work from home, it is easy to solve this problem by popping up to the school with it. But every time you do this, they don't experience the natural consequence of their forgetting. This does not encourage them to self-regulate and find a better system of remembering. More importantly, you don't teach them to build their resourcefulness and solve this situation themself.

Instead, ask your child if they know what they would do if they got to school and realised they had forgotten their lunch. Slowly develop this conversation. Draw out a number of options from them. Check in with them the next day to finish the discussion. Once you confirm that they know how to solve the 'no lunch' problem, they will be more resourceful, and you won't have to deliver forgotten lunches to school anymore. In the same vein, when they complain about being bored, encourage them to find things to do inside or outside instead of you finding something entertaining for them, like giving them a screen.

Be careful of texting solutions

Our ever-present mobile phones make it easy for parents to overdo their help if they're not careful. If your child has a habit of calling you whenever minor problems arise for them, don't pick up your phone and answer every time they call. Ask them to text if they feel they urgently need help. You can then screen problems and selectively respond when you think it is necessary. Sometimes the text equivalent of a shrug is useful. You might reply 'how frustrating' rather than offer a solution. Reduce the frequency of your responses over time and increase the interval between your child's message and your response: give them a chance to sort out their problem on their own before getting back to them. Let them remember you are busy, not simply waiting for a chance to make their life perfectly smooth all of the time.

Teach them to solve their problems

Children don't simply know how to solve their problems. They need to be taught. During their early to mid-primary years, begin teaching them practical problem-solving skills they can apply to their current situation and then to other similar circumstances. This is a step up from the simple brainstorming of options we have described in regard to forgetting their lunch. Teaching them to solve their problems involves coaching them how to approach any problem. Here's how you can get started.

Make a deliberate decision to mark a problem they present to you as the first one they will fully take the reins on. Once your child has explained this problem to you, empathise with how annoyed, frustrated or disappointed your child might feel. Then ask them to describe the outcome they would like most. Now you can coach them to come up with some courses of action they could take to get there.

At first, be mindful that your coaching is to prompt your child to realise that a range of different solutions can get them to their desired outcome.

You might guide them to consider some initial alternatives and, after that, have them think of some further possibilities on their own. It is tempting to jump in and make a definitive suggestion at the start, because as a parent with years of experience you may see the way forward quite clearly. However, it's critical that you apply the brakes and tutor them through the process, rather than putting all the work into generating or choosing the problem-solving ideas yourself. Beware of inadvertently entrenching yourself as their main problem-solver.

Let's discuss an example. Imagine your child is putting together an outfit for book week. They could join with their friends, who are planning to go as characters from *Charlotte's Web*, but turning up as Templeton in their grey t-shirt and handmade rat ears is not an exciting prospect. Or they could put together a different costume to be a book character in a book they genuinely love and can talk about easily.

If they are befuddled about their options, help them do some simple problem-solving to make their choice by helping them think through the alternatives. Never pressure them to choose your preferred option because this would take away from their ownership of the problem-solving process (particularly if you were highly involved in the creation of the rat ears and would love to see your efforts on stage).

At some point, they should decide on the best option and put it in place. Later they can review whether they were happy or not with the outcome their decision achieved. Remember that sticking to this process means mistakes are inevitable: learning from them is part of the path to building their resourcefulness. Over time your child will slowly learn and accept that there are no perfect solutions and missteps will happen along the way. This will ensure they can face life with some independence and realistic expectations.

We revisit how to help children problem-solve in depth when we look at worries in chapter 14. That section is particularly useful for supporting your child with thorny friendship problems and other complex dilemmas that can cause distress for tweens and teens.

Teach them to accept what they can't change

How pleasant life would be if everything were solvable. But there are some situations we must simply grit our teeth and live through. And there are some goals we must simply let go of when our skills don't match our dreams. Only some of us can become professional ballerinas or basketball champions.

There are also situations that are unfair – life is often that way. Of course, everyone is deserving of the same opportunities and no one should be discriminated against, but not everything is perfectly fair all of the time. Even though you were five minutes late because you were doing extra shopping for your sick neighbour, you can still get a parking fine. Even though you worked harder than anyone else on the assignment, if you misread the criteria sheet, you can still receive an average result. There's no invisible courtroom making sure things are always fair and just. And even if there were, things would still go wrong occasionally. (Have you seen *Law & Order*?)

Happiness lies in knowing what you can and should change, and what you need to accept.

Happiness also involves changing your reactions to circumstances and their outcomes, so they don't affect you so much. Don't be sour about your failed ballet or basketball career and focus on what you enjoy about your current occupation.

Teaching your child to know what they need to accept and what they can change is a critical element of resourcefulness. Sometimes it is a good idea to encourage your child to not keep airing their grievances about what did not work out and deliberately move on. We revisit this in chapter 13 when we talk about parents and children chatting about their day's events.

It is also important to let your child move on from any past problems at school. Thinking their school still owes your child for failing to make them class captain three years ago chips away at a healthy relationship with the school and diminishes their trust and respect. Try to encourage your child to shake things off rather than dwell unhelpfully on events in the past. Think of this as a type of karma – if you and your child accept that the school won't always be perfect, the school might also be more forgiving of your child's imperfections (and those of the parent who raised them!).

Respect

Respect is the consideration we show to other people. It involves showing appropriate regard for people who are authority figures, like teachers or the police. It's also following the explicit or implicit rules of the environment we are in, such as not speaking in a cinema or following the family rule about not touching your sibling's belongings without permission.

Respect is not limited to our behaviour toward authority figures or following social conventions. It also involves showing regard to anyone by being appropriately considerate of their rights and feelings. It's asking people about their day, rather than just speaking about your own experience. It's allowing others to shine when their time comes by listening to their stories too, and genuinely congratulating them on their good news.

Respect and anxiety

Anxious people's temperament and overwhelming emotions may not predispose them to develop the skill of respect. Often they don't mean to show poor respect, but they can be so concerned about themselves and their feelings that they don't ask about others. Their conviction that they should always have success or their belief that others expect them to be triumphant can leave them unable to accept others' success. This can lead them to want to dominate games in the playground or only do activities they prefer or in which they stand out.

The regular adjustments families often make to suit their anxious child can encourage them to expect to be the centre of all considerations. They might even expect teachers or coaches to adjust their expectations to perfectly suit them, even though they sit in a class with 24 other students. And while the child might be temporarily satisfied by other people's adjustments, this means they do not gain the confidence that comes from knowing they can generally fit in with others without always being accommodated.

Other signs that anxious children have not developed respect are:

- They show poor attitude and behaviour in class or at home.
- They believe their needs and feelings are more important than others', even when they are in upper primary school and should not be so self-preoccupied.
- They tend to focus only on themselves and show little interest in other people and their needs.
- They show disregard to people they should be somewhat deferential towards, such as their parents, grandparents or teachers.
- They are rude when their requests are refused. They might send their parent multiple insolent texts or refuse to speak to them for a time

when they ask for trendier school shoes and the parent doesn't buy them immediately.

Strategies to increase your child's respect

In our clinical work, we find that anxious children are sometimes rude to their parents when they have been over-catered to through the parents' extreme responsiveness. Parents do this via lots of praise, prioritising the anxious child's needs over those of the rest of the family, and overdoing friendliness to the child. It's an understandable response intended to make the child feel less anxious, but it reduces the parents' demandingness and expectations as well. As a result, anxious children often don't step up to responsibility as much as their non-anxious siblings because they aren't expected to: they might be assigned fewer chores or their family might allow them to frequently get their way. This is particularly true if they are a sensitive director, which we discussed in chapter 5. Any rudeness on their part can also be excused more than similar insolence from their siblings.

Such well-intentioned allowances can significantly hinder the child's development of respect for others. This impedes them socially, making it harder to them to fit in with and be accepted by others. When they are impolite or insolent, their behaviour is often blamed on their anxiety. This is an inaccurate assessment if the child is being rude simply because they have been over-catered to and have not learnt how to be sufficiently respectful. Their anxiety becomes a red herring for the true cause of their conduct.

It is essential that parents keep working on their child's respect to ensure that they are ready for the classroom, lecture hall, workplace and their personal relationships. It's helpful to ask yourself: 'Would I want the behaviour they are showing now, such as refusing to do their share of cleaning up, in an employee of mine?' or 'Would it be okay if my co-worker took their bad mood out on me or turned huffy when I politely disagreed with their suggestion in a meeting?' or 'Would they be a loving partner if they sulked every time they didn't get their way?' The answers will prompt you to give them a consequence for not showing sufficient respect. Here are some further ideas.

Don't centre your home around them

When you first bring your child home as a baby, your household needs to revolve around them. But slowly, your home should become less child-centric and require them to fit in more with you and the rest of the family. Don't allow one child to get the best of everything all the time – the last slice of cake, the choice of the movie, the best position on the couch – or to dictate their wishes – what you have for dinner and who sits next to them. Make sure everyone is catered to at different times and don't spend too much time justifying why their sibling got the last piece of pizza. Remember that the more you try to explain and give attention to their so-called grievances, the more they are encouraged to sing *I've Been Wronged* on high rotation.

Don't try to be their friend

Be warm and caring towards them, of course. But try not to act as or suggest you are their friend. Being their pal makes parenting tougher, particularly in the tween and teen years when they might become somewhat rebellious and actively push back against doing what they *need* to do, instead preferring to do what they *want* to do. If you are their 'friend' in these years, this often-tricky time becomes even trickier because they don't think of you as having any authority over their behaviour.

If you maintain a loving *and* appropriately demanding parenting approach from birth to their young adult years, you are likely to have a positive relationship with them when they are an adult. That's because you have grounded your relationship in mutual respect.

Remember you are in charge

Are you having trouble convincing your child that you are the one in charge? Do you often have to remind them who is the boss? Do you regularly have to say, 'I am in charge'?

> *If you have to convince your child of your position,*
> *you haven't established it well enough*

You need to work hard to change the situation. The first step is to pull back on sweetness by not overdoing the praise and attention that might have led your child to think they are the key player in your home. The second step is to set up your home environment to encourage respect.

Make clear rules about acceptable behaviours that show basic respect for others in your household. Your rules are permanent – put them up on the fridge if you wish. You might make rules around voice volumes, considerate movement through the house and adherence to bedtimes. Include rules for when your child visits friends or relatives and at the supermarket; remind them of these rules when you're on the way to those places.

Set up routines: the before-school routine, the after-school routine, the bedtime routine, and the weekend or holiday routine. Specify the time your child goes to bed, who has the first bath or shower, and what your child needs to do before they get to turn on the TV or gaming device after school. Make sure the bedtime routine is followed regardless of who puts them to bed. When they stick to their routine consistently, there won't be many arguments about what they would prefer to happen. Consider introducing a behaviour chart: if your child does everything in the morning routine and is ready for school on time, they earn a gold star. Change the reward as they get older and make sure the reward earns your child something they enjoy. When they are in pre-school, each gold star could earn them a brief game of catch with you in the backyard after school or a quick stop-off at the playground in the park on the way home. As your child learns to delay gratification, let them collect their stars to earn a more substantial reward: five gold stars might allow them to choose a special outing for the family on the weekend. Keep up the chart as long as it takes for them to internalise the behaviour in their routines.

Introduce regular chores for them. This gives them a sense of control in a way that fits in with you and your household. They need to do what you expect of them – clean up the kitchen after the family have had breakfast – to do what they would like to do – play video games on Saturday afternoons. If they want to do more of their preferred activities, have them take on additional responsibilities. If they are bugging you to stay up later in the evening, let them earn this by making their school lunch each day.

Give them effective instructions. The way you ask them to do something and tell them how to behave is more than half the battle in getting them to comply. You must sound firm – not pushovery or plaintive. Gain their attention with eye contact if possible. Get down to their level when they are small. Give them a clear, calm instruction: 'put your shoes in your room'. Say 'please' if you wish but don't sound like you are begging, or let it seem as if their status is higher than yours. Avoid phrasing your instructions as questions. 'How about packing your toys away now?' sounds like you are asking them what they would like to do, not giving an instruction. If they don't do what you have asked, repeat the instruction in the same way, without raising your voice. (Yelling will make them tense and possibly bring on poor behaviour.) When they comply with your instruction, praise them. When they don't, give them a consequence.

When they are rude or don't follow your instructions, give them a consequence so they learn to behave with respect.

The most effective consequences are brief, fair and unemotional for both parent and child. Such consequences do not rely on guilt or shame for the child who has made an unwise choice.

When your two- to nine-year-old child does not comply with your instructions, tell them this means they must go to Time Out. The Time Out place is a relatively boring and safe place near you with no screens close by. It could be a chair, the bottom stair, a rug in the hallway, or even a seat in a shopping centre. Don't send them to their bedroom because you can't keep an eye on them there and your purpose is not to isolate them. Tell them they need to sit quietly in the Time Out place for one to three minutes, depending on their age. Ignore complaining and whining and if they run off, bring them back. The more they refuse to sit quietly, the more they don't yet respect you as the person in charge. Mastering Time Out helps them learn this.

When your child is over nine years old, a Chore Set is the preferred consequence. If you remove your child's phone or wi-fi privileges for a week or a month, time drags and both of you may remain angry for the duration. A Chore Set is shorter and less emotional. When your child refuses to follow your instruction, breaks a ground rule or is rude, they lose all privileges until they complete a chore you set them to do – something that is not part of their usual chore responsibilities (unpacking the dishwasher), but a larger or less regular activity (washing and vacuuming the car, weeding a section of garden or cleaning windows). Calmly say, 'You have not done as I asked, so I'm giving you a Chore Set. All of your privileges are removed until you get two buckets of weeds from the front garden. Give me your phone and I'll return it when you're finished.' If they go to their room and sulk, that's fine. Eventually they will want their phone so they can tell their friend what a terrible life they have, but they need to weed the garden to get it.

If you would like to learn more about Time Out and Chore Sets, Judith's book *The Bonsai Child* includes a comprehensive discussion of these techniques and many of the strategies listed in this section.

Be consistent

Your consistency is essential for these strategies to work. Every time you (inadvertently) reward your child's wilful actions – letting the rules slip because you are busy and tired, not giving a consequence because you are already running late – you encourage them to repeat their behaviour because they see there's a chance you might be too busy again and are likely to accept it once more. Being consistent is sometimes annoying and tiresome, but your attention here will build a more satisfactory relationship for the two of you, and a much happier child. Your hard work now will yield abundant reward in the days to come.

Responsibility

Responsibility is an extension of respect. Being responsible involves shifting your focus beyond yourself and your own needs to think about others and their needs, and doing what you can to help make their life pleasant. It is also being accountable for your actions, admitting to mistakes, and doing what you can to make amends when required.

It's important to understand the link between responsibilities and rights. Everyone has certain rights to live their life broadly as they choose, but those rights come with responsibilities.

> *As children become older and their rights increase,*
> *their responsibilities should equally increase.*

This ensures they do not simply get the good things of growing up – their own smartphone, the freedom to go out with their friends – without the not-so-good things – doing a share of the laundry, walking the dog when it's raining, cleaning up the kitchen after Sunday lunch with extended family.

People tend to feel better about themselves when they are contributing members of their group. If they are considerate of everyone else and pull their weight, they feel that they belong, they matter, and their contributions count. It is no coincidence that performing random acts of kindness is often suggested as a way to generate endorphins and lift our mood.

When a family over-caters to a child and allows them to avoid responsibility through poor behaviour, that child will likely miss the chance to enjoy the satisfaction and self-confidence that come from knowing they belong to the people who matter in their life and contribute to their happiness.

Responsibility and anxiety

When parents perceive their child to be anxious, they tend to absolve them of responsibility, particularly if the child reports not feeling up to their tasks. These parents risk their child failing to realise that they can step up and meet their responsibilities.

Signs your anxious child may need help to develop their sense of responsibility include:

- They look at life through the prism of 'what's in it for me?' and 'why should I . . . ?'
- They always prioritise their own needs and rarely return the favour when others do something nice for them.
- They refuse to do chores in your home.
- They don't take constructive criticism well and become emotional, blaming the person giving them feedback rather than their own poor performance or mistake.

Strategies to increase your child's responsibility

It is essential for your child to step up and carry out their responsibilities if they are to grow up and become a well-functioning adult. By behaving more maturely they start to become more mature, and you will allow them to do more adult-like activities because you can trust them.

When they take on appropriate responsibilities, they will feel a sense of pride in themselves and their contributions to the world. They won't dwell too much on what the world doesn't do for them. By becoming mature, they will understand that their contribution to others in the world is equally, if not more, important than what others do for them. To paraphrase JFK, 'Ask not what your community can do for you – ask what you can do for your community.'

The strategies we have already discussed to build respect also work here because responsibility is an extension of respect. Rules, routines and chores help your child develop their responsibility and understand that a good life comes from good choices.

We recommend you take the following steps as well.

Encourage them to be grateful

Make sure your child develops gratitude for what they have and what people do for them. Teaching your child to be appreciative of the many good things in their life now increases their chance of future satisfaction.

Have them use basic manners and always say please and thank you. Make sure they give adequate thanks for gifts they receive from others.

Make sure they recognise what you do for them and show some level of appreciation. When they want a lift to their friend's place or help with their homework, insist they ask you politely for this assistance.

> *Have them do something for you in return almost every time they ask you to do something for them.*

Have them take in some washing from the line, so you have time to drive them to their friend's place. When you are cooking dinner and they ask for help with their homework, say you will help them but you'll need their help first to chop the vegetables.

This is not being petty. You are teaching them to be thankful – simply encouraging them to be appreciative and emphasising that they should not expect everything to be done for them. It also gives them some skin in the game: if they aren't willing to cut up a few vegetables to get on the right track with their homework, they are developing expectations fit for a mini empress or emperor.

Allow all school consequences

Don't protect your child from consequences given to them by their school. If they've done the crime, they need to do the time. Even if your child tells you that they didn't deserve the detention, don't step in to try and make the teacher change their mind; they don't give detentions without considerable thought. When your child receives a consequence, it's a sign they are showing an unruly streak and need help to improve their attitude.

Think back to your own childhood. On occasion, nearly every one of us practised some creative excuse-making to get out of trouble by concealing the true nature of what happened. This is not a sign of evil; it's a sign of resourcefulness. You might feel secretly proud of their skill, but don't reward their creativity and elaborate vindications by believing them. The odds are that the vape they were caught with was not 'my friend's that I was just minding'.

Even if your child genuinely wasn't involved or was the only one who got caught, we still suggest you don't save them. Life isn't always fair – sometimes you get caught in the wrong place at the wrong time.

Likewise, allow them to feel the consequence of their own disorganisation. Let them learn that if they let themself get behind on an assignment and hand it in late, their mark will be reduced. They need to know their action or inaction has consequences. In this way, they learn to take responsibility for their decisions and behaviour.

Well-meant but misjudged parenting actions can prevent a child from sufficiently developing the five essential skills. Without them, an anxious child will become even more worried and prone to losing their cool. To some degree the child's worry is justified. Without essential skills they aren't as equipped as their peers to cope with life, because they haven't been able to develop age-appropriate abilities.

When parents see their anxious child lacking maturity and coping skills, many tend to step in with more help. Ironically, their ongoing protective actions further prevent the child from developing these essential skills and worsen their anxiety. And so the cycle continues.

Your child will benefit from learning all the skills discussed in this chapter. Indeed, your whole family will benefit because your child will become more pleasant to be around and more confident in themself and their capabilities.

> *Teach your child to like living in the world as it is,*
> *and you will encourage the world to like them back.*

The rewards will be felt for years to come.

Now that you know the five essential skills your child needs to get on the right track to maturity, it's time to examine one of the trickiest challenges they face growing up today – using screens and technology. Let's get that sorted in the next chapter.

CHAPTER 11

Getting technology right

Technology can cause more arguments between parents and children than anything else. But unless you plan to acquire a DeLorean time machine and transport your family back to the eighties, you will eventually have to let it into your home.

In chapter 4 we looked at the opportunities technology provides to keep us informed and connected. We also highlighted its challenges and the lure of its virtual drip-feed of feel-good chemicals that keeps us staring at our screens. We know that the benefits of technology – including the chance to bond over social media and further develop our sense of identity – can easily be dwarfed by its drawbacks. Without noticing, we can move towards unhealthy habits of performing socially connecting activities on a screen instead of catching up in real life. Or we can lose our power to concentrate on what we are doing by constantly interrupting our focus to pick up our phones to check apps, live feeds and notifications.

We also discussed how technology can make our anxious tendencies worse. We can become dependent on immediate answers and instant affirmation from loved ones or our social media friends to the detriment of our patience, our ability to endure temporary self-doubt, anxiety or boredom, and our resourcefulness.

We may try to escape uncomfortable feelings by looking at our phones when we could be more actively involved in our surroundings, interacting and conversing with people who are physically present. But turning to our devices to soothe ourselves can actually fuel our anxious preoccupations. We also risk becoming less capable of maintaining a conversation (with all its natural pauses and occasional awkwardness) and truly connecting with others when we choose our devices instead of the people we are with.

But all is not lost. This chapter will help you make sure your child's relationship with the screens in their life does not curtail their wellbeing or social development.

Without a good plan, expect the worst

Many parents approach technology in the home with naive optimism. Too often they imagine managing their children's use of phones and tablets will be straightforward. They think, 'I'll let Blair get a phone, and I'll make sure I don't let them on it too often.' Or 'We'll buy a tablet, and Addison and Charlie can share it.' Their intentions are understandable but rather deluded about the addictive nature of these devices. It's like saying, 'I'll buy a packet of Smarties and only have one.'

Judith's colleague, educational guidance counsellor and mental health practitioner Machelle Flowers-Smith, has a useful analogy to illustrate the effect of allowing your children access to technology. She likens any internet-enabled device to a swimming pool. Most kids want one at their place: they're fun and offer almost limitless entertainment. But pools are also dangerous. There are good reasons why legislation ensures they are sufficiently fenced. Even when pools are restricted appropriately, they remain a potential source of danger. Fences and rules about when to go near the pool give parents a sense of safety, but there is always the potential for young children to evade supervision and use all of their creativity to get to that alluring blue water.

We also believe that technology can be dangerous if children are not adequately supervised and taught how to use it safely. When an internet-enabled device gives your child access to the world, it also gives the world the potential to access your child. When you believe installing child-safe protection software will keep them from harm in this environment, you place too much trust in the world and your child. You are also kidding yourself if you imagine you will be able to permanently station yourself next to your child to make sure they always use their device appropriately.

In case you think we are going over the top with these warnings, consider some facts. Studies conducted around the world regularly identify dangerous impacts of technology on young people's wellbeing; the link between screens and emotional difficulties is becoming clear. For example, the more 13- to 15-year-old girls use social media, the more they are likely to have poor mental health in terms of depressive symptoms, self-harm and reduced life satisfaction.

A large longitudinal study of 12- to 15-year-olds, which accounted for existing mental health difficulties, showed those who spent more than three hours per day on social media faced double the risk of experiencing poor mental health, including symptoms of depression and anxiety. Adolescents who watched four or more hours of TV, movies or YouTube per day were three times more likely to be diagnosed with depression, social phobia or severe worry episodes than children who viewed less than two hours per day. Students who rated their family's household TV watching rules as 'lax' described more instances of depression over the previous week than those with average or strict parental guidelines.

Young people aged between 14 and 17 who use screens for over seven hours a day have a greater risk of clinical depression and anxiety compared to those who use their screens for one hour a day or less. They are also twice as likely to lose their temper and 46% more likely to be unable to calm down when they are overstimulated.

Other research shows that parenting is affected as well. Parents report that children who use screens daily for seven hours or more are harder to care for than children who don't. These parents report that the more hours their child uses a screen, the more likely they are to do things that really bother the parents and spark their anger. It's possible that the child's behaviour encourages the parent to give in and allow them to use the screen they demand, and this is why the children are on screens for such a long time. But we remain concerned that a child who is almost permanently in front of a screen in the home is far less likely to learn compliance and fit in with the rest of the family, which might set off a vicious cycle of poor behaviour and screen use.

Before you start hunting down that DeLorean and googling 'time machine operations manual', the news is not all bad. Educational screen time, including using computers for homework, is associated with positive learning outcomes and does not negatively affect mental health. And children who overwatch TV are not affected if they also spend sufficient time playing sports, exercising and participating in cultural activities like visiting museums or attending plays.

But parents and educators are right to be concerned about the bad news on technology. And almost everyone needs screens these days for education, work or to organise their social life, so your child will need to learn how to manage their device usage. This will involve considerable effort on your part as well.

Never fear. This chapter will help you prepare your child to make the most of their screen time and enjoy it without detriment to family harmony.

Be prepared to do the work

We have often seen parents lose control of how their child uses technology because they are unaware of the degree of effort it takes to really keep an eye on it.

When you allow your child to use any new device or app, set aside four weeks to monitor how your child uses it. Initially, they are likely to test your boundaries and try to get extra time on the device or do away with some of the rules we suggest in the next section. You will need to keep holding the line here. Even determining whether your child is mature enough to have a new device takes effort.

Everything we encourage you to do in this chapter involves work on your part, particularly when you are finding your feet and setting up good habits. We recognise this will sometimes appear tiresome. But just as you would not take your four-year-old to the pool without planning to supervise them closely, or let your 13-year-old sign up for an ocean swim race without any open-water training, you should not introduce them to technology and leave them on their own.

*If you don't put in the work
to make your child ready for technology,
be prepared for their screen habits to become unhealthy.*

How to introduce screens to your child

The steps we describe here show you how to introduce any screen into your home and methodically manage its use to benefit your child.

Don't allow screens for very young children

Think of this as putting the fence around the pool. Children are drawn to water: without a fence to stop them, they may accidentally tumble in. The risk of drowning is high until they are old enough to handle themselves near water and be safe. Technology presents similar risks: screens are sparkly and exciting, and you need to keep your child away from devices until they are developmentally ready to use them without detriment to their potential.

What are the risks to their future? The earlier you introduce a child to a screen, the greater they are at risk of decreased cognitive performance and heightened developmental delay. Young children are also likely to be more behaviourally inhibited if they overuse screens. That's because they choose screens instead of learning how to interact with the people around them.

Children under two who use screens have greater risk of delayed development in their gross and fine motor skills and their problem-solving skills. This is because devices don't offer them any actual activity to develop their muscles and gross motor skills or any real-life problems to practise on. Many experts advise that children under five should not have easy access to a phone or tablet because screen use can replace opportunities for play that develops their physical and imaginative skills.

We go further and suggest that you do not allow access to any personal device (phone or tablet) until they are seven years old. We have two reasons for this. First, we think that by handing children under this age a phone, you can stunt their natural desire for creative play and their joy in the wonders of the world. Second, developing a child's ability to self-soothe when upset due to frustration or disappointment – even in the midst of a tantrum – must take priority until they are at least seven. This will be more difficult to achieve if they are distracted by screens. We stress the importance of this: children must be able to regulate distress in the absence of a screen if they are to function well at school.

Our clear message here is to make sure you do not give your phone to your young child to easily amuse, distract or soothe them. We understand this can be difficult when you need to get something done and your toddler constantly interrupts you, demanding your attention. You give them your phone to play with so they will leave you in peace for five minutes. We get it. But before you do this, think very carefully about what it means they miss out on.

Your child will focus on your phone instead of anything else that may be happening around them. If you are outside, they will look at the screen instead of the other children or birds and dogs they meet as you push their stroller around the park. When you give them your phone, you deny them this chance to engage with the world. You also suggest that what surrounds them at the time is not interesting enough to maintain their attention. The park will seem insufficient – when in fact it offers more than enough amusement.

Encourage them to engage with the world. If your child grumbles or starts to cry because they aren't as entertained as they would like, you may still be tempted to give them your phone, particularly if you are in a place where their cries may disturb others or be embarrassing to you. But resist the phone solution whenever you can.

We know this will be difficult at times but plan to always bring something – a few books, toy cars or building blocks – that will amuse your child. You might think these are not engaging enough, but they are only lacking when compared to the dancing pixels of moving images on a smart phone. If your child is not used to that level of colourful engagement, toys and books will usually satisfy them.

The real challenge, of course, is not giving in to the convenience of the phone. There will be times when you are tired, your child is playing up, and it is simply easier to give them your phone. We know there will be trying circumstances where giving a screen to your child is the best you can do. Another option is to be selective about when you keep your phone with you. Perhaps you have a watch or dumb phone (for messages) that you wear or carry when you are out with them that has no easy access to Facebook, YouTube or ABC Kids apps. You can be reached if necessary but you are not tempted to engage a bored child with the tantalising options your phone presents. This will be easier for you if you deliberately put your phone away and engage with your child. They will become more demanding about access to your phone if they see you constantly staring at it when in their company. Placing your phone out of easy reach is helpful for both you and your child: it prevents temptation and allows you to make the most of your moments together in the joyful years when they want to spend time with you.

Not interacting with your phone when you are with your child could benefit their health as well. Researchers in Taiwan found that mothers' screen time with three-year-old children was associated with incidence of ADHD by the time children were eight years old. This is a sharp reminder for parents to restrict their own screen use when spending quality time with their children.

We understand that you will probably want to be responsive rather than demanding of your child to learn tolerance. You want to respond to their boredom or irritation with the kind gesture of giving them your phone to distract them. But this is when you need to be appropriately demanding. You are starting to build your child's self-regulation and resourcefulness here with skills for managing their mood and learning to amuse themself.

If you do give in, be aware that this quick solution to your current problem will have a knock-on effect. Your child is likely to simply ask for your phone the next time they feel they need distraction, and cry when they are left 'stuck' with their blocks or books which now pale in comparison – and you will be back where you started.

Another option when faced with a bored child is to engage them in whatever you are doing. This will make them feel part of the action and build their skill in coping with activities that offer less immediate excitement than a screen. Point out things to look at, express your own wonder at what you see, ask them if they see the ducks, sing songs with them, or ask them if they can make the sounds the ducks (or dogs or birds) make. At the supermarket, involve them by asking them questions: 'We need some potatoes – you tell me when you see them.' Or have them play predictive games like how many steps it will take to walk the produce section. This is preferable to letting them be distracted by your phone as you push them around the aisles.

Remind yourself that the environment itself will often be interesting enough for your child. When they are moving – in their pram or on a bus – there will be an abundance of people, buildings, dump trucks or a passing train to look at. Letting your child stare at a screen denies them the ability to enjoy the moment and be a part of the community. It also raises the bar for what is interesting enough for them to look at. Make sure you take every advantage of what their environment offers to gain their attention without turning to the phone.

Determine your child's readiness for each device or application

We can't count the number of times we have been asked: 'How old should my child be to have their own phone?' But there is no conclusive research that clearly demonstrates a definitive age for a child to be ready to have a phone or tablet of their own, so we don't want to suggest there is. Soz! Even Bill Gates, co-founder of Microsoft, was strict about letting his children have a cell phone – reports say he didn't allow it until they were 14. We think he knew full well the power and allure of technology and decided to keep it out of his kids' childhoods for as long as he could.

There is a huge variation in maturity and skill in children within each age group. To say that when a child is eight or ten or fourteen years old is the right time for them to have a phone or tablet is to risk putting a device in the hands of a child who is not ready for the responsibility required to manage their use of it.

Consider the pool analogy again. You would be comfortable to let your child use the pool without your supervision when you are confident they can swim safely and get themself out of trouble. You would also let their friends use it with them once you're confident they have similar skills and that peer pressure and silliness would not put anyone at risk. These decisions depend on your assessment of their maturity.

Your child's maturity is also a fundamental consideration when deciding they are ready for their own screens. Without self-regulation and responsibility, they will lack the skill to manage their time and activity on their device. Unless your child has sufficient maturity and common sense to manage the temptations and potential dangers of screen use, they are at some risk. And if your child has not developed sufficient respect for you, it will be difficult for them to follow your rules around their technology use.

When you consider your child's readiness for each of the following devices and activities, assess their maturity and respect rather than setting a particular age for them to have access. Consider whether they have developed the maturity to manage their own self-care – cleaning their teeth, showering and doing their homework – without your prompting most of the time. Being able to calm themself down, listen to others, see a situation from different perspectives, and view themself as part of a household where there is give and take are also indicators of increasing maturity.

Access to their own phone

They need to earn a phone rather than receiving one on a pre-specified date such as their birthday or the beginning of high school. The way they earn it is to display a level of reliability for a sufficient period that proves to you they have the necessary maturity to manage their own phone.

This means they need to willingly do their fair share of chores without pushing back against their responsibilities and without constant reminders from you. When they first ask for a phone, sit down with them and offer a way forward for them to eventually earn it. They can achieve this by doing regular household chores for others, like vacuuming every Saturday morning or preparing vegetables and setting the table for dinner each night. If they are to be excused from a chore at regular times – perhaps they are not required to help with dinner on Tuesdays because they have an evening piano lesson – agree on this and note it in your weekly plan. If you do not have a clear weekly routine, you leave the way open for them to tell you they are 'too tired' or 'have too much homework' to do their chores. We recommend you set your weekly schedule of chores in stone so it is clear that it's non-negotiable.

The time it takes for them to demonstrate their maturity can be anywhere from a few weeks to months or even a year. Don't give in to nagging or sulkiness, or the claim that everyone else has a phone and they are the only one who doesn't. It is better to rely on your common sense rather than their desires. This is another situation when being demanding of them to show sufficient maturity trumps being responsive to their preferences. Their claim to be the only phoneless member of their class might also reflect their resourcefulness rather than the truth. Kids have been using the 'everyone else has it' line forever.

There are also situations when you might want your child to have a phone because you want them to be able to contact you immediately. Perhaps they have started to take public transport or walk to school on their own. The same rules to determine their maturity apply. Getting to school under their own steam is in itself a demonstration of maturity – you might propose it as an incentive. Alternatively, you could consider non-smartphone choices such as a dumb phone which permits calls and texts only, or a standalone smartwatch with a small screen which makes internet activities relatively unfulfilling while allowing them to call you.

When your child uses their phone primarily as a social device – even if you initially bought it for them for safety reasons – they should pay for their phone plan by taking on additional responsibilities. If it is part of your plan, they can reimburse you. Again, link their increased responsibilities to their additional rights in the form of more household chores as their means of repaying you. By taking on extra tasks to extend their use of their phone, they prove their maturity by demonstrating that you can trust them to use it for socialising in a balanced and healthy way.

Access to a computer or tablet for schoolwork

Your child will be required to use a computer or tablet at most schools. Conditions of access will be subject to the school's technology policy which could include use of school-issued tablets or laptops. If this is a game changer for you, be sure to check the school's policy before you enrol your child. Don't worry – if your child's school allows Bring Your Own Device (BYOD), you can insist on certain rules around that device, which we discuss in the following section on managing limits for school devices.

Access to gaming

Require your child to earn their access to gaming apps installed on their phone or gaming device, just as they initially earn the right to their phone. Don't buy them a gaming device until you are sure they will respect your rules and do as you say; avoid buying one simply to gain relief from their pestering. When you know they are sufficiently mature, buy one only as a significant gift like a birthday present, or allow them to contribute to the purchase with birthday money or through doing extra chores, like helping you clean the fridge and pantry. Be aware that children can often access gaming through websites; they don't require a specific gaming device or app. This means you will need to keep an eye on their online activity to ensure they are not gaming at times they shouldn't.

Access to social media

You must manage multiple risks when your child's phone or computer becomes the portal to their social life. These include excessive use at night at the expense of their sleep, a mistaken belief that they can multitask, more friendship fights, possible cyberbullying, and the chance that a stranger will attempt to befriend them online for nefarious reasons. Your child on social media is exposed in a way they weren't when they were simply watching Netflix or playing games on their own.

We define social media as any image- or video-streaming apps which include discussion and sharing options, such as TikTok and Instagram, or apps which allow for group messaging, like Snapchat or Discord. Simply put, any app where people socialise.

We suggest you do not give your child access to social media until they are 16 years old. We have good reason for this. Social media has the chance to wreak havoc on friendships if used badly. We know that school relationships are often most fraught in the early high-school years, particularly in late Year Seven, Year Eight and Year Nine. We think it is dangerous to give your child access to social platforms which have so much capacity to negatively impact friendships, particularly when they still don't have the maturity to manage their use. In this we adopt a similar recommendation to Jonathan Haidt, whose book, *The Anxious Generation*, shows the potential dangers of screen use and social media on a generation of children.

Think very carefully before you give your child access to social media. We encourage you to take a two-step process here. First, reflect on the health of your child's friendships before you even contemplate letting them start to use social media. It's a bad sign if there are still extensive daily dramas and ever-changing loyalties and disputes in your child's peer groups. This usually shows that their friendships are not yet settled and stable enough to withstand the added pressure of the day's minor tiffs escalating with endless commentary and friction overnight. Your child might tell you that having social media will be some sort of magic panacea to make these dramatic friendships more stable. Tell 'em they're dreaming. Social media only works when all players are mature, and friendship loyalties are able to withstand minor tiffs and hurt feelings.

Second, have them earn their first social media account by taking on additional responsibilities to build and prove their maturity. If you allow them a web-enabled device at age 13 or in their first year of high school, ask them to demonstrate further maturity by taking on extra responsibility to gain a social media account when they reach 16. In addition to the responsibilities they have taken on to earn their phone in the first place, you could require them to make their own and their sister's lunch every school day, or walk their brother to the bus stop to show they are mature enough to have access to social media as well. Alternatively you might require them to do some regular volunteer work, perhaps by mowing an elderly neighbour's yard or baking for them to show they are ready for their first social media app. Of course, they also need to have followed your rules in the early days of using their phone. (More on this below.)

These are not arbitrary requirements we've thought up on a whim. Their willingness and capability to take on these responsibilities shows their commitment to manage their time and be considerate and caring of others. It sets them up to use their screens maturely and respectfully, which provides essential proof to you of their readiness to engage in an alluring new social world. Their capacity to focus on the new responsibilities you have set them is a maturity prerequisite for this phase.

Access to headphones

These days, headphones automatically come with most new devices. We recommend you give similar consideration to letting your child use headphones as you do with the devices themselves. It's important that you establish clear rules about when and where using headphones is acceptable.

There is good reason for this. When we wear headphones, we block out the world around us and deliberately focus on an audio feed. This sends a non-verbal message to the world as clearly as spelling out DO NOT DISTURB across our foreheads. It discourages others from speaking to us and allows us to fully immerse ourselves in a phone conversation, an engaging podcast or our favourite song, rather than our surroundings. So much so that it becomes an effort to switch our attention to a person or situation in front of us and prioritise them over our audio.

We recommend you make a rule that headphones are not to be worn in your family living spaces. We also strongly suggest that headphones should not be used when doing chores in shared areas such as the kitchen.

This is important: we lose the 'empty' time we need for our creative thinking when we are distracted by listening to audio while we do chores or go for a walk. Empty time is why we have so many ideas while in the shower – it's free from distraction. A TikTok trend for silent walking (as if it is a new thing!) has arisen because people have discovered the joy of taking in the sounds of our surroundings while feeling present in the moment. Losing ourselves in a non-stressful activity lets us develop natural ways to calm ourselves. Encourage your child to do this; also think about doing it yourself.

Manage strict limits from the beginning

Children want to stay in the pool forever, but adults know there comes a time to get out. To ensure children don't get too tired, cold or sunburnt, adults set rules like 'no swimming for more than an hour at a time' or they allow them to swim only at certain times of the day, so they don't overdo it. Applying similar limits on technology use ensures children are able to enjoy it sensibly and safely.

When your child has demonstrated they have the maturity to have a personal phone, tablet or PC, set up a strict agreement with them about the rules for their use of the device before you even head for the store. Sit down with them and establish the guidelines they need to observe to be allowed to get and keep the device. Make sure you include the following rules in your list.

The 'parents are in charge' rule

While your child lives under your roof in your care – when they are a child, tween or teen – they live by your rules, their screens are subject to your rules, and you have the authority to manage their time on their screens. Regardless of whether a device is a school-issued computer, their phone, their tablet or the TV in the kids' rumpus room, it is still subject to your directions. They should always adhere to the rules you have set and should promptly turn off a device or give it to you without whining or grumbling excessively when you ask them to hand it over.

> *As long as they remain a child,*
> *you remain the screen master,*
> *in charge of all devices.*

This applies even if they bought their phone themself from the money they earned in their part-time job, or their iPad was a gift from their other parent – devices are under your control when your child is in your care. And you should be able to remove them at any time without creating a major altercation.

If you don't see this as fair or can't see it working in your family, consider a scenario where your 16-year-old gives an older friend some money to buy a bottle of alcohol for them or is given one when staying with their other parent, returns home with it and starts swigging from it in your living room. Would you think, 'I can't insist they don't drink it because they bought it themself or received it as a gift.' Or would you step in and insist they stop and give the bottle to you?

It's no different with their phone or other device. If the way they are using it is causing them harm or harming others – gaming into the night and losing valuable sleep, using apps known to put them at risk of grooming, or staring at their phone instead of interacting with the rest of the family at dinner – it makes sense for you to remove it from them. You are the adult, and you oversee their actions for their own good.

Insist on their respectful willingness to stop using any device – TV, computer, tablet or phone – when asked. Give them a five-minute warning and listen carefully to the language they use and the respect they show you when it is time to switch off the device or put it down. Show zero tolerance for disrespectful actions or language. If they display rudeness, they forfeit future time on the device and must do a Chore Set.

Do not try to enter into deep discussion with them when you remove a device because they failed to follow the rules for its use. Such discussions are often inflamed by anger and frustration; your child will not be receptive in that moment to a reasonable or thoughtful chat. Save any follow-up talks for when the conversation is more likely to be calm.

Of course, your screen manager role will change when they turn 18 and contribute equally to the household by completing an adult share of chores and responsibilities. But even then, everyone watches the TV in the lounge – they have no monopoly on it. And they must be considerate with their use of screens, such as keeping the TV volume at a reasonable level, or not turning their bedroom into a silent gaming retreat where they spend the entire weekend. If your adult child can't follow household rules, or their unhealthy or inconsiderate screen use creates an unpleasant environment for others, it's time to reconsider whether they can live with you.

The maximum daily screen time rule

Set clear limits on how much time you allow them to spend using screens in total. Passive screen use is linked to reduced literacy and lower school results. Findings from the Murdoch Children's Research Institute show that children aged eight and nine years old who watched more than two hours of TV a day had poorer school results in literacy and numeracy when they reached ten and eleven years old. German research has shown that even the presence of a TV or computer in children's bedrooms is linked to lower grades, particularly in Maths, and particularly for boys, who often have reduced impulse control. Too much screen time appears to prevent children from doing other important activities, such as their homework, reading or physical play.

How much time is healthy for them? We believe children and teens should limit their use of portable screens (phones, tablets, laptops, gaming devices) to between one and two hours a day. Until they reach their teens, we recommend you set the limit below one hour. This does not include homework or watching TV on the couch with the family.

We imagine your eyes are rolling – 'Yeah, right, Judith and Danielle. No problem.' Before you think we are advocating a return to life in the 1980s, consider that this means children's total screen time across a day is still likely to exceed two hours. There are only so many hours in a day and if you allow up to four hours or more of screen use, this will take time away from essential activities like homework, meals, exercise, chores and sleep. A maximum limit of two hours online is more than reasonable for your child, and they are likely to spend less than this on days they are involved in after-school activities. When you impose a limit, you train them to notice how much of their time is spent on screens and to strategically consider the best way to use their screen time.

In school holidays, keep in mind that children need to move their bodies after spending 45 minutes on an interactive screen. While you may set a higher limit for holidays that allows them some additional screen use, aim for this to be later in the day and leave enough earlier time to enjoy screen-free recreational activities like outside play, learning to cook, playing a musical instrument, spending time on scrapbooking or other hobbies, or reading printed books. If you are home with them, ensure your child spends an equal amount of time moving their body in outdoor exercise as they do online and make sure their screen use is not in lengthy sittings to encourage an active, balanced approach to how they spend their time.

To make sure they adhere to the maximum daily time limit you set, we suggest you create a screen use diary with your child to track the time they spend across all their devices – this is easier if they don't have access to a lot of devices. Most devices now have settings which allow you to track usage across activities; this makes monitoring relatively easy via 'screen time' on an Apple device or 'digital wellbeing and parental controls' on an Android device. Take note of how much time they spend on gaming, social media, streaming services (streaming on a laptop or tablet rather than shared viewing on the family TV) and news channels (which can also become addictive due to the dopamine and oxytocin injections they induce). Keep your response to their use calm and curious throughout.

Check whether basic self-care (eating, showering, brushing teeth) has taken place without your instruction. Some children can become so absorbed in their screen-based activities that their hunger will go unnoticed, particularly if their day starts to become anchored by screen use rather than normal routines and responsibilities like breakfast, getting dressed, going to school, attending swimming training, doing their homework and having dinner with the family.

Their daily demands may vary considerably week to week, due to extracurricular activities and changing school responsibilities; in the lead-up to a cello exam, dance eisteddfod or maths test, balancing preparation with the temptation offered by screens will be more fraught. Plan to make sure you review their screen use diary before and during these more stressful periods to check they are still managing their responsibilities and time well. Week 3 or 4 of the school term is ideal for this.

To help with managing their time on individual devices we suggest you consider the following ideas.

TV rules

When your child is young, they should ask you if they may turn on the TV. Make a rule that they need to complete certain tasks, like having their breakfast and making their bed, and engage in a productive activity that will consume a good part of their day before they get to watch their TV shows. When they ask to watch TV, they should have done what they know they need to do; you can check this is the case before you let them turn it on. If they are a tween or younger, make sure they have done some physical activity, spent some time entertaining themself (playing with LEGO or colouring activities) and any chores they are required to do (walking the dog, putting out the plates and cutlery for dinner) before you let them zone out in front of TV. This rule still stands during school holidays; require them to have done all of their chores before they start the fun part of their day. This will likely take some monitoring, but it's worth it. They can lose some of their self-regulation skills if you allow them to be completely unregulated and do only what they want during their school breaks.

Now that watching TV can be done across multiple devices and apps, it can be an isolating experience when a family's viewing preferences become disparate and exclusive. Watching shows in isolation removes a major source of family togetherness and connection.

We encourage you to deliberately watch TV as a family – particularly include teenagers you don't see as often as you used to. *Gogglebox* shows us how watching TV together promotes discussion and lets us find shared joy and mutual interests. Choose shows to suit the ages of your family and include lighthearted comedies or David Attenborough documentaries that will keep everyone interested. Time spent watching these shows together is not part of your child's screen hours for the day – it's time connecting with their family.

School device rules

Many parents lament that the school device or BYOD brings technology into their home. Make a rule that homework must be done first and then the school laptop or tablet must be put away. Limit any time your child spends on the device apart from homework and manage the apps they install on it the same way you would for any other device. Remember: you are the parent, and you are in charge. Schools will back you 100% here.

When your child begins to use the device at home for their schoolwork, set them up in a shared space such as the dining room. This allows you to keep an eye on them and check they are not gazing at YouTube videos when they should be doing their Maths homework. Once your child is in high school and they've proven their maturity, allow them to do their homework in their bedroom with the door open. You might also encourage them to apply a setting like focus mode while they are doing homework or study, so they are not tempted to open apps or interrupted by notifications which will distract them from the job at hand. Remind your child that they will get better results from their time studying if they are in the deep concentration that comes from not being interrupted and losing their train of thought. Different device types and operating systems (Android, Apple) offer slightly different settings and capabilities that can be switched on to pause apps and silence alerts and messages.

Don't allow a child under 16 to keep their device in their room overnight. When they've finished their homework, have them leave the computer in a designated location to charge.

If you allow them to use their school device for leisure, for the first five days set up a screen use diary so you and your child can collaboratively monitor how much time they spend on this.

Expect to be tested while your child begins using the school device at home. It's important you stick to your guns here. Your child will try to push your limits and it's important not to catastrophise about this. Remain calm and consistent.

Phone rules

Set a rule for the maximum amount of time your child may spend on their phone each day in the school week and on Saturdays and Sundays, when you might allow them increased (although not unlimited) phone time. If they cannot stick to this limit or observe your household rules, consider switching them to a dumb phone without internet capability.

If you feel your mental and parenting load is already at capacity, make a rule that allows your child to use their phone for a specified period once they have completed their other responsibilities, perhaps for 30 minutes before dinner, after homework and chores are done. This is a simpler way of limiting their phone use.

Be aware of the tug of your child's friends' social and emotional needs and how this can affect how much your child may wish to use their phone. Our desire to care for our friends and be there for them when needed is core to our sense of connection and wellbeing; most children want to connect with their friends after school. But keep in mind that if you allow your child to continue their online conversations late into the night, this will affect their sleep, their mood – including their anxiety – and their capacity to put their best into their schoolwork the next day.

Gaming rules

Before your child even unwraps the console, set up your house gaming rules. Stick to similar rules as the ones you have already made for watching TV, using their computer after their homework and using their phone. The door to the room they game in should remain unlocked and ajar. Make sure their gaming stays within the agreed time limit: use a timer or set a reminder on your phone at the start to check they adhere to it. Even within the designated limit, make sure they can switch off their game within minutes if you ask them to. If you find their gaming becomes out of control when they use their device independently, go back to closely monitoring their use to refocus them.

Allowing your child to play games within limits can be beneficial –

it might even act as an incentive for them to do some study. Australian research has shown that a small amount of video gaming on weekdays and weekends for children aged 11 to 17 was associated with better NAPLAN scores in reading and numeracy than no gaming at all. Unsurprisingly, gaming for more than four hours a day was associated with poorer results, but an hour or so on school days, and one or two hours on Saturday and Sunday seemed to be the sweet spot.

The study suggested that children were likely do their homework more studiously if they knew they were able to play a game when they finished. Additionally, these children were able to stop playing their games after one or two hours when requested by their parents. This suggests that they were developing healthy self-regulation and that their parents were providing a home environment to support that.

For good gaming hygiene, nominate one or two days a week when your child does not play at all and must relinquish gaming's dopamine highs in favour of off-screen sources of amusement. This is important for children and adults: it's best for everyone in the family to have days when they don't play video or phone games.

Don't forget to make a specific no-gaming rule on days when your child is sick and stays home from school. If they are ill enough to stay home, don't allow them to game or use any personal device – you don't want them to see more potential for joy in a day at home gaming than going to school. To encourage them to go back to school, home must become boring quite quickly.

Be clear that they will need to earn each new game they want to play or buy via chores or part-time work. And do not be afraid of permanently removing access to a game if it prompts them to break your rules. Remember: your house, your rules.

Social media rules

Starting to use social media is a milestone in a child's online interactions, so it's important to be careful with the limits you place on the first social app they use. If you withhold access to social media until they are 16, your child will likely possess the maturity to handle it well. In this case, you may be confident they will not need to follow all the rules we list here. However, if you allow your child to use social media prior to that age, we recommend you adopt all of the following suggestions.

When your child first creates their account, insist they set up appropriate parental controls and privacy settings, and tell them these particular settings must remain for them to continue to have access. Once the account is set up, load their new social media app on your own device under their name and login so you can observe their activity. Be prepared to spend considerable time and effort in the initial month observing the conversations they engage in. The level of attention you give to their usage can diminish over this time. We recommend you set phone reminders to alert you to do your checks at specific times.

- In week one, let them find their feet for three days while they set up friends and accounts or topics they wish to follow, then check every day.
- In week two, check every second day.
- In week three, check twice.
- In week four, check once at the end of the week.

Make sure your child understands that you will read their interactions on the app and discuss their contributions and the responses they receive with them for an initial 'shadow period' of one month. This is non-negotiable. Choose times for these discussions when they are not likely to be hungry or tired, so they will be comfortable to sit and talk through your observations and their experience in a relaxed way. Once you see they are handling their use of the app in a caring and thoughtful way, you can gradually step away and allow them their privacy.

Use this shadow period whenever they begin to use a new social media platform. With each new app, you will see a flurry of excitement and use followed by a more settled pattern. After the shadow period, move into a maintenance period: conduct spot checks during months two and three; set a calendar reminder for yourself to do these. We also recommend spot checks on their activity in the lead-up to exams, year parties, and at the end of the first week of school holidays. If your child arcs up about the invasion of their privacy, remind them that they are creating a digital footprint that will live with them when they go for their first and subsequent jobs and that you are supporting them to make sure the record they create is one they will be comfortable with in future.

You are checking to see the types of messages and sources your child interacts with. You may choose to keep an eye on a couple of peers you see as intrusive or domineering; also look out for these traits in your child. While you won't shadow them long term, doing this at the start is a valuable test of their mature use of the platform.

The most important matters to discuss with your child are likely to arise during their first month using social media. Ask if they have felt annoyed, angry, overwhelmed or bored with what they have read or seen on the app at any stage. If so, what did they do? Did they use their device to do something else or did they turn to a non-screen activity? The shadow period provides the perfect opportunity for you to discuss any tricky feelings they noticed and how they reacted to any unhealthy messages they encountered. You want to be aware of anything your child has seen that might cause them angst. Wait until you see examples of these types of unhelpful messages before you bring them up. Also talk to them about their feelings of urgency to respond to others and make them aware of the kinds of circumstances when it's helpful for them to slow down their responses.

Pay attention to the level of FoMO you see in your child after using the app, particularly when you see conversations about a social event your child wasn't invited to or other group activity in which they weren't included. Children who experience high levels of FoMO are less able to manage social media without becoming anxious. If you need to reduce your child's FoMO, normalise it by talking about how feeling left out is normal and that they can't expect to be included in everything. But also encourage them to assess whether friends are true friends if they play politics with events, which we discuss further in the next chapter. Remember, to overcome FoMO, a person needs to miss out on being involved in events or chats from time to time and realise they can survive this and are still liked by others.

Check how they express their feelings in their app usage. Think about whether you can see any patterns in their exchanges.

- Do they seem to be more friendly or rude than usual in particular conversations?
- Does their tone depend on the time of day?
- Are they able to ignore some messages?
- Are they inclusive in their responses?
- What appears to tempt them to be exclusive, domineering or dismissive in conversations?
- Do they boast? If they do, what form does this take?

- What do you notice about the frequency of their posts?
- Ask how they feel when their messages don't receive a response.
- Ask how much time they spend thinking before they respond to messages which contain an element of conflict.
- Do they seem affected by images their friends post, like underwear shots or provocative body posing? Do they talk about how they feel when they see these posts?

Discuss anything you have noted with your child in a non-confrontational and curious way rather than telling them your thoughts. You may not be familiar with the app they have chosen, or even social media itself, and it could feel alien and wrong to you. Use common sense and empathy when you speak with them about it.

There is a sweetener for your child in the shadow period. By the end of it, they will have earned their privacy within the app. When you're satisfied they can handle themself safely and sensibly, you can remove the app and their login details from your own device, and they can feel free to set a new password.

Once your child is accustomed to using one social media app independently, they will want to use more. If you have chosen to allow your child access to social media before our recommended age of 16, we urge you to limit their number of social media apps to two until they reach that age. Once your child reaches their limit, a new app means an old one has to go. The best way is for you and your child to work out which of their current apps are worthwhile, and which ones dampen their mood or steal too much attention for them to maintain a healthy on-screen off-screen balance.

Do not be afraid to withdraw an app if you can see your child is not mature enough to communicate wisely on it or if they circumvent your requests to observe or check in on their usage during the first few weeks. Give them a 48-hour warning to alter their use and if they do not, remove the app. Busyness is the enemy of vigilant parenting; set yourself a reminder on your phone to do this if you need to.

If you allow your child to access entertainment apps like TikTok, Netflix and YouTube, negotiate the terms of when they can use them and suggest that they make them available on one device only so they are not tempted to access them elsewhere. Be aware that they can access these platforms on web browsers as well, so you might need to keep an eye on your child when they are using any device.

Apply ongoing rules

When your child shows sufficient responsibility using their devices and you have done the intensive management we recommend when they begin using a new app, you can focus on your ongoing rules. If we return to the pool analogy, people are required to abide by rules like 'no swimming after nine at night', 'no diving in the shallow end', and 'keep noise to a minimum'.

Your ongoing screen rules should be anchored in your family values. Sensible rules are not unnecessarily controlling: they will continue to support your child's development of self-regulation, balance their screen time with healthy activities, and improve their real-life communication skills by ensuring they do not fixate on screens in lieu of family time and socialising. Not setting rules or not giving your child consequences when they don't comply with your rules could increase their likelihood of developing anxiety because of unhealthy and fixated screen use. This is particularly pertinent to already anxious children whose wellbeing can be affected if they routinely turn to screens to block their tricky feelings and worrying thoughts.

Here are the ongoing rules we suggest.

Hand over screens on request

The first rule is that they should hand over their device(s) to you at any time. If you request that they give you their phone or tablet for a consequence, or ask them to stop their Minecraft game for dinner, they should do it when you ask. It would be helpful to give them a three-minute warning, but this is not always practical.

> *If your child cannot give up their device or game on request, you need to take it from them until they respect your rules.*

If you cannot get them to put down their phone or stop playing a game, you have a bigger problem. This is not only screen addiction: your child lacks respect for you or has real difficulty with self-regulation. If this happens, take their phone or game from them until you are confident they will return it when asked. You may need to get professional assistance to achieve this, which we talk about in chapter 15.

No screens on wheels

We have already recommended you don't allow your child to use screens when they are young and you are in the car or on the bus, so they are able to engage with their surroundings. We suggest you maintain this rule as your child grows older. Sitting in a car together is an excellent opportunity to catch up on the day and converse in unpressured side-by-side, eyes-on-the-road chat. Make use of this time together. Allow them to accept that every moment in their life does not need to involve five-star entertainment.

We recommend you set a rule that no screens or headphones should be used in the car at all – by your child or teen, or even by your partner.

> *You become the taxi driver*
> *when they look at their phone instead of interacting with you.*

You show kindness by driving them where they need to be; they show rudeness if they ignore you and stare at a screen. It shows a lack of respect for you and is not a good habit for them to form. We believe this rule should apply to all passengers (including the friend you are driving to the train station as a favour). Also limit your own speaker calls to those that really must be made at the time.

You might make exceptions to this rule when you are on a long journey. But remember there is some value when kids occasionally need to create their own entertainment: being bored in the car will prompt them to chat amiably, play silly car games, sit with their thoughts, fall asleep, or engage with whatever is going on outside the car.

No screens overnight

There are many studies documenting the danger of leaving screens in bedrooms while children and teens should be sleeping. Have your child return every handheld device to you about an hour before they go to sleep. (We believe it is not good for adults to have tablets or phones charging next to the bed either, but we will leave that up to you.)

The danger is that even people who are otherwise sensible will reach for their screen in lieu of getting to sleep. There are times when all of us have probably scrolled on our phone in the dark when we feel tired and should be sleeping. It's not just your child's ability to be responsible that matters here. Any parent who has confiscated their child's phone will have seen how many notifications and messages from friends arrive at all hours of the night.

Multiple studies show that when phones are accessible in their bedrooms, children's and teens' screen use interrupts their sleep. There also appears to be a direct link between teens' night-time use of their phones, poorer sleep quality and reduced mental health. So we believe you should not allow your teen to have their phone in their bedroom to ensure it does not rob them of sleep, nor reduce their general wellbeing and ability to focus and learn.

Consider making an additional rule that children, particularly primary-aged children, do not use screens in the morning. Watching TV or looking at an iPad are magnets that make it difficult for your child to drag themself away to get ready for school. It's better that they play with blocks or toys if they have free time.

No screens in family time

Deliberately set occasions for screen-free family time. Consider a physical gimmick like a phone jail (it could be a cardboard one) that everyone uses before sitting down to dinner. An effective rule is to say that no devices are to be used at the dinner table or in family moments, like a large family get-together or during a shared meal with family friends at a restaurant.

Be careful that your child is still not somewhat connected to their phone at these times. Don't allow them to keep their phone in a pocket (buzz buzz), nor in audible distance (beep beep) and not in view (I can just reach forward), because the movement, sound or even sight of a screen can cue a person to focus on its presence. Even smart watches can be distracting (don't get us started on watches that light up in movie theatres). Ask your family to turn off notifications during screen-free time.

We also suggest you adopt the screen-free three (or two or one). This is a scheduled number of hours at a particular time on the weekend, such as Sunday afternoons between two and five o'clock, when the whole family puts aside their screens and does something else. The activities could include bushwalking, going to the beach, playing board games, or reading books in the backyard with cushions, blankets and snacks. Your choice will depend on the age of your child – screen-free time might be Sunday lunch followed by a few board games. Start with 60 minutes, then try to extend it. Everyone needs to experience screen breaks to give us space in our week. Even if your family doesn't do this specifically, make sure you set aside time to rediscover the joys of nature or the pleasure of disappearing into a printed book.

Children are responsible for their screen costs

Make sure your child accepts responsibility for their phone and tablet, including their upkeep and replacement costs. If they have smashed the screen, they should pay to replace it. If they want to take out insurance, they should pay for it. If they don't have a job, they can do additional chores for you to earn the money to pay for insurance or repair. This teaches them respect for their belongings.

Start them on a pre-paid plan for their phone and app purchases so they can't run up huge bills. Don't give them your credit card number or password to make purchases. Stay informed about what they have access to and what you can and should contain in terms of their online spending. And be aware that many apps use clever techniques to get a child hooked on purchasing add-ons that can easily lead a usually sensible child to make unwise decisions.

Make sure your child understands they will have to pay for any purchases they make on their phone. They will not be blasé when they know that they will bear the cost of any Uber rides and snacks they order online. Be careful with what you permit them to have access to in any case.

Manage problematic behaviour

It is important to give your child a consequence when they do not follow your screen rules. We recommend Time Out (for younger children) and Chore Sets as discussed in chapter 10. Your consequence should be brief: don't be tempted to take their phone from them for a week because preventing them from communicating with their friends for long periods can be harmful. When you give your child a Chore Set, remember to match the difficulty of the chore and the time it is likely to take with the severity of their misdemeanour. Even grave transgressions can be followed by a concise period of intense effort. The strongest of consequences – perhaps for lying about the presence of adults at their friend's party or stealing money from you – might warrant a day or an entire weekend of work such as cleaning out, or even painting, the garage. Once your child has completed the Chore Set, the matter is over. You have dealt with it effectively in a way that most tweens and teens prefer.

If they exceed your phone use limit or use their phone outside their permitted times, give your child a consequence of reduced screen time the next day or at a time when you can monitor their use. Remember to include this when you first draw up ongoing screen rules.

Your child might muster all of their resourcefulness to try to avoid your consequences. If you tell them they need to put their device down and do a Chore Set because they have been rude to you, they might report a big assignment or group project they now can't do now because you have cruelly removed their tablet. Think well of their resourcefulness but don't reward them for their sneakiness. Most importantly, don't change your mind. Give them a Chore Set that will take 15 or 30 minutes and then they can get back to their assignment. Your child's respect for you is more important than their schoolwork because it is fundamental to the health of your relationship. Ensuring they learn to be polite trumps their homework every time.

If you didn't set adequate rules at the start and your child's screen use is already drifting out of your control, don't feel you are stuck. Getting them back on track is not a lost cause.

> *You can change your rules at any time*
> *because you are the parent,*
> *and you are in charge.*

It's your job to create an environment in your home that is responsive and demanding enough to encourage your child to thrive. The message you want to convey is that there is a time and place for device use. If their devotion to their devices is causing them, their studies or their family relationships harm, you must address this. It will not be easy and will take concerted time, effort and modelling (by both parents, whether you live together or not).

We cannot stress too strongly that managing screen problems involves the tough stuff of parenting. It is likely your child will think you are unfair, and your relationship could become angry and tense for a time. Keep the bigger picture and your long-term goals for your child at the top of your mind. Sometimes a 'mean parent' is the most loving parenting of all.

Plan for potentially risky screen activities

Using technology exposes your child to a range of behaviours and outcomes that you need to consider and plan ways to deal with in advance.

Screen dependence

Children develop different types of screen dependence. If you don't set any limits, they simply develop bad habits, so introduce limits now. Review our recommendations on setting limits and ongoing rules earlier in this chapter and start afresh.

If your child's screen obsession is more advanced, you may need professional help. It's serious if your child refuses to stop using their device and is aggressive or abusive toward you when you tell them to put down their phone or stop gaming. Or if they are unwilling to go to school because they want to game, or not sleeping because they watch YouTube videos or text their friends most of the night.

Therapy is only useful when the person receiving treatment is motivated to change their situation. They must recognise that some element of their behaviour is not helping themself or others. They also need to be sufficiently determined to do the hard work of altering their actions to produce change.

Typically, children aren't keen to decrease their screen use – it's parents who see this as excessive and problematic in their child's behaviour. Children need sufficient maturity to see the effect on them or their studies. They also need the necessary motivation to do the work to change their habits. Therapists can sometimes encourage children to understand this, which can in turn spark their desire to change, but parental limits on screen use will always be required for their efforts to succeed. Once these limits are in place, a child will be more likely to engage in and benefit from psychological help to further develop their skills in areas such as assertiveness, social interaction or challenging perfectionism. We look at ways to get the most out of therapy in chapter 15.

If a child is not motivated to change their screen use, it will usually be the parents who need to get therapeutic help, either in addition to or instead of their child. Some parents aren't strong enough to be consistent with their rules and need assistance to implement them or manage the way their child responds when they place firm boundaries on screen use.

Pornography

Before you say that your child hasn't seen porn or isn't likely to see it, consider that 90% of children aged 8 to 16 have seen online pornography. As they become older, they become more curious, and it is natural for them to want to google 'penis' or 'breasts' or 'sex'. Generations ago, kids needed to put in more effort to find a magazine and purchase it or go through Encyclopedia Britannica to find pictures of naked bodies. Today it's easy and the range of material they can access is limitless, including images and videos most people would consider hard core. What's worse is that there are many immoral operators out there who take terrible advantage of children's curiosity and can easily manoeuvre a child into a situation where they are exposed to harm because of their naivety.

Pornographic images or videos are often not an accurate depiction of consensual sex, a respectful relationship or normal types of bodies. They are also often disrespectful to women. Online pornography is designed to excite viewers sexually so they want to watch more. It can make people doubt their own sexual confidence, question whether they are 'good enough' in their sexual relationships and create an unrealistic impression of the age and type of person they are attracted to.

Being overexposed to pornography can have dire results. Younger teens may develop serious fears about sex, which can be accompanied by obsessive-compulsive cycles. A teen watching illegal underage porn may become sexually aroused. Danielle treats teens who have started to worry about their own sexuality and morality when they have been exposed to material they feel they should not be aroused by, such as acts they don't necessarily identify with their own sexuality (homosexual porn) or which they view as immoral (violent or paedophilic porn). This sets off fears that there is something 'wrong' with them which can easily lead to OCD-type responses. They may start to double check whether their reaction is genuine by watching porn clips again. This can lead to triple checking and before long to nonstop checking of the material, often resulting in extreme angst in the child or teen.

Extreme or violent porn can desensitise teens and cause them to become impervious to the joys offered by caring and reciprocally enjoyable sexual relationships. They may become disregarding of both parties' right to be in an equal and consenting sexual relationship, which will affect their ability to find genuine, sustainable pleasure in their sexual experimentation and experience, both on their own and with future partners.

There are some great resources prepared by experienced specialists to help parents navigate this tricky topic. We strongly recommend Maree Crabbe and David Corlett's *It's time we talked* (itstimewetalked.com) and Susan McLean's *Cyber Safety Solutions* (cybersafetysolutions.com.au).

Sexting

Sexting – sending sexualised images, sexually explicit photographs of oneself or sexual messages – is becoming increasingly common. Talk to your child to forewarn them of potentially tricky situations and risks here. If your child receives a sext, let them know that laws in Australia state that a person who asks for, accesses, possesses, creates or shares sexualised images of someone under 18 could face criminal charges. It doesn't matter how the image gets to their phone; they are responsible for it being there.

This means they must take evasive action if someone sends them a sext. Help them solve the problem of what they should do. Prepare them in advance, by saying, 'At some point a girl or boy you know might send you a picture where they are naked or not wearing much. Look at it for less than a minute, then delete it. Do this every single time.' Let them know that you understand they might feel uncomfortable showing it to you or telling you about it – what's important is that they delete it.

Also tell your child that if they receive sexual images or messages regularly from a particular person via text or social media app, they must bring it to the attention of an adult they trust.

Technology has changed the environment for young people to explore their sexuality and parents need to be mindful of this. Your child is likely to be tempted to take sexualised photos of themselves and consider sharing these via text or other messaging apps. Consider not allowing them to have their phone with them in the bathroom or bedroom while they are under 16; this is an effective way of curtailing the temptation to experiment with these kinds of photos.

When your child begins to form a close relationship with someone and may start to use text messaging and social media for expressions of intimacy, they need to know who they can talk to about this safely. If they feel they can't speak about it or the person they are involved with tells them they can't tell anyone about the relationship, let your child know this is a clear red flag that means they *should* speak to someone trusted, particularly someone they believe can cope with the potential trickiness of the situation. If this person is not you, they may be an aunt, an older sibling or the school counsellor. Nothing that goes on between two individuals should be so completely private that they can't talk to someone they trust about it.

Tell your child it is very easy to end up in an unhealthy online relationship if they don't talk about it with other safe people in their life. Ask them to chat to you about it or identify people they would feel comfortable talking to. Don't take offence if your child chooses to talk to someone other than you. Your parenting is not on trial here and – as you will know from your own childhood – there are many times when you don't want to talk about something, particularly sex, with your parent.

The websites mentioned above in regard to pornography are also useful sources of further information about sexting and being safe online.

Manage your own screen use

It's important to consider your own screen use in the context of helping your child develop a healthy relationship with technology.

Don't contact your child too much

Try not to contact your child on their phone during a school day or when they are with their friends. Your calls or texts take them out of the moment when they should be focused on their schoolwork or enjoying their breaks. The only reason to send your child a text during school hours is if you need to change a meeting time. Be precise and avoid any additional conversational banter.

We suggest you never message or email your child with your negative feelings – particularly not to have the last word in an argument! This is not the way to have emotional conversations: have these in person. If ever you feel you must, wait for six hours before you send a strongly emotional message. And be prepared for your child to reply with even stronger emotion. That's why we say . . . don't do it if you are trying to win an argument.

We also suggest you avoid texting your child to reassure them you love them or to confirm that they love you as a typical part of your day. Don't send them heart emojis or messages of love for no particular reason. They should not need this form of pumping up when they are busy elsewhere. Predicting their emotional needs makes them less autonomous in the moment. Frequent and unprompted loving exchanges via text are often a sign that either you or your child need too much reassurance and are somewhat dependent on each other. Even when doing exams, they should not be dependent on a text from you.

Responding to your child's texts when they are at school or work, or out with friends is also unhelpful. If they rarely text you, there is no problem, but if your child texts you every day to tell you their friend or teacher is annoying them, or that they are feeling unwell or bored, it is a clear sign their phone has become a kind of umbilical cord enabling them to stay attached to you. This undermines your child's ability to connect with others in the moment and to cope with the minor daily challenges and disappointments that are thrown their way. It can lead them to have more fears about real-life social occasions where they are without your back up.

Model healthy habits

Think about your own relationship with your tech devices while you consider the effort involved in helping your child develop healthy screen habits. We've talked about screen dependence in relation to your child, but what about you? Are you rarely without your phone in your hand? Could your phone use be getting out of control?

Dr Brendan Meagher, a Melbourne psychologist, has identified the following questions as important markers of potential phone dependence. These apply to adults and children – but let's start with you first.

- Do you think you spend too much time using your mobile phone?
- Has your mobile phone use caused problems in a relationship?
- Do people say that you spend too much time on your mobile phone?
- Does the time you spend on your mobile phone stop you from doing other tasks?
- Have you tried to cut down your mobile phone use?
- Have you used your mobile phone while driving or crossing a road?

We suggest an additional question. Would you be willing to rationalise the number of apps on your phone and remove the ones that take up too much of your time?

If any of these ring true, we suggest you actively try to curb your phone use to be a good role model for your child. There are apps to help you do this – yes, we recognise the irony in this suggestion, but sometimes an app can help us to spend less time on apps! Otherwise, move the time-wasting apps off your phone or use the built-in tracking function to see how much time you spend on particular apps.

The recommendations in this chapter will help you help your child develop a healthy relationship with their tech devices and live their life free from domination by the black mirror. But there are other relationships that can make your child or teen's life feel either wonderful or awful – their friendships. Let's look now at some general principles to help make friendships less anxiety producing for them.

CHAPTER 12

Getting your child friendship ready

We are all part of a village, and you can help your child be ready for the interactions that come with day-to-day village life. This chapter shows you how to develop their ability to make friends and be a good friend.

Our relationships are one of the cornerstones of our quality of life. Even so-called solitary activities usually involve regular communication with others. Although you might sit alone at your desk, your work may often involve reading emails from others and responding in return. When you read a book on your own, you engage with an author's point of view, or a narrative focused on interactions between characters.

Because human connection is central to our lives, it is no surprise that relationship difficulties can strongly influence a person's wellbeing. Bad blood between family members, friends, colleagues or neighbours can significantly affect our lives. Having a manager you don't get on with or a co-worker who is rude or indifferent can completely change the way you feel about your job and your daily work satisfaction. In fact, it is hard to think of any environment where your interactions with other people don't make or break your experience, be it your home, a classroom, a family gathering or a party.

To truly equip your child for life, you need to make them ready for all types of connections and exchanges with other people. This preparation includes guiding your child to become someone most people enjoy interacting with in any situation.

This is particularly important for children who are anxious. The worries of many people, particularly those with social anxiety, are based on their prediction that they won't be thought well of by others. When your child feels prepared for a wide range of relationships and social interactions, they will also feel confident to go out into the world.

They also need to acquire the conversational skills to make them good company. When people enjoy speaking with them because of their warmth, humour, interest in others or unique take on the world, they are likely to feel at ease in interactions. They are likely to have fewer fears about facing social situations when they are equipped with the skills necessary to comfortably participate in conversations.

But becoming good company is still only half the groundwork they need. You must also prepare them to cope with tricky situations likely to happen in their interactions with any of the eight billion people they could potentially meet – with all their differing personalities, variations in status, their off days, contradictory opinions, power moves, and generational and cultural divides.

Of course, a person with great social skills and ability to handle tricky interactions can still feel anxious about meeting up with people and mingling with them. They might feel this way because of unwarranted self-doubt, false perceptions of the way others experience their company, or a degree of perfectionism about just how interesting, entertaining, and caring they need to be with other people. They may also have distorted memories of past exchanges and incorrect beliefs about the lasting effect of minor conversational slip-ups. Here our focus is on building your child's skills in making friends, so they are more confident coming into and leaving social exchanges.

Help them be easy to like

In an ideal world, everyone would accept your child exactly as they are. And thankfully society is becoming more tolerant than it used to be. But you cannot rely on this always being the case.

Your child will have an easier time in the company of others and be more acceptable to a wide range of people if they display 'likeable' traits. So which character and behaviour traits have psychologists identified as making a person likeable?

Self-acceptance

Broadly liking ourselves forms the foundation of our likeability. We need to feel confident of our right to be in a conversational space, our right to express our opinion, and our basic worthiness as a person.

To help your child feel this way it is important that you show them love and acceptance. One of the simplest ways of doing this is forming a loving attachment with your child by spending time with them, giving affection to them, and talking to them in a caring way.

It is also important to show you accept both their strengths and their weaknesses. Applaud and praise them for the things they do well. But don't shy away from acknowledging the times they don't do so well. Normalise this: if they play poorly in a soccer game and come off the field saying they were terrible – and they were – don't rush to praise to make them feel good again. Simply shrug and say, 'Yeah, sometimes that happens. But you kept going and showed fantastic persistence. Good on you.'

When you show comfort with all aspects of your child – their strengths and weaknesses – you show you truly accept them.

This acceptance is a more loving form of parenting than only acknowledging their triumphs. It means you love your child for who they really are, not the perfect version of them. This will assist them to slowly develop self-acceptance.

Self-confidence without self-focus

It is important for a person to be confident, but not to be so confident that they are annoying. Admittedly, it's hard to get the balance right. Many parents, when driving their child to the town of Self-Esteem, can inadvertently go too far and end up in Boastville.

Main Character Syndrome (MCS) is a term that might help parents think about this. A person who has MCS thinks they are the protagonist of any situation they are in. They think they're always the most important person in the room. They are self-centred and think mainly about their own needs when talking to others.

Imagine a conversation between two friends, Sidone and Jo. Sidone says she has some good news. She's just been promoted to area manager. Instead of offering congratulations as her first impulse, Jo replies, 'Really? I thought I was in line for promotion last week, but I didn't get one.' This suggests she is thinking of herself, not her friend, which is classic MCS behaviour.

Main Character Syndrome is a pop-psychology term. In the therapy room, a psychologist might describe the trait as relating to characteristics of narcissism or entitlement. Nonetheless, as psychologists we find MCS useful because it describes traits most people can easily identify. And while parents might be hesitant to describe their child as narcissistic, they can easily pick when their child is starting to behave like a main character.

Parents encourage their child to think they are the most important person in the household when they make them the centre of the family by letting the child's needs trump everyone else's. Or when they allow the child to dominate most conversations, especially if they permit them to take the spotlight in the typical interplay between siblings vying for airtime.

Some parents completely focus their attention on their child's performance on the field or on the drama stage, rather than valuing others. At sports matches, they might enthusiastically praise their child, but not even comment on the goals or runs scored by other team members.

MCS is not just an annoying trait. If a child genuinely thinks they are the main character in every situation, they are likely to be overly concerned about how they are perceived by others because they believe they always stand out and everyone is looking at and noticing them. This can bring on anxiety about their performance or any social situation.

To make matters worse, children who focus only on themselves are not likely to be able to go along with the conversational flow. They tend to be rather boring to talk to because their contributions are usually self-centred, even self-congratulatory, and they lack self-restraint. They might indeed stand out, but for the wrong reasons.

Children become more self-focused at certain developmental stages (hello teen years!) but be careful not to allow a momentary trait to last longer than it should. There are ways to encourage your child back into the village of Everyone Matters. Teach them from an early age to ask questions of others, like 'how are you?' together with a follow-up question. As they become more conversationally skilled in their late primary years, gently tell them when they're being a little too self-focused. Make sure they stick to conversational themes and not just talk about themself. Let them learn through feedback in your home, rather than wait until they become rejected by a peer group because they are 'full of themself'.

As they grow older, ensure your coaching occurs in private, never in front of others (not even your partner). Your child will be receptive to one-on-one discussions if they know they are protected and can trust that you are not sharing what is said with everyone. If you give them feedback in the presence of others, they are less likely to actively listen and accept what you tell them because they may feel exposed and self-conscious – or even ashamed – with others looking on.

Empathy

Your child needs to be okay with who they are. They also need to be okay with accepting the people around them. This involves being aware that others sometimes feel differently, think differently, and experience events and shared situations differently to them. In short, your child needs empathy.

Empathy is essential to being good company. When we tell someone we have had a bad experience, we want them to be caring toward us. When we tell a friend we lost our grandmother's engagement ring or grandfather's war medals when moving house, we want them to acknowledge our feelings and offer some sympathy. We don't expect them to change the subject immediately or go straight into a story about the time they lost their phone for an hour.

Having empathy makes you good company because people feel they can be themselves around you. Your friends know that when they tell you something deep or important about themselves, you won't laugh at them or use the information cruelly in the future. An empathetic person will listen, show care rather than pity, and take it upon themself to respond to their friend's needs at the time. Their empathy urges them to do what they can to make the other person feel better, rather than solely focus on their own needs.

Children are born to be naturally empathetic. From a young age, they notice their parents' facial expressions and mirror these or anticipate what the parent is likely to do next. This primes them to notice other people's feelings. We see toddlers hug each other when they fall over or go and find an adult to help their friend because they recognise their buddy needs assistance.

You can't necessarily teach empathy, but you can encourage it by regularly making your child aware of other people's experiences and feelings. When you read a book or watch TV together, ask your child questions about what they think the characters might be feeling. As they become older, make them aware of the nuances in emotions and encourage them to become less black and white in their thinking about people. You might note that even the 'baddie' is human and might feel hurt when people say mean things. A classic example of this is Professor Snape in Harry Potter: at the start he is depicted as a nasty character, but he ends up being brave and compassionate.

You can encourage your child's empathy by asking them how others might feel as a result of their actions. If your child breaks their sibling's toy, ask them to imagine what their sibling might feel. Have them brainstorm ideas of ways to help their sibling feel better by way of apology. This is a more empathetic consequence than simply saying the word 'sorry' which they might not truly feel.

Occasionally let them know your feelings and reactions. When you talk about your day, mention that your co-worker had a tough time, so you made them a cup of tea. If your neighbour has their pet pass away, encourage your child to think of nice things your family can do for them.

When you encourage empathy in your child, remember they need good boundaries as well. They must not feel responsible for everyone's feelings or become overwhelmed when learning to be empathetic. Some children easily become burdened by a friend who wants their constant support when going through a rocky period.

Anxious children often believe they need to help people all the time. Your child can end up being the one everyone turns to; consequently they can become swamped by an overwhelming sense of responsibility. When they believe putting themself last will make others like them, they can give disproportional conversational care to others through attentive listening rather than contributing. Over time, their friendships may become one-sided as they continue to focus primarily on their friends' needs. Remaining likeable in this way can easily get out of hand, particularly when a friend who faces genuinely difficult situations has become reliant on your child's shoulder to lean on.

Encourage them not to take on care of their friends as their perpetual responsibility. Give them ways to recognise when their caring is becoming too much for them by taking up an excessive amount of their time or energy. This may occur when they feel weighed down by responsibility for a friend's problem yet have no idea how they may help them. Or when they feel obliged to constantly look after one particular friend's needs at the cost of maintaining other friendships. Let them know that in these times, they should seek advice from a trusted adult. Make them aware that it is often more caring to support their friend to find proper help because fixing problems can take time and multiple resources.

Being interested in people

These days most parents make sure to spend time with their child and chat to them. Parents do the lion's share of the effort in these conversations: they continue to appear interested in what their child has to say even when the story about what happened in the playground handball game has gone on for some time and has no end in sight.

This is important. You need to be generous while your child finds their feet conversationally. But there is a point when you need to step back from overdoing your efforts and allow your child to step up conversationally. This is essential for them to get on in the world beyond your home because others will not be as enamoured of your child's self-focused chatter.

The excellent television program, *Love on the Spectrum*, is about people with autism socialising and finding love. The dating coach on the show, Jodi Rodgers, teaches participants techniques to help them sustain a conversation when they first meet someone by actively asking questions of the other person as well as speaking about themselves.

Many of us need to learn these skills, not just people with autism. It's particularly important for young people who have not been required to do much in conversations other than talk about themselves. Start to teach your child critical conversational skills when they are as young as six or seven years old to help them form genuine connections with other people during exchanges.

As they grow older, coach your child how to show authentic interest in other people and put deliberate effort into keeping others involved in discussion. When it is just the two of you, make sure you are not the only one asking questions. When talking to your tween or teen, use the three-question rule to encourage them to ask you something. Ask them three questions and then give some space for them to ask about your day. Don't fill every conversational space with another question for them, as this won't happen with their peers. Occasional periods of silence teach your child to come up with their own questions and to realise that pauses during discussions are normal.

Teach them easy conversational topics they can turn to with most adults: 'How has your day been?' or 'Have you got a busy weekend planned?' For younger children, try 'What have you been doing this morning?' Informal conversations with peers often start with an observation, so encourage your child to observe and refer to their surroundings. They could make a comment about the weather, the wall decorations, or the noisy street they are walking down. Explain the art of non-confrontational questions: 'What is the flavour of your yoghurt today?' is a gentle query that doesn't try to tease out particularly personal information. Make sure they understand that some people are shy at first and open questions will help them expand on their responses. If they were to say what they watched on TV last night, a good follow up would be, 'I haven't seen that show yet. What's it about?'

Let them practise involving others in conversations. Have a roster for family members to take turns at keeping conversation flowing at the dinner table, with everyone expected to help. Perhaps have a rule that each person must answer with more than a single word and must occasionally throw questions back to others in response.

Teach your child how to recognise times when another person is not interested in talking. It's important for them to be able to tell whether a person they approach is inclined to chat in that moment: one-word answers that give away little information usually mean that the other person doesn't want to talk. Let your child know of instances when this has happened to you, but you knew not to take it personally. Tell them the words to use to extricate themself from the situation: 'You seem a bit busy now – we can chat later,' or 'Nice to see you. I'm going to see how Liora is going.'

Check that your child is actually listening in conversations. Quiz them on what they've learnt about other people in their time together. If they seem to have learnt nothing after spending time with their grandparents, prompt them to ask a few questions next time.

Being interesting to talk to

Think about the people you most enjoy spending time with – the ones who can make you laugh out loud, entertain you with a great story, or who consider life in a different way, like Luna Lovegood in Harry Potter, or Kramer in Seinfeld. There are ways to encourage your child to be just as engaging, so people will seek their company.

Start by encouraging them to be interested in the world. People who are attentive to and knowledgeable about what's going on around them tend to be more interesting to talk to. Encourage your child's curiosity by talking about and being involved in your neighbourhood. On daily walks with your young child, chat about what you see, such as newly planted trees, and the birds and pets in your area. When your child becomes older, encourage them to engage with world events and politics by watching the news or reading the newspaper in a café together. Chat about the stories and ask them for their opinion. To keep them involved, don't judge their opinions as being 'right' or 'wrong'. Be curious about why they feel that way rather than shutting them down with a dismissive comment. This will develop your child's skill in being able to expand on their reasoning for their beliefs and help them learn to debate ideas.

Young children often have difficulty getting to the point in stories, and you can accommodate that. But as they get to mid primary, encourage your child to keep talking while also helping them to focus on their important points. Do this through questions like 'Why was it funny?' and 'What did you enjoy most?'. This will help them not ramble on.

Take the time to teach your child how to tell a funny or interesting story about their day. Encourage them to use an engaging start and a relatively quick way of getting to the point. You can coach them by telling stories together to someone else. When you both come back from the shops, team up with your child to tell another family member about something interesting that happened. Plan it by first asking them, 'How are we going to say it?' This will help them understand how to make the most of their story.

As they become older, make sure they don't download their entire day to others without pausing for breath or asking for any input or mutual discussion, as this will make them less interesting. Every now and then, be frank, perhaps with a twinkle in your eye: 'This story seems to be going on a long time – is it going somewhere anytime soon?'

Discuss films and shows you've watched together. Ask your child to nominate their favourite character or funniest scene. Have them give the show a rating out of five and justify it. Ask them how they would describe the show to someone who hadn't seen it in three sentences and without giving away the plot. Let's face it, talking about which TV shows we are binge-watching is a common topic of conversation these days! After they tell a story, be sure to allow someone else to have a turn so your child doesn't become too accustomed to being in the spotlight – they are not performing a one-person show.

Sense of humour

Most children love having fun. Don't overlook the significance of how much fun a person is to be around in their relationships with others.

Recent research from Florida Atlantic and Concordia Universities sought to understand the link between a child being fun and their likeability and popularity. It specifically looked at children in late primary school when their need to have fun typically increases alongside a growing emphasis on peer status and reputation.

The researchers found that a child being considered 'fun' was an important predictor of their social success, namely their likeability and popularity. Even when they excluded other factors known to be associated with popularity, such as pro-social behaviour, leadership skills, physical attractiveness and low levels of aggression, children who were regarded as fun to be with were more likely to have good standing among their peers.

So, what makes a child fun? Fun people are good company because they're enthusiastic and engaged but also able to control their zest such that they don't always dominate a space. They don't necessarily seek the spotlight – fun people get into the spirit of events, are more cooperative with those around them, and tend to draw others into their amusement. They are good humoured and see the funny side of things, often making a joke or laughing easily at other's quips. This doesn't necessarily make them the class clown, but means they help make any situation enjoyable or bearable for everyone by not dwelling on problems or being negative about what's happening.

Fun people are also more likely to show resilience and resourcefulness when faced with challenge. They are likely to embrace new experiences and not just follow the same old pattern where they can predict and control the result.

Some parenting approaches end up damping down children's fun side. Giving children predictable lives and guaranteed outcomes can lead them to not embrace change or seek new experiences. Even the toys parents choose can help build children's sense of fun. Toys like blocks and empty boxes are far better than single-purpose toys that have limited versatility in creative play. Prop boxes in drama rooms contain common objects, simple costumes and pool noodles because these encourage children to use their imagination.

There are ways to bring out the fun in your child. Embrace novelty: occasionally have family dress-up dinners where everyone wears clothes and eats food of a certain colour, or acts and talks like pirates or robots. Set times to make daily life an adventure: have the family do Saturday chores in costumes you can easily create (a tiara clean-up morning) or play some loud music to dance to as you each gather your laundry and tidy up. Play fun games like charades or create outfits out of items in the recycling box. At dinner, ask everyone if anything funny or interesting happened that day or that week, and get them to tell the story.

Try to see the funny side of mildly annoying things to encourage your child to take the same attitude.

Deliberately choose to show them funny, age-appropriate TV shows to bring out a good sense of humour in them. We like *Bluey* and *Horrible Histories* (the latter is good for their history knowledge too), but any clever TV comedy you can both enjoy is good. Be careful of shows like *The Simpsons* until they are mature enough – some parents have found the rapscallion Bart can exert too great an influence on their child's behaviour and attitude.

Ability to be part of the team

It is important for your child to experience the glow of the spotlight, and it's even more important for them to learn to be part of the support crew. Judith's first career was as a high-school drama teacher, and she knows firsthand how drama helps students develop skills in creativity, empathy and communication. High-school drama allows teens to assume a wide range of different characters and emotions at a perfect time to help them slowly develop confidence in expressing their own personalities.

Studying drama also allows students to be in the spotlight and learn to be self-assured when all eyes are on them. It's not only the lead roles that help students develop confidence and capability; many support roles in school performances develop equally important skills.

In musicals, the group of actors who form the chorus onstage often don't have speaking roles. They need to work together – singing, dancing or quietly being in the background – to provide a sense of spectacle. Most musicals also need a backstage crew to paint sets, set up props on and off stage, and perform unheralded work, such as makeup or front of house. And being in the stage band is critical to the musical, yet often gains little attention.

Many students see greater value in having a speaking role on stage but being part of the support crew also enables children to thrive. Being in the chorus gives them the experience and confidence boost of being on the stage without the pressure of carrying the show. Those who work behind the scenes or in the orchestra enjoy the camaraderie of being part of the performance without the burden of the spotlight. Taking on roles which support the lead actors teaches children to fit in with others and to let others have their moment in the limelight as well. Everyone needs to pitch in to accomplish a common goal; there is no room for show ponies who insist they remain the centre of attention or that the group cater to them. Most of our working and family life involves this type of teamwork. Even the most talented singers and actors have learned to be comfortable with their moments in the background.

Knowing they can participate in a performance for an audience without being the centre of attention gives anxious children confidence and helps quell any fears they may have of standing out for the wrong reasons.

Children should also be able to cope when the spotlight isn't on them in life, and their sibling gets more attention than they do. Every child deserves special birthday attention, and parents have no need to say sorry to siblings on these occasions. If parents feel they need to apologise, it doesn't bode well for the miffed child's co-operation skills and ability to be good company.

Children who don't take part in school performances need to learn teamwork skills in other ways. Encourage your child to play a team sport so they learn how to work with and support others. When they are 'good sports', they reap the benefits of belonging: whether they win or lose, they do so with others, and the pressure of victory or defeat does not rest on just one person.

As often as you can, ensure siblings work together in activities like cooking a meal or cleaning up the kitchen. Make sure everyone takes turns to lead family discussions about activities you will do together, such as the games you will play on Sunday afternoon, or how you will celebrate dad or mum's birthday. You might say, 'Hey Joseph, why don't you help us decide which sport we'll play in the park?'. Other times you could assign support roles, such as nominating one child as timekeeper to help everyone be ready for school on time.

Being inclusive

Children don't need to include everyone in all of their games or invite every child they know to their party. But it is beneficial for them to develop a natural inclination to include others. It shows kindness and encourages people to feel more comfortable in their company.

Remember there are two different motives for friendship. Some people want popularity, and some seek intimacy. Those who strive for popularity usually do so at the expense of someone else, through relational aggression. Children who do this often pick on different kids on different days to diminish that child's status and cement their own position of power. These children strategically reject inclusivity.

When a person's goal in making friends is intimacy, that closeness is sometimes formed by encouraging another to mutually dislike someone else. Psychologists call this triangulation: becoming chummier with one person by bonding over a shared dislike of another. It's the easiest way in the world to form a connection. You might become closer to your co-worker by kvetching about your manager. In the long line at the post office, you might briefly bond with someone over how slow the person behind the counter seems to be. Right now, your child and a schoolmate are likely forming a better friendship by complaining together about how annoying their nagging parents are (see, they actually needed your nagging all along!).

It's not realistic to expect your child to be a loving friend to everyone all the time. Every now and then, intimacy in one relationship is enhanced by sharing the frustrations of other relationships. Most of us occasionally double dip and complain about our friends or partner to our co-workers, and later complain about our co-workers to our partner or friends.

But to do this regularly is not good for true intimacy. It displaces real conversations and truly getting to know others. If your child is overly reliant on this technique to be friends with someone, it stops them getting to know other people in their class because they and their best mate have decided that everyone else is awful. This exclusion will disadvantage them if their best friendship goes haywire and they need to look for another child to hang out with at lunchtime. If your child is inclusive and kind to others, they will form a wider friendship base from which to draw company.

Encourage these qualities in your child. Show them how to be inclusive when you are with them. If a family disagreement results in divided opinions, try not to let your child know about it so they don't form an unhelpful 'us and them' mentality. Don't complain about their school, their teacher or a classmate to them, and make sure you don't encourage this type of conversation by asking, 'How was that annoying classmate/teacher of yours today?' Stay open with your questions and pay as much attention to their friendship joys and successes as their challenges.

Do all you can to be warm and supportive of your child's friends and talk about any tricky qualities in others without demonising them or picking their personalities apart. Chide your child when they use derogatory terms like NPC (non-playable character) to describe someone lacking in social skills. Remind your child that most people feel out of their depth in some social situations, and that when this happens to them, they will hope to have someone there who is kind enough to include them. Tell them that karma is kind to those who are kind.

Giving friendships time to develop

It is important to teach your child that making friends is easier when they are broadly affable early on and then slowly let their opinions shine through. The more initially appealing people are – by not running their personality or opinions up a flagpole – the easier it will be to form friendships, even in schools where children and teens have freedom to dress and express themselves how they choose.

It's also important that they don't overshare too early. People often do this in an attempt to create instant intimacy. But when a child tells a potential new friend about their anxiety, or how their last friendship ended, they can overwhelm them. They risk being thought of as 'hard work' and may be overlooked in favour of someone who does not seem to expect support for their personal issues on a first meeting.

> *Remind your child to go slowly –*
> *there's no need to impress new people right away*
> *or form instant friendships.*

Tell them that most new acquaintances won't be interested in hearing about their personal life and frank opinions until they have also had a chance to talk. It may take a couple of encounters before either feels that a friendship will develop.

Being comfortable with the slow pace of evolving friendships might seem unnatural to a child, although less so to teenagers. Adjusting your child's expectation of instant closeness will help an over-sharer hold back and allow them to be less fearful or unnaturally show-offy with new acquaintances. Let them know it is important to keep some aspects of themselves close at first, and deliberately and wisely choose who to tell certain things to after allowing some time to get to know them. If they don't do this, they risk their intimacy not being respected, even to the extent that personal vulnerabilities may be cruelly broadcast to others.

Develop their friendship-making skills

There are some very practical ways you can encourage your child to develop their friendship-making skills. Try these.

Let them practise their skills in familiar environments

Many parents worry excessively about their child making friends on their first day of pre-school, primary school or even high school. Help them prepare by practising their connection-making skills in a range of situations, so they become good at meeting others and increase their confidence. Have them play with other kids at the park or playground; let your child initiate this. When you take them to parties and family gatherings, let the kids simply find each other. If you want to be involved at first – perhaps by introducing them – you can. But try to involve yourself less over time. Remember, you will not be in the playground at school; they need to become fairly self-reliant when starting an interaction with another child.

If they are reluctant at first, offer to stand near them as they play with another child or children they don't know. Then slowly move away. Stay within viewing distance but deliberately move further back each time so they become less reliant on your presence to help them approach new friends.

If your child is not comfortable to play with others without your assistance, teach them the friendship-making skills detailed below.

Teach them the basics of making friends

Some children instinctively know how to make friends, but others don't. You can help by teaching your child the basics.

Give your young child the following tips to help them connect with playmates:

- Start by mimicking other people. Sit where they are sitting and do what they are doing.
- Ask another child if they would like to play together and, if they agree, copy what they do. If they run to the monkey bars or swings, run with them.
- Be a good listener. Always make eye contact when you talk to a person to show confidence and interest in them.
- Be generous. Offer to share a toy or treat you have, take turns in activities, listen to their preferences for games, be gracious when their performance is the best at the time. No one wants to play with a sore loser.
- Be assertive if another child doesn't play fairly or share properly. Everyone involved has the right to enjoy play.
- If another child is mean, move away and befriend someone else.

Give your older child or teen these tips for starting conversations with potential friends:

- Make eye contact with people so you can see who seems open and friendly.
- Show interest when others are speaking by matching your facial expressions to their expressed emotions. Nod your head to encourage the speaker to continue.
- Try a neutral, easy topic of conversation at first, such as what you are both doing at the time. Questions are easy ways to get another person involved. At lunchtime, you might say, 'I've got my favourite sandwiches, chicken and tomato. What's in yours?' Or in class, ask if they are interested in the topic of the lesson.
- Encourage the other person to talk a little about themself, so they will then feel inclined to listen to you in return.
- Don't fall into the trap of trying to find things in common with someone you have just met; this puts pressure on you to work too hard – it's unnecessary and you may end up talking too much in your attempts to find shared experiences or interests.
- Look for 'breadcrumbs'. Listen to what the other person says and ask

them more about it. People drop clues in conversation that indicate topics they are comfortable talking about. When someone says, 'I was so busy yesterday', they give you permission to ask what they were busy doing. (You can help your child practise this in a lighthearted way by pretending to meet them for the first time and starting a conversation which includes strategically placed clues for them to detect. Let them practise following your breadcrumbs as you speak.)
- Let the other person contribute equally to the conversation. Try not to say more than three sentences in a row to ensure you don't dominate.
- Try not to show too much emotion when you initially talk with a new person. Remember you are trying to encourage conversation, not take centre stage or create an impression you are hard work to be with.

Let them learn from their sibling relationships

Your child's relationship with their siblings (or cousins or neighbours if they are an only child) can help ready them for the ups and downs of friendship. The love–hate dynamic of these relationships prepares children for the playground and friendships beyond the family.

Most siblings can't help but compare themselves and their achievements because they are in such close proximity to each other. This is similar to school friends who all get the mark for their English essay at the same time or learn who got on the A team for debating together.

Often this comparison is strongest when report cards come out. Emma's grades may have improved greatly, and her teacher's comments are more glowing than those given to Noah, her more consistent sibling. Or Ethan might have received a C for Science while their sibling, Mason, received an A.

When you receive comparative feedback on your children, avoid trying to level it by immediately stepping in with some comment about how Ethan is more responsible with taking out the bins. This is pity praise, and if he is over eight years old, he will pick this up as a desperate win. This will make him feel worse.

Instead, be matter of fact when Ethan says he did worse than Mason. Maybe agree, nonchalantly, that Mason is better at Science *right now*. You could say, 'You can't be best at everything. That's okay.'

The truth is not cruel. What's cruel is to make children think they need to win all the time in life. Your child can't be best at everything. And the sooner they accept this, the better off they will be. They will also be less anxious about their minor mistakes and not as likely to dwell on future comparisons where they don't come out on top.

Siblings can also pick at and bully each other. If a younger sibling cannot get their older sibling to play with them, they know they will still get their attention by annoying them. Bonus points if they get their sibling to yell at or hit them – then they can let their parents know how mean their sibling is. This becomes a huge win if it gets them sympathy from their parent and their sister or brother ends up in trouble.

Your child is likely to have classmates who will also be prepared to simply annoy them to get attention. Help them be ready for these peers by showing them how to deal with sibling problems at home.

Remind them they can't make someone play with them or be their friend

Sure, they might want their sibling to hang out with them, but they can't force them to. Likewise, they might want to be friends with a particular group at school, but they can't force that either. Making and being friends is a mutual decision. It's not necessarily fair – but it's life.

Give siblings the same consequence for joint misdemeanours

If they can't agree or choose to fight, they should each receive the same outcome. So, if the argument started over which TV show to watch, they both bear the cost of the TV being turned off for ten minutes. If they argue over the use of a toy, take it away from them for five minutes, then give it back to see if they can play with it cooperatively.

Teach them to ignore annoying behaviour

Given they will both receive the same consequence, it is in their best interest to ignore their sibling's attempts to bother them. Coach your child how to do this: suggest they move to another room or say something neutral and unemotional like 'you might be right, and you might be wrong' to show their sibling they don't really care.

Let them sort squabbles out

Unless quarrels become physical and may potentially cause harm, you are best to let them work out a solution. Every time you step in, you stop them from learning negotiation skills or ways to de-escalate tension.

Take preventative action

Keep them busy and separated at times they usually argue, such as when they are tired or bored, but slowly oversee this less as they become older. Encourage them to cooperate by offering a reward if they work together, like letting them watch TV after they clean up the kitchen together.

Equip them for times they are on their own

In an ideal world, your child would always have someone they could play with at lunchtime. But this will not always happen; sometimes they will find themselves without their friends. Even if they have a wide friendship base, there will still be times when they can't find someone to play with. To prepare them, encourage their ability to amuse themself without needing to be with others.

Schedule time when your child needs to find things to do without your company. Take them to the council library and let them browse the books themself. When you dine out with adult friends, have your child bring a book or game and let them amuse themself, rather than always bringing them into the conversation. The more they can do this, the better they will be ready to be good company for themself when alone. When reading, manners should not be dropped; teach your child to ask if it is alright to read a book when they're with company. Books shouldn't become a way of avoiding conversation with Aunty Meredith or Grandpa.

To confirm your child has the resourcefulness to solve a 'no friend at lunchtime' situation, ask them what they would do if they didn't have someone to hang out with. Give them some ideas, such as going to the library, exploring the school to find a quiet lunch area, taking a book, cards or art tools with them, or doing some form of exercise. Discourage spending time in the bathroom on their phone; Danielle's experience shows that many who choose to do this end up feeling inadequate and anxious, with no sense of accomplishment. The library or exercise are both far better options.

Show them how to manage inevitable friendship problems

There will be days when your child comes home and tells you their best friend was mean to them, or they had an argument with their mates. Their tear-stained face may make you want to go to that child's place and exact vengeance, John Wick style. But of course, you can't.

First, accept that all friendships have ups and downs: you can't protect your child from this. Understand that disagreements do not necessarily involve bullying. Behaviour must involve three elements to be considered bullying: deliberate targeting, regular occurrence and a power imbalance. A friendship disagreement does not usually qualify as bullying.

When your child is upset, it is important to offer them initial support. Listen to their story and show empathy to their plight. Perhaps suggest some alternative views of what happened – their friend might not have meant to be mean in what they said or might have been having a bad day which put them in a grumpy mood. By doing this, you reduce the likelihood that they will view the friendship disagreement as permanent or personalised. You don't need to get to the bottom of the issue immediately; given time, your child will deduce the real reason for their disagreement.

Have them think through what they could do if the behaviour happens again. Depending on the situation, they could have a range of responses: clearly stating to their friends how they are affecting them, letting the matter go and deliberately changing the subject, or even moving away from the person or group for a time.

If the problem persists, seek assistance from the school by talking to your child's teacher or year level coordinator. Remember to work amicably with these people – it is in their best interest to help all children and their counsel will be invaluable for all parties to move on.

Parents and their child's friendships

Parenting is sometimes a lonely job. You may not be as close to work colleagues as you used to be because you no longer have time for out-of-work catch-ups. Your own friendship groups may feel more distant now that your lifestyle has changed and no longer matches that of those who don't have children. The responsibilities of parenting can be so consuming that you barely have enough energy and space to catch up with yourself, let alone time for meeting up with old friends, particularly those who you think might not understand your circumstances.

Parenting is also a more intensive job today, with parents far more actively involved in raising their children than in previous generations. This can significantly affect their social life: there is research that shows parents born after 1960 have 51% fewer friends than those born before. Some parents hope that when their child goes to school and makes new friends, they will also become friends with the parents of their child's schoolmates.

However, parents who become over-involved in their child's friendships can inadvertently cause their child social harm. The following guidelines will ensure you avoid this.

Don't pressure your child to make friends or the 'right' friends

Some parents view their child's schooling as a chance to network and meet the 'right' kind of other parents. While this might extend their social connections and improve their business contacts, it is not helpful for their child at all. Children have enough social pressure as it is without parents placing more on them by insisting they make friends with the 'right' kids.

Be particularly careful not to pressure your child to be friends with the popular kids who have popular parents. If you want to make friends with those parents, do your best at parent gatherings but don't expect your child to help pave the way for your social circle to expand in your desired direction.

Remember that befriending the popular kids can occasionally involve dealing with some strong and sometimes manipulative personalities. The right friend for your child is the one who likes them and treats them well. The 'popular' child may be the worst friend for your child, just as the popular parent might be the worst person for you to aspire to have as a friend. Popularity in itself can reduce opportunities for socialising with a newfound friend: if they are always invited everywhere by everyone, they may not have much time for you.

Also take care not to pressure your child to be invited to a certain number of birthday parties. Some parents virtually tell their child they are not making enough friends. Different children need different numbers of friends: it is particularly awful to suggest to your child that their friendships aren't up to scratch, or that their low popularity is embarrassing. This can directly cause them to feel inadequate and suffer social anxiety.

Judith has helped children overcome feelings of social inferiority arising from this kind of behaviour. In one clinical situation, a parent claimed their 12-year-old daughter didn't have friends. When the child objected and said she did have friends, the parent countered with, 'No, you don't – not real friends.' The parent may have meant to help their child, but their response was intensely hurtful for the child to hear. We suggest you seek assistance for friendship problems only if your child brings up friendship as a concern, and you and the school determine it is an issue. Otherwise, leave the matter be and let your child slowly find their friendship feet.

Show kindness in your friendships with other parents

Occasionally a group of parents dominates a year like a *Mean Girls* clique. You may have come across similar alliances in a workplace, a mother's group, a fundraising committee or any environment where some adults are keen to form a power bloc that places them in charge. While it may reflect the politics of the playground, it is not okay. Be aware of this dynamic and don't become part of this type of cruelty, even if the in-group accepts you. Don't play their game in WhatsApp discussions or social media comments to fit in with them. Be aware that they can easily turn and do to you what they do to others. Instead of joining in their behaviour, do the opposite. Deliberately seek out and engage with parents who are left on the outer at school events and model the inclusivity you wish to see in your own child.

Parent and child friendship groups

Imagine your child has met a great group of kids at their school. When you meet their parents, you all get along beautifully together. Saturday afternoon barbeques become a regular occurrence. There's even been talk of going to the same beachside location for the next summer holidays. This would be fantastic for everyone involved . . . wouldn't it?

Be careful. Children often grow out of their friendship groups, particularly in early high school. This is fine for a child if they find another group of friends, but often their parents aren't happy because they had started to rely on their child's previous friends' parents as part of their social life.

Although your child's choice may come at some cost to you in this situation, try to maintain those friendships without your child's involvement. Invite a few of those friends for coffee during the school day, or out to dinner one night. This allows you keep up your connection with them without forcing your child to be friends with kids they no longer connect with. True friendship with other parents will transcend your children's friendships.

If your child has ongoing concerns about making friends or the dynamics of their peer group because of their anxiety, we urge you to consider the more targeted strategies described in the next two chapters or seek professional assistance. Let's look now at how to deal with the day-to-day problems and pre-emptive worries that children often experience.

CHAPTER 13

Helping your child face day-to-day challenges

Parents often inadvertently grow anxiety in their home through actions they take with the best of intentions. This chapter shows you ways to approach your child's daily challenges that help minimise anxious thoughts and feelings.

Now that you have read the preceding chapters, you know how to help your child become more resilient, self-regulated, resourceful, respectful and responsible as they mature. You've prepared them to use technology productively and within limits, and you're doing the groundwork that will see them form positive relationships with others throughout their lives. You're ready to start stepping back a little to allow them to step up.

But what happens when the new school year is about to start and your child is worried they will be separated from their friends, or they didn't get the role they wanted so badly in the school production of *Annie*, or they are visibly upset because they've missed out on an invitation to a classmate's laser tag birthday party, or they are crying because the 3D working volcano they have spent the last fortnight building for the Science competition has just collapsed? In these moments you will no doubt want to make them feel better immediately. You could call the school and ask the teacher to engineer the class lists, or speak to the musical director or the birthday child's parents, or roll up your own sleeves and make that Science project erupt again.

With this in mind, we have written this chapter to give you practical strategies to cope with day-to-day challenges. These are the times when your child is confronted with something difficult – a past, present or upcoming event that is worrying them – or when you are worried about how they will face a challenge. These strategies are designed to prevent their minor troubles or tricky feelings becoming worse and leading to ongoing problems for them. (We speak about more complex challenges in the next chapter.)

Each strategy will help you to help your child feel slightly better in the moment while they face their uncomfortable feelings and become more willing to meet the challenges that cause such feelings. When they learn how to positively manage their tricky moments, they become stronger, more resilient and able to face future challenges. This will prepare them to live an interesting and fulfilling life.

Our strategies make sure your child is not rewarded for their fears through the secondary gains we spoke about in chapter 8. They also encourage your child to reach their potential primarily through their own efforts, not via other people's adjustments and allowances. This makes them less dependent on other people's continual support.

When they face challenges

In the lead-up to a challenge – the first day of school, exam time, a NAPLAN or school admission test, an audition, or a school camp or sports day – many children become nervous about how they will manage when the time comes. So do many of their parents.

But parents often worry more about how a child feels in the days and moments leading up to the challenge than how they will perform during the event itself. Parents grapple with questions like 'How does my child feel about what will happen?' and 'Are they frightened about how this will turn out for them?' or 'Is this worry making them feel awful?' and 'Should I try to get them to talk about their feelings to help them feel better?'

These are perfectly reasonable questions and represent understandable parental concerns. Your child is about to face a challenging experience and you want to help them. But the way some parents act on these concerns is not so helpful. To quell their own fears that their child may not cope, they might ask their child about their mood and zone in on the child's feelings with questions like 'How do you feel about your exams?' or 'Are you nervous about starting school?' Most children – apart from the most confident or blissfully chilled – will say they are a bit nervous or worried.

When they hear this, some parents tell their child that they will ace the test, or surely get the role, or make heaps of friends on their first school day. All of these false reassurances can build the child's hopes unrealistically or add further unwanted pressure on them because of their parent's apparent prediction of success. The child might also learn that expressing their fears can result in extra parental attention and may even allow them to escape their upcoming challenge. This can be an incentive for them to focus intensely on how they feel if past experience has shown this will deliver consoling hugs, special treats and parental permission to get out of fulfilling a few of their usual responsibilities in a bid to make them feel better in the moment.

There are better ways to help your child in the lead up to events.

Turn down the focus on feelings

Once you know your child has a tendency toward anxiety, you are likely to discuss it – a lot. You may often ask them if they feel anxious because you want to make sure that worry is not adversely affecting them. This is understandable.

But regular discussion about feelings tends to amplify those feelings. This is particularly true when anxiety is often mentioned in general conversation in a way that suggests it is always hovering about and can be expected to visit regularly.

Instead, turn down the focus on fear and similar feelings. Deliberately try to be comfortable about your child's daily challenges. Talk to them about what is coming up in a way that encourages curiosity, rather than fear and dread. Keep your discussions low key and focus more on what the situation requires them to do than how they feel about it.

Increase opportunities for casual conversation

Make sure your conversations with your child do not centre around their potential problems or your own worries. Find more opportunities to have undirected, less serious conversations with them. Keep checking in with them in an unconcerned manner.

There are several good ways to do this. Do some chores side-by-side with your child to encourage casual chat. Visiting the supermarket or hardware store together can also encourage the sort of low-key conversations that bring some tweens and teens out of their cone of silence. And have them put away their phone and headphones when you are in the car together, so these devices do not block opportunities to chat casually.

Determine the importance of their challenge

It's important to determine what is truly a big deal and what is hyped up as a big deal but is not for most children. (The hype is usually simply clickbait.) Starting school is a big deal; the sports carnival is really not a big deal.

Try to remain moderately chilled about their normal school activities. You do not need to have a deep conversation before each task they do at school. You don't want to overwhelm them with heavy conversations which amplify their emotions and bump up fearful anticipation. Instead, ask them about their upcoming day or week using broad questions like 'What's on the agenda for today?' or wait until they bring the topic up themself. Try not to discuss their feelings about everything; focus on what they need to do in the short term and how this fits with their larger goals. When discussing the sports carnival, focus your comments more on their house colours costume and the camaraderie of the day, rather than the race they are running. When discussing their exam timetable, talk practically about their plans to keep up their fitness and take healthy breaks alongside their study sessions, rather than concentrating on their pre-exam feelings.

When your child faces a larger challenge, such as starting the school year or a new sport, be upbeat in your conversation, yet try to remain a little low key. 'School starts in two weeks – have we got everything you need? Do you have enough notebooks?' is preferable to, 'How are you feeling about school?' or 'Are you excited about school starting?' delivered with a look of concern or hesitation. Remember, your fear can instigate their fear. You want to project serenity and composure: don't let your nerves lead them to think you believe they have serious faults or that you doubt their capabilities.

Don't predetermine disaster

It is important to stay open to your child's ability to face circumstances you think might be tricky for them. Allow them to face situations like being put in a new class without their best friend or with the teacher they don't like, or being placed in the camp group with children they don't know well. Avoid predicting disaster and keep an open mind about the likely possibility that they will cope and learn from the experience. Even if the outcome is suboptimal – they don't make great friends with their camp group – they will feel more confident going into similar situations in future, because they have learnt to face and cope with them in the past.

Don't try to pump them up with confidence

Be careful not to pump them up with prefabricated confidence before a new experience: this can signal potential danger. Imagine if your friend said to you before a party with work colleagues, 'Before we go in, I just want to let you know how much I believe in you and how amazing I think you are.' Sounds reassuring, but it's not. The over-the-top encouragement makes it feel like you are going into a nest of vipers – is it a party, or an interview with Anna Wintour or Gordon Ramsay? Likewise, pumping your child up too much with talk of their impressive qualities as you drive them to their first taekwondo class can make the prospect sound more dangerous or scary than it is.

Don't do their work for them

If you or your child are worried about their History project result or even their homework, you might be tempted to step in and help them to ensure they do well. But if you do most of the work, the extent of your assistance suggests you think they can't do it themself. You can support them and coach them, yet still insist they do most of the work. Make sure you develop your child's academic confidence and independence, not teach them to over-rely on your help. If you have over-helped them in the past, slowly reduce your assistance and take on a coaching more than a doing role.

Don't sit with your child while they do their homework. Some children in upper primary still want their parent to sit with them as they do their work. While this seems harmless, the parent often offers regular praise and reassurance without realising it. This won't help the child to develop academic independence. Be confident that they will come and ask for your help if they need it.

Don't expect perfection
When you look at their Maths homework or hear them rehearsing their speech for the debate or practising their saxophone piece for an audition, be careful to keep your own perfectionism under wraps. Try not to correct every mistake they make and trust that their teacher or coach is best placed to tell them where they can improve.

Don't allow mental health days
We are not fans of 'mental health days' (see chapter 8). Children can feel rewarded for missing school because they get to decide what they do at home. Many end up spending the day gaming, scrolling on their phone in bed, or watching movies on the couch. It's not hard to see that this might prove to be more attractive than going to school.

Being away from school for a few days can often make it harder for your child to fit in with their classmates when they return. When they miss out on classroom activities, lunchtime discussions and in-jokes, they find it more difficult to get back into the groove of peer friendship. This can diminish their sense of belonging. Sensitive children in particular can be more reluctant to go to school after mental health days because they become convinced that others don't like them. This can be especially significant for long-term school refusers.

So don't let your child miss a school day for no reason. Even if they say they aren't doing anything in the final week of term, or don't want to go on cross-country day because it is 'boring', we recommend you insist they go. Be nonchalant about their 'hard' or 'tedious' life. Just as you have come to accept that you must go to work even on the days you don't want to, your child also needs to learn to face this aspect of normal life.

If they are genuinely bone tired and want to stay in bed, they may be doing too much. Pull back on some of their extracurricular activities or what you allow them to do on school nights. And check they are not sneaking their phone into their room at night because this can reduce their sleep quality.

When they are nervous before challenges

You hope your child will remain relatively calm about any approaching challenges. But they may – like any of us – experience some nerves and trepidation. If they mention fears, the following steps will help.

Listen to their concerns

When they tell you about their concerns, listen carefully and summarise them. Help develop their emotional literacy by naming the emotion you pick up: 'It sounds like you are a little nervous about school camp next week. Is that right?' Be precise and accurate when you describe what you think they feel. Deliberately use words here like 'sad', 'flat', 'uneasy'; steer away from expressions like 'anxious' or 'depressed' which can assume too much or overwhelm a child by making their feelings seem stronger than they are.

Let them know their feelings may be due to excitement

Make them aware that their feelings of fear might be connected to excitement. This is particularly true before they begin activities which are genuinely new for them, such as starting school for the first time. There is not much difference between our physical experience of fear and excitement; both can involve butterflies and a fast-beating heart. You might say, 'It could be nerves, but I imagine you are a bit excited too.'

Empathise with them

Show them you understand their feelings, particularly if they start to feel overwhelmed by their experience. 'Yes, exams can be nerve-racking. I think nearly everyone worries about them, particularly if they want to do well.' Or 'Most people are a bit nervous and excited about their school camp.'

Determine their particular worry

Ask if they are worried about anything in particular. You want to find out if their fear is general – they are worried because they haven't experienced the challenge before and are uncertain about how they will handle it – or specific – they are worried because they might miss you when they are away on school camp, or they might not be able to sleep at their sleepover, or they might not make any friends on their first day at school.

It's common for children to worry about speaking in class, just as many adults fear public speaking. If this is your child's concern, normalise it by telling them that everyone worries a little about speaking to a group. Practical suggestions – like looking at people when they speak to them or sweeping their eyes across, or slightly above, faces when speaking to a group – will help. Tell them the test of success for their speech or their 'show and tell' presentation is simply doing it – not doing it perfectly. Have them practise with you a few times to give them confidence. But leave feedback to their teacher: if you give them improvement tips at this stage, you will likely make them self-conscious. Remind them that the only way to become more confident about speaking in front of their class is to do it; avoidance only makes it harder the next time. Just as when they learned to ride their bike or tie their shoelaces, they can't skip the awkward and uncomfortable stages.

Keep these ideas in mind when your child is facing particular worries:

- Don't give false assurances to make them feel immediately better.
- When you understand their particular concern, say something that reduces their expectation or fear without making false promises. A false promise would be, 'Don't worry, you'll make heaps of friends on your first day.' It would be more helpful to say, 'Yes, that thought can be scary. I bet there are a few kids who feel the same. Even if you don't make lots of friends right away, I wonder what you will really enjoy on your first few days and who you will get to know? I guess we'll find out in a week.' Or 'It's normal not to sleep well when you're at your friend's house,' or 'Most kids miss their parents a bit when they first go to camp.'
- Show them you are curious about the outcome of their challenge. 'I can't wait to hear how it turns out. You'll know how it went by the end of tomorrow!' Then encourage them to be similarly open to challenge. 'I wonder how much sleep you will get,' or 'I wonder what you will like most about camp.' Additionally, try to remind them of times they have coped well in similar circumstances, such as when they had less sleep when they had an ear infection, yet still managed to do full days at school.
- Remind your child it can be fun when the unexpected happens. 'I remember the time I went on camp, and it rained half the night and when we woke up, our blow-up mattresses were afloat on a river of

water in our tent. My friends joked we should have gone to sleep in our swimming costumes!' The message is that surprises make life fun and create great stories. Most importantly, let them know that they will cope if something unpredictable happens.
- If your child asks you to reassure them directly about what will happen, try not to do so. If they ask, 'Do you think I will do well on the exam?', tell them you don't know, as you don't have a crystal ball to predict the future. Let them know that if they practise a healthy approach and prepare well, it's likely they will do okay, and the more exams they do, the better they will get at handling them. With camp, let them know to expect some challenges, some fun experiences and some unpredictable moments.
- Children seek reassurance in subtle ways. They might make extremely emotional statements in a bid to get you to reassure them. 'I'm going to fail!' is a declaration most parents will immediately want to deny with 'Of course, you're not going to fail!' Instead, tell your child that their concern about failing means they care, and this feeling will spur them on to put in an appropriate amount of effort beforehand. Let them understand that their fear of looming disaster is nothing more than their mind's way of urging them to work hard.
- Regardless of which methods your child uses to get your reassurance, the best comfort you can offer is that no one knows exactly what will happen and that they will get through the experience whatever occurs. Emphasise a 'let's see what happens' or 'what an adventure' approach to facing the challenge.
- Focus on their big-picture goals – getting through their first day of school or being able to swim – as opposed to their current feelings. Be matter of fact: anything new involves a somewhat awkward first day. Remind them they can't skip bits of the experience – they need to go through it all. This is what makes them stronger to face the next challenge, which may also be difficult at first but will eventually be rewarding.
- If your child becomes fixated on adverse outcomes, remind them of times they've been strong and tricky situations they've faced. This is where you pull out the stories of past difficulties, such as that time they ran into the tree on their bike and had to have stitches. Remind them of their bravery in these moments and that they are likely to

show similar strength again when things don't work out just as they would like.
- Try to make your conversations about your child's nervous feelings relatively brief. You want to move on fairly quickly and not give their fears too much attention. Try to shift your conversation and focus elsewhere – perhaps play a game in the backyard or enlist their help to start making dinner.
- Talk a little about the effect of mood on predictions – happy feelings make us not as likely to be negative, and bad moods tend to make us find fault with everything and sense impending danger at every turn. Try this example: work out how many traffic lights there are between your house and school and, if you are running late and stressed, ask them to predict how many red traffic lights you will get. Have them predict again when you are on time and again on a day when you are early and relatively chilled. This will demonstrate how our mood often influences the way we *think* the future will go. When your child realises that things go well or not, regardless of how they feel about what will probably happen or their current emotions, they are likely to conclude that there is no point in obsessing about events they can't control. More importantly, they will see that they typically cope with what happens, even if it turns out to be the worst predicted outcome – 15 red lights!

Reduce the performative elements of their challenges

Don't amp up the stress of an upcoming challenge for your child by inviting a cast of thousands to witness their performance. If it is their very first day of school, don't invite the extended family and the lady next door and her dog to accompany your child on the way there. The more people present, the more it hypes up the event and risks increasing your child's nerves. If you or your family or friends really want to observe the occasion, contain it by having a morning tea the week before school starts for everyone who would like to be part of the event. This will also serve as a trial run for your child to get dressed in their new uniform, so they can show everyone. You could make it fun by making lunchboxes for everyone to have a picnic in the backyard, providing an opportunity for your child to practise opening their lunchbox.

Likewise, don't invite all and sundry to be spectators when your child starts playing a new sport or learning to swim. Be there yourself for the first day and, should you wish, gradually bring family and friends to observe and cheer them on when they have developed some skill and confidence.

During their challenges

Imagine your child is at their first day of primary or high school or doing their most difficult exam. As much as you want to not think about it at all, you can't help but imagine worst-case scenarios. What if they don't like the school? What if they don't like their teacher? What if they bomb out on the test? If they are at their school camp, you might think, 'What if they're cold and don't have enough warm clothes?' or 'What if they are missing me terribly and need a quick chat with me to feel better?' or 'Surely the school wouldn't mind if I just check they are coping?'

Children don't need to be facing a milestone for this kind of parental thinking to kick in. If your mind tends to worry easily, you might think of everything that could go wrong – your child might not like their lunch, they might eat their lunch but still be hungry since they didn't have much for breakfast, that mean kid might pick on them again, they might get out first ball in cricket, they might forget their lines in rehearsal ... With thoughts like this on repeat in your brain, you might find it hard not to call the school for reassurance, or email or text your child directly if their school allows it.

Our advice? In a word, don't. Resist the urge to call the school or contact your child. Calm yourself and let them face their challenge. Be confident that the school will call you in an emergency and if there's no emergency, best let your child get on with what they need to do. (If you don't feel able to do this, chapter 14 will help you manage fears you find hard to let go.)

Don't respond to their texts during school time

If your child texts to tell you their bus was late, they've forgotten their lunch, and their friends are annoying them, don't reply. Texting you takes them away from being in the moment. And if you race up to school with their forgotten lunch, you won't develop their skills in coping and resourcefulness. Ignore those texts and trust the school and your child's ability to face minor challenge throughout the day without leaning on you.

Don't rush to pick them up from school

Similarly, don't act on your child's pleas to pick them up from school during the day. Trust that if they are genuinely sick or upset, the school will contact you. It's likely your child is trying to escape some aspect of their school day – their slight boredom, the difficult topic in their Science class, or the awkwardness of navigating friendships.

When their challenges are over

When you see your child after a big day, it's no wonder you can hardly wait to ask them about every part of it so you can verify that nothing went wrong. Perhaps you do this even when they have simply had a normal day. They might regularly face a barrage of questions from you as soon as they get in the car.

In your haste to make sure nothing went awry, you may not be interested in answers that indicate things went relatively well. When you ask if they liked the questions on the exam and they say yes, you may not examine this further because of your eagerness to learn the outcomes of other potential problems, like what happened with the friend they'd argued with the day before.

Remember we are dealing with human nature here. We all like to feel needed and useful. When a parent and child reconnect after school, it's understandable that the parent wants to know what happened in their child's day. But this ostensibly loving impulse can steer parents in an unhelpful direction because the emotional reward for the parent (feeling needed) is greater when they can help with things that go wrong than when the child copes independently and doesn't 'need' their parent to solve anything for them.

We do the same thing with our friends. When we catch up with a good mate, we often run through what's been happening in their life to find something that gives us the chance to offer our support and wise counsel. When we hear their job is going well and their partner is fine, we comment briefly – 'Great!' – and move on because there's not a lot more we can offer. But when we find out they're in a dispute with their neighbour over a damaged fence that might end up in court? 'Ooh, tell me more! I can probably help!'

Of course, talking through problems is often beneficial. But only when it is done in a helpful way. When we only look for or discuss what doesn't go well, we focus on our troubles and skip over the good things. We talk solely about the bad stuff in our lives when we're with those friends and family who direct conversations in a pessimistic way in an effort to help us. We risk over-examining our problems and, over time, friendly catch-ups can make us feel miserable.

When a parent continually cycles through topics with their child looking for problems, the child can become used to focusing on what's bad about their day, no matter how minor. Children learn that reporting problems brings them more conversational attention and parental care than reporting good things, so they produce problems almost on demand. In fact, many children come to know what their parent seems to want and walk out through the school gate with a ready list of problems that make their relatively good day seem much worse than it really was.

So how do you turn this around?

How to talk about their day

The first step is to stop your worry molehills turning into mountains by not catastrophising about what happens to your child outside your care. (More about this in the next chapter.) Instead, lead your conversations into positive territory.

Begin with broad questions

Start with an oldie but a goodie: 'How was your day?' or 'How was it at Grandma's?' or 'How was training?'

If their response is positive, be affirmative with your reply: 'Fantastic!' or 'That's great.' Then try to go further to massage their good experience. You might ask 'What happened?', 'Did Grandma put lots of raisins in her apple crumble for you?' or 'Did you think your performance was better too?' or 'Who else got on the team?' Remember to pay equal, if not more, attention to their good moments as you do to their disappointments. Another way to encourage your child to focus on what went well is to ask everyone at the dinner table to say what was the best part of their day as a means of catching up. This is far better than delving into your child's fears or your own problems and anxieties.

If your child doesn't report anything difficult, don't assume there's something they aren't telling you. Hold back from the desire to find out everything that's going on in their lives to reassure yourself. If they say that their day was good, trust that it was.

Don't give your anxious child more attention than others

It is easy to be much more attentive to your anxious child than to others in your family. This can happen when you allow their experiences to dominate conversations, or you fall into a habit of questioning them at length about the parts of their day which often make them nervous. And perhaps your chilled offspring don't seek to download their experiences daily. Attentional inequality does not benefit anyone. Deliberately involve all family members in conversation and ensure that everyone shows respect to each other when they are speaking. If you have an only child, insist they ask you about your day as well as telling you about theirs. They should not expect to be at the centre of every situation. Don't put your conversational camera into portrait mode to focus on one child only; leave it on the standard setting for everyone.

What to say when they report difficulty

Imagine your child gets in the car or walks in the door after their school day and tells you that something negative has happened – they didn't get the place on the debating team they had their heart set on, or they're not sharing a room with their three preferred friends on the Canberra trip. When this happens, you might be inclined to put things right for them. There are a number of ways you could do this.

If you respond, 'Oh, honey, I am *so* sorry,' you suggest to your child that you are somehow responsible for what has happened. Over time, they may come to blame you for sending them to that 'stupid school' as the cause of all their day-to-day difficulties, including those that every child experiences at any school.

If you occasionally offer a treat like an ice-cream or chocolate, you'll do no harm. But if every difficulty warrants an immediate reward, they won't learn how to face challenge without needing compensation.

If you call their school and attempt to fix the problem by urging the debating coach to rethink their team selection or asking the Year 6 coordinator to reassign room groups, you question these people's professional judgement. You also attempt to solve your child's difficulty on the spot without the need for them to do anything at all. And that's not helpful for them in the long term.

If you tell your child how unfair the decision is – or claim the debating coach has no idea of talent, or single out a member of the team as unworthy of their place because of their inferior debating skills – you risk turning your child's temporary upset into anger. Anger is a strong emotion, which helps us feel more powerful and justified in our position. But it is not helpful for your child to become angry because it also makes them feel like a victim.

If you let your child avoid their difficult situation altogether – allow them to stay home for a few days so they don't need to face the kids who got on the team or offer to fly to Canberra yourself so they can stay with you instead of their designated roommates – they don't learn to become resilient in the face of disappointment or difficulty.

All of these approaches are understandable because your child is hurting, and you are stepping in to make them feel better. But you cannot fix their problems forever.

When you immediately resolve your child's day-to-day difficulties,
you are not really helping them
because they do not learn how to face their challenges.

Help them by being by their side and supporting them, but don't take away their challenging situation.

How to teach them to manage disappointment

When your child experiences disappointment, begin by doing exactly as you do when they report nerves ahead of a challenge. Listen to them talk about the situation. Name the emotion they describe. Empathise. Normalise their response to let them know their feelings are understandable and you can see their side of things.

To teach your child how to manage their disappointment, proceed to offer some alternative points of view on their circumstances, particularly if you think your child may be catastrophising. If they think their new teacher hates them because they reprimanded them for trying to retrieve a ball from a restricted part of the school, reframe the situation. Suggest the teacher might have been worried about their safety and explain how worry sometimes turns into anger. Tell them about a time you yelled at them because your fear when they nearly ran out onto the road turned into anger. Urge them to stay open minded about their teacher. Over time, ask them to come up with different ways of looking at their situation instead of offering your suggestions.

Encourage them to stay open to the likelihood that their disappointment will be temporary, and they are best to wait and see what happens. (We look more closely at this in the next chapter.) Remind them that everyone – kids and teachers too – experience short-lived bad moods, which can make them tricky to deal with at the time. Explain to your child that their own mood may even have influenced their behaviour in the moment and that the teacher may have been responding in turn to the way they were behaving at the time. Alternatively, your child may have catastrophised the moment as being worse than what it was.

When their responses to challenges are more complex, consider the following strategies to teach them how to cope.

Show them their situation is not 'unfair'

Today we overuse the word 'unfair', often in situations that would more accurately be described as disappointing. When someone does not get on the Maths Olympics team or doesn't do well on the Geography assignment they worked hard on, it is disappointing but not unfair. A situation is genuinely unfair when someone is disadvantaged – for example, when a person who uses a wheelchair is unable to go on the school camp because the grounds cannot accommodate them. This is inequitable and therefore unfair.

The problem with inaccurately using the word 'unfair' is that it misrepresents the reality of life, which is that we are not always the lucky ones, our efforts do not always take us in the direction we hope, and we don't always end up with our preferred outcome. Everyone's life has swings and roundabouts, and if a child thinks their every disappointment is unfair, they will also feel deliberately targeted and less likely to get over a situation quickly. Gently correct them when they use the word 'unfair' and replace it with 'disappointing'. Then, after empathising with them, encourage them to accept their circumstances and move on.

Show them how to accept their situation

When we face difficulty or disappointment, we pretty much have two choices – to accept it or change it. We mentioned this in chapter 10, but let's look at it again in the light of managing daily challenges.

Sometimes we face tricky circumstances that we can't do anything about. When you want to be in the cool group at work or school, but you're not wanted as a member? You must accept it. When you want to be in the basketball team but you're not a natural and you're passed over in favour of taller players? You have to accept it. When you want to come top of the class or get that promotion but someone else pips you to the post? You have to accept it. When you want to marry George Clooney but some unbelievably intelligent, attractive, internationally renowned human rights lawyer beat you to it? You have to accept it. When you want to marry Amal Clooney but some unbelievably intelligent, handsome, award-winning movie star and director beat you to it? You have to accept it.

It doesn't feel good, but it is the best you can do. If there is truly nothing you can change, then you have to accept your circumstances – or forever live with unresolvable anger or sadness that detracts from your wellbeing. The earlier your child learns to accept their circumstances, the better.

One of the simplest ways to teach your child acceptance is to demonstrate it yourself. When they are faced with a situation they cannot change, support them with empathy but don't do anything that will take that situation away. Avoid directing them into another unhelpful emotion like anger. Turn down the volume on the topic by not bringing it up or discussing it extensively. Limit your chats and, when you think you've given the subject enough airtime, deliberately focus on something else and encourage them to do the same.

Acceptance doesn't mean glum resignation. We can always change our reaction to disappointment. Acknowledge your upset and deliberately move on to accept what has happened. This is much better than ruminating on a slight or transgression, which leaves you focused on the past rather than putting your best into the future.

Show them how to change their situation

If your child misses out on a one-off opportunity, such as being dux in Year 12 or going on the Year 10 Space Camp, they must accept the outcome and move on. But some opportunities offer a second chance. Your child may make next year's debating team, or they might be named goalkeeper for the next game. When this is the case, your child can take action to potentially change the result if they try again. In these circumstances you can help by teaching them to solve the problem of why their performance wasn't up to scratch. Understanding this will build their resourcefulness.

Your child can decide how to change their situation by simply reflecting on their performance and their preparation and then determining what they might do differently the next time. If their situation involved selection of some kind, they could also speak to the person who made the decision.

For example, your upper-primary or high-school student can speak to their coach or teacher to find out what they need to do to reach the standard needed to get on the team next time or what they could have done in their essay to get a higher mark. They could even ask their teacher to help them better understand a criteria sheet so they know what is required in the next essay.

You can coach them how to have that conversation. Talk to them about choosing the best time to approach the teacher – before or after class, or at lunchtime. Help them formulate the best way to ask their question: 'Could I speak to you, please, to help me understand what I could do better next time?' Teach them to take the right tone so they understand they are likely to receive the most helpful response when they are respectful rather than accusatory or sullen, and show they are keen to learn how to improve. To help them practise their approach, take the part of their teacher in a role-playing exercise and teach them how to accept the constructive feedback they hope to receive. Give them tips that children won't naturally be aware of: nodding their head while the other person speaks shows they are attentive and receptive, taking notes allows them to reduce uncomfortable eye contact while being told what they need to improve. Also remind them to thank the person for their time and feedback.

Of course, there are some situations your child absolutely should change. They must not accept being persistently targeted and bullied. Coach them how to use a calm and confident voice to tell the perpetrator they don't like what they are doing and ask them to stop. If the situation continues, tell your child to speak to their teacher about it. If they say they can't, seek their permission for you to speak to their teacher or school counsellor. Don't rush up to the school bristling with anger; it is surprising how often parents concerned about their child being bullied go on to bully school staff with ongoing demands and threats. Instead, book an appointment so you have time for a useful discussion. Be open minded about what your child says has happened; so far you have heard only one side of the situation.

If you worry that a disappointing or distressing event may have a lasting effect on your child, you are likely to ruminate on it unhelpfully. Resist the urge to discuss the situation at length with your child. Instead, talk about it briefly using the listen and empathise strategies we have described. If you involve your child in constant re-examination of what has happened and how they feel about it, you will most likely make them feel worse and prevent them from moving on. Support that continues for too long can easily turn into unhealthy rumination.

Ensure your child is coping by continuing to check in with them now and then. Don't directly question them – 'How do you feel about your disagreement with Olive now?' – because this approach will keep them thinking about the disagreement. Instead, offer them conversational space in times when the two of you are alone, perhaps cooking a meal or walking to the shop together. If you allow some silence to occur, they are likely to take that opportunity to bring up anything that's troubling them. Trust this will happen rather than worry that they are keeping some deep, dark problem from you.

Also be aware of our protective human tendency to catastrophise. Just because your child did badly in the Maths test doesn't mean they will end up homeless. Just because they had difficulty connecting with someone in their first week of school doesn't mean they will be a loner for the rest of their life.

Be curious and open to the future, not fearful of it.

If you find it difficult to keep worries – yours or your child's – under control, we give you a clear step-by-step strategy to help with this in the next chapter.

Don't give your anxious child special powers

Anxious children often get special considerations. This is an understandable act of care by parents who want to help them, but it can accidentally give them control of the household and encourage them to remain anxious, so they can retain their position of power. To gently push back against this, try the following strategies.

Don't justify bad behaviour

Some people believe that children – particularly anxious children – find it difficult to maintain a positive mood all day. These people think this is why some children, after needing to keep their behaviour and emotions in check at school, come home and vent their negative feelings on their parents and siblings in the form of rude or aggressive behaviour. This belief is completely false.

If your child can behave well all day and then can't with you, the problem stems from their expectations and respect for you, not their overwhelming feelings. It is not okay for your friend or partner to take out their frustration on you, and it is also not okay for your child to treat you as a receptacle for their bad moods or frustrations.

Insisting your child immediately cleans their room when they come home from school might be a big ask. But insisting they treat you and other family members with respect? This is a minimum expectation. Don't excuse regular bad behaviour as the result of tricky feelings. Respond calmly and consistently with a non-emotional instruction or consequence.

Don't let their needs dominate your family

Avoid rewarding your anxious child with extra control in your family because of their feelings or preferences. If they ask to be dropped off last at their primary school after their sibling gets dropped off at high school, and this is not convenient for you, don't do it. Remember they need to fit in with the family. Prioritise helping them overcome their desire to control the driving plan each day by not giving them their preference every time.

Don't reward them for not participating in activities with their peers

Avoidance should not be more entertaining than participation. If your child chooses to hang out with the adults in the kitchen at parties rather than join in the action, make sure the kitchen is boring enough to encourage them to think that better things might be going on outside. Keep the conversation focused on adult interests like politics or work and try not to allow others to pay too much rewarding attention to your child. Stand with them near the children playing, so your child can watch the games and understand that they are missing out. Perhaps point out a low-key way they can join in.

If they are too nervous to participate in the swimming or Auskick activities you signed them up for, don't whisk them away to have a milkshake and biscuit nearby. Sit and watch the class with them – don't entertain them on the sidelines. You want them to want to join in, not believe that the best fun is to be had by escaping.

How to cope with difficult feelings

Anxiety and disappointment are not the only feelings that can adversely affect the wellbeing of adults and children. Others that can cause us trouble include envy, FoMO, flatness and boredom. As we explained in Part A, these feelings can be related to anxiety. Let's look now at ways to deal with these emotions.

Envy

We can feel envious when someone else has something we would like to have. When a friend is appointed to a leadership role or is promoted with a pay rise, those of us who also desire (or have desired) these things may experience envy.

This emotion can be tricky to identify. We typically don't want to admit that it's envy which sets off our feelings of personal failure or self-doubt when someone else (even an influencer we've never met) gets something we want. Parents can become envious when they see another parent (or that parent's child) enjoying success of a kind they also value, or a co-worker achieving goals they hoped to achieve before becoming a parent.

Danielle's RIC technique is an effective way to identify and manage your feelings of envy.

R – Recognise your feeling

Recognise your feelings of discontent and displeasure as envy if, on reflection, you realise you are reacting to someone you know, or know of, having something you desire or once wanted.

Speak to a trusted person about your feelings. Choose that person wisely – your choice should be someone who is likely to help you feel better, not judge you or make you feel like a failure. Explore your feelings in your conversation. It doesn't have to be a serious discussion – you might end up able to laugh about the situation. Do not judge yourself for the way you feel. Experiencing envy helps you re-evaluate what you really hanker for in your life.

I – Identify your triggers and goal

Something has triggered you to react this way: your feelings will be related to a goal that you aspire to achieve. Feeling envious when you learn that someone is achieving or doing something you would like for yourself – scoring a free ticket to attend the rugby with a generous work associate, or being invited to join mutual friends at the preview of a new movie – indicates that being invited to participate in social gatherings is an important goal for you. This would mean that people who constantly talk about their social successes – the friend who spends most of Monday telling you about the amazing time they had on the weekend with their new partner and their friends, or the clique of former schoolmates who relentlessly regale the group chat with accounts of the fabulous parties they attend – intensify your envious feelings because they appear to be realising your goal while your life seems horribly dull in comparison.

Rather than dwelling on the difference between their lives and yours, it is important to identify the goal you wish for yourself which they appear to be achieving. Once you are confident you know what your goal is, you will be in a position to decide whether you are better to try to avoid the situations that trigger your envy or whether you could try and overcome your envious feelings by checking, and possibly refocusing or changing, your goal.

C – Check your goal

Now that you have identified your goal, check whether it is realistic for you. Is it a truly worthwhile goal for you? If it is, and you believe you can achieve it, you may be able to overcome your envious feelings by taking a different approach to realising it. Perhaps you need to work harder or differently. If your goal is to become a competitive amateur hockey player, you may need to do some additional training to up your game to make your local over-40s team. If your goal is to enjoy an active social life every weekend, perhaps you could be more proactive in your friendships and be the one to initiate more get-togethers rather than waiting for others to make the first move each time.

If you check the goal you have identified and realise you really can't meet it, don't be tempted to try to hang onto it. An unrealistic goal will continually disappoint you because you won't accomplish it. This will make you feel worse about yourself and more envious of others. If you find your goal is not realistic – you want to be an all-round high achiever but you realise you can't perform your current job, plus raise a young family, plus get a PhD, plus run a marathon later in the year – change your approach given your current circumstances. What can you prioritise now that will bring you some satisfaction? Could you achieve a subset of your goal if you train to run five kilometres and take part in a fun run instead of the marathon this year?

If you are stuck in a situation where you can't change your approach and envy keeps eating away at you, try to think of ways to reduce the triggers that bring the feelings on. Unfollow the former work colleague whose Instagram posts show them checking in to the Qantas international business lounge almost every week or unsubscribe from real estate market updates while you're at a stage in your life when you can barely meet your rent costs. Understand that your current circumstances mean you have to let some goals go for a time. Remind yourself of this when something triggers your envy.

You can adjust this approach to help your child, who is unlikely to be able to independently identify their emotion as envy. When you see they are upset by what appear to be envious feelings, talk to them to draw out their emotions and help them understand that what they feel is envy. Then normalise it, so they also understand that everyone feels this way at times. If one of your children becomes upset when their report card shows mostly Bs and their sibling is dux of their year, explain to them that there will always be situations where other people, including their siblings, do better than them. Suggest they focus on their own lane and help them come to terms with the outcome by not dwelling on a comparison of their results with their peers'.

Encourage your child to consider and perhaps adjust their goal. Ask them if they think their aim to always match their friend's or sibling's achievement is helpful. Would they do better to focus instead on carefully choosing where they want to put their effort and working steadily for a set time each afternoon to improve in that area? Ask them to think about their goals to determine which are the most realistic and which are the ones they value most. When they've done this, they may choose to focus more on their effort grade than the results in their report card, or they may decide to invest more time in drama practice or soccer training. Encourage them to think about whether they are better to define their efforts relative to others' or alongside their own previous performance. Could their efforts yield other gains, such as becoming stronger when facing challenges?

FoMO

FoMO is a type of envy with the added sting of being excluded. How you treat FoMO depends on the situation. Is it a one off? Or are you or your child dissatisfied because you are often excluded from friends' catch-ups? If so, you and your child would be better off finding more inclusive friends. If this is not possible, you might both have to put up with your FoMO and learn to cope when it happens. You need to decide whether some friendship with this group is better than no friendship at all.

If you or your child feel you do not have enough friends, your FoMO might be set off simply by seeing social media posts of people spending time with others. Some of us can slip into a pattern of spending too much time on online connections, allowing them to substitute for more satisfying real-life connections. This can become a vicious cycle: we feel lonely or low, spend time with an online audience, feel momentarily connected again, yet forfeit our time and skill for nurturing our real-life relationships. If this sounds like you, invest some time and effort into making more face-to-face friends.

Sometimes you may find your friendships are not as plentiful as they used to be, particularly in the early child-focused days of parenthood or later in life when your children are starting to live more independent lives. Children can also go through tricky times when they don't easily find a group to fit in with at school. As we have suggested, encourage them to brainstorm worthwhile ways of spending their lunchtime on their own during these periods.

Also remind your child (and yourself) that not all gatherings with friends are as much fun as social media smiles suggest. Sometimes when groups catch up, people put more effort into their Instagram photos than actually enjoying each other's company. In fact, some people may wish they were you, in your pyjamas, watching a movie on the couch with your family instead of participating in a supposedly social situation that in reality is not fun at all in between the selfies and group snaps.

Remember that social media produces envy and FoMO for many people. If these feelings affect you, it is probably best to step away from your apps or move them to a single device like your iPad and make a deliberate decision when you invite them (and FoMO) into your life.

Flatness

Life can't always be busy and exciting. Sometimes you feel flat simply because yesterday was fun and today is not (particularly when it is the first day back at school or work after a holiday).

The most effective treatment for a low mood is to get busy and find a new focus for an hour or two. We humans feel better when we have a purpose to direct our energy toward. It's best to manage our flat moods with activities we enjoy that give us a sense of accomplishment. Even small tasks like cleaning out a pantry shelf or stocktaking your wardrobe and donating some clothes to charity can help, as can working toward more long-term goals, like learning a new language or musical instrument, or involving yourself in a hobby like gardening or playing a sport.

Some ideas you and your child can consider include:

- Low level – colouring in or colour-by-numbers painting, tidying your desk, practising a new piece of music or a song, going to the local shops for a coffee and brief exchange with someone there (which builds a sense of belonging to your community), going for a walk outdoors or doing an online exercise class.
- Medium level – knitting a jumper for your dog, reading a book (perhaps for a book-club discussion), researching a holiday, going to a museum or gallery, starting a language or jewellery-making course, joining the local soccer or gymnastics club, or going surfing or fishing if there are beaches nearby.
- High level – going on a holiday, building an art portfolio and gifting a piece of your art to a friend or exhibiting your work, joining a choir to sing Handel's Messiah in front of an audience.

Boredom

We are not good at handling boredom these days. Get on any bus, tram or train and see how most people prefer to stare at their phone rather than sit with their thoughts or occasionally chat to the person who ends up sitting next to them (although these random pleasant exchanges have a positive effect on mood and often relieve boredom). At home, we often scroll through social media while we watch a TV show. Even when we are with others, many of us have a habit of picking up our phone to get a hit of excitement rather than listen to everything our friends or co-workers are saying.

Learning how to cope with being slightly bored supports our creativity, allows us to have some downtime and encourages us to be more engaged in the less frenetic yet still meaningful aspects of life. But we need to practise the skill, or we will continue to pick up a phone or tablet as soon as things slow down. This is as true for children as it is for adults.

Think about situations in which you can practise being comfortable with being bored. Try to be mindful in these moments; notice what is around you and how you feel in those surroundings. Release yourself from the urge to be entertained and reduce any tendency to multitask while doing slightly monotonous tasks. Start with short periods without picking up your phone – standing next to the jug as it boils – and move on to longer stretches of time – taking the train to work or waiting for your child outside their school. Go for a walk without headphones and simply look around you, particularly at a beautiful time of day like sunrise or sunset. When you have time alone, eat a meal without watching TV or scrolling your phone and notice the tastes and textures of your food.

Allow yourself to have unproductive moments of contemplation. Moments of rest allow us to recover from overload just as sleep does. Keep practising until you are better at calming your mind.

Allow your child to be bored. When they tell you they are bored, don't suggest activities to them that will displace the feeling. It's a good idea to discuss boredom with them and frame it as a healthy part of life that sparks independent thoughts and solutions. You want them to develop their creativity and ability to sit with their thoughts. Let them come up with something to do that does not involve screens. We are not talking here about prolonged boredom which is unpleasant and associated with extended periods of low mood and no activity. This is about parts of the day which lack zing or excitement and that children (and adults) complain about.

When they blame you for everything

Your child or teen will reach a stage when everything that goes wrong in their life – everything! – is your fault. This usually happens around the tweens and teens: the intensive individuation years when your child is trying to become an adult overnight and you insist on bothering them by hanging around the house and being their parent with your stupid rules and other tiresome expectations. Or you inconveniently insist on sending them to a school that requires them to turn up five days a week and do boring stuff like lessons and homework, assignments and exams. Everything is just SO MUCH WORK and ALL YOUR FAULT. This happens with many children, but anxious children in particular tend to regularly see their parents as culpable for their daily woes, potentially because their parents have gone to great lengths in the past to remove any obstacles or difficulty in their life lest they increase their child's anxiety.

These are the years when your child might come home and blame you for something that happened at school: 'That stupid school you send me to gave me a detention today.' They may constantly bring up an alternative school – the one you cruelly don't let them attend – as a better option. Their preference might be an alternative, arts-focused school where the kids are 'way cooler', the state school which is 'more chill about uniforms and everything', or the independent school that has 'the amazing drama centre with the recording studio and better subject choices than the dump you send me to'. They take every opportunity to bring up this option and point out that the school they attend – that you callously insist on – continues to ruin their life.

They might blame their daily disappointments on this terrible school: 'If you'd sent me to Average Grammar or So-So Hill State High School, I would have made prefect.' (Subtext: it's all your fault.) Even if they haven't come up with a preferred alternative school, they might still bring up their daily challenges to disagree with you about the things you insist they do (i.e. go to school).

To a certain degree they behave this way to help them feel separate and independent from you. This is normal – most of us did it when we were this age. But when children lament their daily troubles this way, many parents are tempted to step in and solve the situation to become close to their child again through triangulation – siding with them at the expense of the school. When a child complains, 'a new prefect at that awful school you send me to gave me a demerit today,' their parent could show their 'loyalty' to their child by emailing the school to insist the demerit be removed, as it was unfair and marred the child's impeccable record. Other parents might choose to defend their choice of school and apologise as if it really is their fault.

The best action you can take is to ask a question or two and ignore what they have said about something being your fault. You can empathise a little with their plight but don't apologise and don't try to solve matters for them. This is particularly true when they are at fault. And if their complaint involves a detention, it usually means their behaviour has veered toward rudeness, and the teacher is simply pulling them up to stop this tendency.

Try a technique Judith describes in her book *The Bonsai Child*: shrug. You can pull a face if you like to show you understand how they feel, but your shrug tells them you think they can cope. Even if they say, 'This stupid detention's stressing me out – if I fail then it's the school's fault!' don't rise to the bait.

Be particularly stoic if they begin to list what they see as your responsibilities to help them. They might ask you to speak to the school and get them out of the detention because they believe they have too much to do, they are frazzled, they can't afford the time and on and on. Show empathy but don't change your position. Say, 'No, I am not doing that; I'm sure it's tricky but you will cope.' Stand firm, even if they start bringing out their big guns: their supposed anxiety and stress. Let's talk about that a little more.

When they use emotional manipulation to escape their responsibilities

Children – and some adults – find ways to use their emotions to avoid their responsibilities. Using our feelings in a calculating way to control someone else's behaviour is called emotional manipulation. A person might tell their partner they feel stressed so the partner will end up getting the groceries for the fifth week in a row to spare them any further pressure. If they really *are* stressed, that is not emotional manipulation. However, amping up average feelings of frustration or boredom into stress to get someone to do something we would simply prefer not to do ourself is emotional manipulation.

A common form of this technique is the defensive retort. Beloved by tweens, teens, and occasionally other family members or co-workers, the defensive retort is often used to effectively turn the tables on criticism.

Imagine your tween says something rude to you and you chide them for their inappropriate comment. They might reply: 'I'm sorry if you *think* that was rude, but I've had a terrible day and I'm still upset.' Or your teen has made a shoddy job of cleaning the kitchen after dinner, and you ask them to do it again. They might reply: 'Gee, I'm sorry I can't reach your high standards, but I'm overwhelmed and stressing with assignments right now and the kitchen is the least of my concerns.'

As these examples show, the defensive retort usually has two parts. The first is a faux or deliberately half-hearted apology which suggests the other person's reaction is extreme or unwarranted. It implies the critic's response was more out of line than the action that prompted it. The second part is a statement of emotional difficulty the person believes will excuse their actions: 'I'm just trying to do my best in the worst week of my life,' or 'You have no idea how stressed and anxious I am right now.'

Defensive retorts are used so often because they are emotionally manipulative statements which work in the criticised person's favour. Suggesting that the other person over-reacted can be effective because if they lack confidence in any way, they will question the legitimacy of their response. A parent might think, 'Hang on, did I over-react? Am I at fault here?' This puts them off their guard. So, when a child has been rude, the parent might question their reaction and re-think how rude the child's retort truly was. This will make some parents doubt themselves and likely back down.

The emotional difficulty aspect is particularly effective because it changes the conversation completely. When the teen is slapdash cleaning the kitchen, they change the subject from their slackness to struggles with their schoolwork. Faced with their child's reported emotional difficulty, a parent's first instinct is to rush in with soothing statements and offers of help, particularly if the child's anxiety or mood has been a problem previously. The child's laziness or rudeness ends up completely forgotten.

Children or teens who use defensive retorts show they're clever enough to adopt such an effective technique and, in a way, good on them for being so inventive! But if they do this regularly to their benefit, they won't learn to cope with criticism and, most importantly, to apologise, fix their mistake and move on. They might continue to use this form of emotional manipulation into their adult years. Most of us have come across a co-worker or extended family member whose mistakes are always everyone else's fault and whose blunders are always due to their hard life or difficult current circumstances. But the defensive retort is not helpful for anyone if it occurs on repeat. Even when a child is genuinely upset, they're much better to learn to discuss their situation with their parents, rather than become surly or lazy and then pull out their big excuse when reprimanded.

What can you do when your child uses the defensive retort? Ideally, acknowledge their emotional situation but don't change your mind about the feedback you gave that prompted their response. You might say, 'It's a shame things are difficult, and we can talk about your school situation in a moment, but first I'd like you to clean up the kitchen in the way I've shown you before.' Or 'I understand you're upset, but it's no reason to be rude to me. Next time come and talk to me rather than show you're distressed through rude comments.'

We are not saying that all children or teens who report anxiety or stress are making use of these emotions. But some tweens and teens, when faced with an unwanted responsibility, bring up these emotions for maximum benefit. And over time they learn to talk about their emotions more than they learn how to do the tough stuff when they need to, regardless of a particular mood or busy week.

Ask yourself the following questions to help you work out whether you should stand your ground when your child deploys the defensive retort:

- Are my expectations reasonable?
- Have I given them a realistic timeframe?
- Can their peers do similar tasks without emotional outbursts?
- Is their reaction reasonable for the task I have set them, or might they be using their emotions to get out of doing something they don't want to do?
- Is their emotional reaction due to their disorganisation and poor choices before now?
- Will learning this lesson and facing a consequence help them to develop their organisational skills or recognise that their actions – or lack of action – have consequences?
- Will the short-term cost – their momentary displeasure – become a long-term benefit by further developing their resilience, self-regulation, resourcefulness, respect or responsibility?

How to disagree with them

Most kids disagree with their parents at times. When you push back against your child's emotional justifications for not fulfilling their responsibilities, it will likely become clear to you that they are simply being noncompliant. Don't overthink this as an indication of their poor character. It's a rare close relationship where people agree all the time. A tween or teen wanting to do only what they choose to do is typical.

You will have confrontations when you need to point out something they are not doing appropriately, and the art of disagreement is fraught. How do you express your opinions so both of you feel heard without allowing your differences to blow up to epic proportions? Here are some important considerations.

Check your fuse before you shout at them

Think about whether you are simply shifting your own frustrations from one point to another. If you have just come home from a trying day with a co-worker or client, you may be almost looking for a chance to shout at someone.

You might have spent your commute building up your irritation with woeful predictions: 'I bet that kitchen is a mess!' And lo and behold, your child has left their plate and toast crumbs on the bench and you have the perfect opportunity to release the frustration you have been holding in all day.

This scenario risks your anger outstripping the gravity of the situation. Instead, deliberately do some form of exercise or pleasant activity to shake off your day on the way home. Better still, address the matter with your co-worker in the moment rather than transfer your bad work mood to your family.

Choose your timing to address problems

If you have been annoyed for some time about your child's reluctance to clean up after themself, don't bring it up on a frantic morning. Instead, find a time when you are both more open to a reasonable discussion, perhaps during the drive to sports training or when you go to a café together after doing the weekly shop.

Schedule family meetings

Family meetings are great times for everyone to raise and sort out any concerns. Schedule fortnightly meetings at a regular time, such as a family meal or Sunday afternoons before you all play soccer in the backyard. Chat through the things you are doing well in addition to those in need of improvement.

Stop the build-up

Michael McIntyre, the English comedian, does a very funny piece where he talks about the mysteries of women's 'tether'. He says that, out of the blue, they will announce that they are 'at the end of their tether' and then get very angry. For anyone to avoid getting to that point, it is important to address minor issues as they come up. The more it builds, the more it blows.

Don't be tempted to deliver TED talks

TED talks are impassioned speeches of about 20 minutes in which a person endeavours to inspire their audience. Many parents love delivering TED-type talks to their children. In a parent's mind these are inspirational moments for their child, but in reality they rarely work this way.

How they usually go is that the parent notices something their child is doing that is not in the child's or the family's best interests. The parent decides they must talk to their child about this. They spend a long time planning their lecture, rehearsing all the good points they wish to make while on the bus or lying awake at night. They might write the speech down in bullet points on their phone. Once they've finished planning, they seize the first available opportunity to say their piece, highlighting in great detail what their child is doing wrongly and why it is a problem. To drive their point home and make sure the child realises it is imperative that they alter their behaviour, the lecture pulls no punches about the doom and gloom that will ensue if this change does not occur.

If a child is spending too much time on their screens, the parent's TED talk might include phrases like, 'You are ruining your future and not appreciating the world!' If siblings are fighting regularly, the talk might veer into: 'One day you'll see how special your relationship with your sister/brother is to you if you are nice to them right now!' If the child is not pulling their weight in the home, the speech might include how important it is to take responsibility and that they will never be a valued housemate or partner if they do not contribute equally to household duties.

When the parent plans their speech, they often anticipate the way they think their child will react. They might expect that after their monologue, it will suddenly dawn on their child how they have been getting things wrong all this time. 'Ahh,' the child will say, 'I now realise how I have erred, and yes, mother/father, I will immediately amend my ways.'

Of course, it doesn't happen this way. Usually, all the child hears is the first sentence or two followed by 'blah, blah, responsibility, blah, blah, future, blah, blah, don't you agree?' And at that point the child will often nod and smile, and the parent will think their carefully prepared eloquence has worked. But it most likely has not. Because the parent delivered a lecture and kids rarely respond well to being lectured. All that effort wasted! Don't despair . . . try the following strategy instead.

Calmly mention your concern – the calmer you are, the more likely your child will react positively. Talk unemotionally about what they are doing: if you display the intensity of your feelings, you risk making them more sensitive and defensive in response.

It's important to only bring up the behaviours that are important to your child's wellbeing and your home's harmony. Once you bring something up, you should see it through; otherwise there is no point mentioning it.

Separate their intent from the effect of their behaviour by asking them for some insight into why they are doing what they are doing. Sometimes they might mean well. If they say their behaviour has good intentions and it's genuine, acknowledge this. Then evenly state the impact on you or the whole family without exaggeration. Starting with 'you always' would indicate you are overstating things from the outset.

Move on to your desire to resolve the situation and ask them if they have any ideas as to what to do. Encourage them to think about it, then set up a time to reconvene to discuss solutions. Give some suggestions if they have no ideas. But ultimately you must reach a joint decision. Treat the problem as something you are helping each other solve. Check in with your child after a period of trying your agreed solution and together assess how it's going and whether any adjustment is needed.

Ignore any emotionally manipulative statements your child may use to shift blame and make you feel guilty. Stick to your definition of the problem. Withdraw privileges if they do not amend their behaviour – if they continue to be late to the car in the morning and making you late too, tell them you will no longer drive them to the bus stop. Alternatively, give a calm consequence – if they do not immediately clean up their kitchen mess when you ask them to, deny them use of their screens or any other privileges until they do a Chore Set, as we described in chapter 10.

This chapter has given you ways to manage your child's day-to-day challenges and the difficult feelings that can accompany them. But every now and then you or your child are likely to have concerns that persist even when you do everything we suggest here. Your tween might have experienced a friendship fight and you have helped them to manage the situation by talking about it as we have described, but they are still extremely upset. Your child's or teen's conviction that they are going to fail their exam might be so great that they can't focus on their study at all. Overwhelming situations such as these need different approaches, which we discuss in the next chapter.

CHAPTER 14

Dealing with persistent worries

Despite your best efforts, there will be some worries that you or your child can't seem to let go. This chapter shows you what to do when your worries persist.

We've discussed ways to minimise daily fears and how to make sure we don't inadvertently amplify momentary feelings of challenge into long-term difficulty. If you follow our suggestions, you will reduce the likelihood of minor challenges looming larger than they should for your child and for yourself. You will also be able to prevent slight hesitations transforming into anxiety.

But we must be realistic. Not everything can be readily resolved. Your child's fears about starting school might be so strong that they return to you again and again to ask you to confirm that it's a school with nice kids who will be friendly to them, or beg you to find out if the teacher will let you stay in class with them for their first day. Your teen's worry about their piano exam might be so burdensome that they are losing sleep and thinking about cancelling it. Your child's genuine upset at being excluded from their classmate's party might mean that a week later they are still asking if they can change their class.

You may be worrying about everything your child is worrying about, possibly even more than they are. Your own fears about the lack of a party invitation for your child may be such that you are having sleepless nights due to your overwhelming concern that they are unpopular. This might prompt you to call the teacher regularly throughout the week to check on your child; you may even consider hiding behind the bushes around the playground at lunchtime to check on their socialising (yes, some clients have told us they do this). It is likely that some of the ways you try to decrease your concern and theirs may not end up being helpful for you or for them. You may both be fixating on your worries in a way that is detrimental to your wellbeing.

When these types of cycles happen despite your best efforts, you need to change your approach. This chapter gives you different methods to release yourself from the tight grip of your worries. Our approach shows you how to work through your own worries and how to help your child work through their worries too.

We know these techniques work because Danielle has developed this model with clients over many years with great success. So much so that it is known as Einstein's What When Model to Redirect Anxiety.

The bubble machine

We've already established that fear is a useful emotion we all experience to help us stay focused and keep safe. Feeling fearful about an actual danger is beneficial because it prompts us to either get away from the threat or prime our body to face it. But, as we have pointed out, our fears are sometimes greater than the situation warrants, and some people are prone to stay in a state of anxiety despite being relatively safe. These people constantly feel that something bad is around the corner, and they tend to zone in on the fear-inducing elements in their lives much more than their relaxed peers.

There's a lot to potentially zone in on. In our minds, we human beings are always saying things to ourselves: we live with a perpetual soliloquy of frivolous thoughts and deep insights about our current surroundings, our feelings about past events, our projections about what may happen in the future, or our daydreams. These thoughts ping at us all day, to the extent that it is sometimes difficult to focus on one thing when our mind is wandering around thinking the myriad of things it does. It is like a machine perpetually producing thought bubbles that float around our head, coming and going and coming again. Sometimes we pause to examine these thoughts; sometimes we simply let them float on by.

There's a never-ending supply of these bubbles. We think thousands of thoughts – perhaps up to 70,000 a day. Some thoughts lead to others, and some stay random and solo. A person walking down the street may be thinking a mishmash of 'What's on this weekend? Aww, that's a nice dog. What's for lunch? Goody, there's a new episode of LEGO Masters tonight. Will I do well in my job interview tomorrow? Damn, these new shoes are pinching. I'll do some washing when I get home ...' Certain situations bring on more thoughts than others. Scrolling through emails, news and social media where we encounter other people and their circumstances can supercharge the bubble machine and prompt us to begin to compare ourselves with what we see.

We mostly give more attention to the thought bubbles that are important to us at the time, such as finding food if we think we are hungry. That thought is likely to lead us to go on to think, 'What do I feel like eating?' and 'I wonder if the corner sushi place is still open?'

All of us focus on different types of thoughts at different times, and we all have different priorities. A person who has recently been thinking about getting a new pet may notice a cute dog and start to think about whether they want to adopt one: 'Have I got time to care for a pet? What would I name a puppy?' A person who loves connecting with others might pass a sportsground and immediately think: 'Is there a game on this weekend and would some friends be interested in going with me?'

Not all thoughts lead to the same reactions for everyone. Even a thought about the outcome of a job interview might not lead to any great examination in people who are more curious than concerned. For these people, the result may not be a big deal. Their reaction to a job-interview thought might be to shrug their shoulders and let the outcome remain a mystery for now, to be determined later. These people are likely to be confident about coping with whatever happens, so they stay chilled whenever those question bubbles pop up.

However, a person who tends to worry will zone in on any question-type thoughts with an uncertain outcome in areas that are important to them. As you will recall, discomfort with uncertainty is one of the key factors in the likelihood of someone developing anxiety.

When this happens, people are torn. Although the worry thought bubbles attract their attention, they are also aware, on some level, that it is too early to think these through because the feared outcomes might not eventuate. Their reaction to feeling torn between attention and concern is often tension in their bodies, which they don't necessarily notice until the end of the day.

When it comes to worries, people respond differently. There are two coping strategies which usually lead to difficulties – psychologists describe these as unhelpful coping strategies.

The first is to dwell on the worrying thoughts to the point of fixation. While worrying thoughts come to everyone, they really dominate the attention of people who are prone to anxiety. This makes what could have been a minor thought bubble, which was originally one of many, become much bigger and preoccupying. Due to its importance and all the additional thoughts that link to it, the bubble looms large and causes increasing unease.

This is particularly true if the thought has a 'What if this (or that) happens?' dimension, or if it prompts the questions, 'What should I do, and will it be the right thing to do?' People who have these questions are often reluctant to examine the worry bubble properly so they can resolve them. They might be hopeful that the situation will resolve itself quickly or that someone else will pop the bubble for them. People who rely on this strategy share their worry with someone else in the hope that the other person will have some advice or be able to take their fear away with a reassuring statement like, 'Don't worry, you're amazing! I'm sure you'll get the job.' (Children often seek this type of help from their parents to deflate their worry bubbles.) While this approach can be healthy if done occasionally, people who use it every time rely too much on others.

The other unhelpful coping strategy in response to worry is for the person to put their head in the sand in the hope it will simply go away. They might immediately turn to Candy Crush or online shopping. People who rely heavily on this method may be masters of distraction, but their diversions, such as binge-watching TV shows or scrolling their social media feeds when they should be studying, are not helpful at all. These actions remove discomfort but the relief people feel when they deliberately look away from their worry is only temporary and does not resolve their concern.

Worries about their child have the potential to crank up a parent's bubble-producing machine into overdrive. The parent who is worried about their child's popularity might become hypervigilant and overly focused on the child's daily social success to pop their own bubbles of uncertainty. When an extremely anxious parent questions their child's social interactions at the end of the day, they can inadvertently cause the child to become more anxious about their popularity than is warranted, simply because the parent keeps bringing it up.

How to deal with troublesome thought bubbles

It doesn't have to be this way. There are better ways to deal with those bubbles that allow them to glide past without bothering us so much that we need to stare at them intently or pop them immediately in ways that aren't helpful at all.

Here is the technique developed as the Einstein What When Model to Redirect Anxiety. It sets out four steps to use when you get a particularly troublesome thought bubble. These steps work with most worries that involve challenges or concerns about preoccupying future events.

Step 1 – Identify your worrying thoughts

First identify the worrying thoughts that are having a detrimental impact on your wellbeing. This involves sorting through the trove of thought bubbles floating around you to find the ones that are bothering you so much.

If you have a feeling of unease about the meeting you just had with your work team, your impulse might be to ask your colleague whether it went well or if what you said was persuasive. This would indicate that you are worried about your performance in the meeting and your worrying thought might be, 'What if I didn't say the right thing?' If you are uneasy about the forthcoming class lists that will show which teacher and classmates your child will have, your worrying thought might be, 'What if my child gets in a class with a teacher they don't like or students they don't know?'

Your worrying thoughts are likely to revolve around what you should do next. If you think you had one drink too many at the party last night and were a bit sillier and louder than you normally are, you might wonder whether you should call your host and apologise, or call a good friend who was there to check that you weren't too rambunctious. If your child didn't get into the class with the teacher they prefer, you might wonder if you should call the school to ask that they be moved, or if that might make their teacher more inclined to dislike your child. Again, you are thinking about choosing the best thing to do. You may have several thought bubbles for this one: 'Should I call the school?', 'What if my child has another terrible year?', 'What if my child never applies themself in primary school?'

> *We sometimes feel strong emotions without being aware of the background thoughts that prompt us to feel this way.*

Our feelings may be a mixture of emotions like disappointment and anxiety. Imagine you have an argument with a family member about a decision they have made to spend Christmas with their new partner's family without consulting you. You may feel disappointed at being left out of their plans, but you also feel anxious and worried about the impact their decision will have on you and whether you will lose that close connection with them as they embark on their new relationship.

Talking or texting with someone you trust about what has just happened can help you put your finger on the underlying thoughts which are sparking your emotions. Imagine you are preparing to move house; after a week of packing boxes, you wake up with back pain. You go to a therapist, and they massage your back to work out exactly which muscles have made it sore. Similarly, there are times when seeking help to massage the experience you have had can allow you to precisely pinpoint what you feel so nervous about.

> *Working out what our deeper worries really are guides us toward the best way to deal with them.*

You don't always need another person's help to do this. If you prefer, you can pinpoint the thoughts causing your worries on your own; this becomes easier with practice. Look for both superficial and deeper worries, because addressing both kinds will be most helpful. This can feel unpleasant, but it takes only a few minutes of your attention. To extract an elusive thought bubble that is making you anxious, ask yourself what you are worried about and write down all the answers that come to mind. Don't be concerned if detecting the troubling thoughts and writing them down feels tricky at first or you can't seem to get it right. Over time you will get better at identifying your worrying thoughts and pulling them out of their bubbles. This will help you progress to the next step.

Step 2 – Classify your worrying thoughts

Once you have identified the thoughts producing your worries, the next step is to work out which type of worry each one is. We call this classifying your worrying thoughts. This allows you to determine the path to take in response to each one.

The worries we deal with here can be classified into two types: 'what if' worries and 'what do I do now' worries. 'What if' worries involve a fear of something terrible happening; they can hold you in a state of dread. 'What do I do now' worries express a need to do something very soon, together with a fear of choosing a 'wrong' response which will produce even more problems. It can be tricky to work out which is which; here are examples of both.

'What if' worries

Most anticipatory worries are 'what if' worries: nothing bad has happened yet, but we anticipate things will go wrong. The following are good examples of 'what if' worries for adults:

- What if I don't get any work next month?
- What if my holiday flights get cancelled?
- What if I don't have anyone to talk to at the networking event?
- What if no one enjoys the barbeque I have arranged?
- What if I don't get the job I applied for?
- What if I can't meet my mortgage repayment next month?
- What if my relationship is not good enough and we don't last the distance?
- What if I have chosen the wrong school for my child?
- What if my child doesn't score a goal in the game today?
- What if my teen doesn't get into the apprenticeship program?

Children and teens also have 'what if' worries. For them, the 'what if' thoughts can be like the following.

For primary-age children:

- What if I can't sleep when I go to my friend's house?
- What if no one sits next to me on the bus to camp?
- What if I disappoint the violin teacher?
- What if I don't do well in the test?
- What if I can't get into the concert band that my clarinet teacher wants me to try out for?

For teens:

- What if I don't have a friend to sit with in my new class?
- What if I don't get the good teacher in Maths this year?
- What if I don't answer every question in the test?
- What if the clothes I have packed for camp aren't cool enough?
- What if I don't get a date for the semi-formal?
- What if I'm hanging out with my friends and they get caught vaping and the principal thinks I'm bad?
- What if I drop the ball in the game today?
- What if I am not smart enough to get into university?
- What if I am not picked for the solo dance performance?
- What if I don't get awarded Year 8 dux?

Remember these questions are only problematic if they are in an area that is important to the adult or child or teen, such as being perceived well by work colleagues, being a good host, being cool enough, or doing well in an exam or game.

A worry looms large
when the importance we place on its future outcome
leads us to catastrophise about it in the present.

You'll notice the last worries on these three 'what if' lists involve fear of good things *not* happening, such as the child's fears about not getting a place in the concert band or the teen not becoming dux. A worry about the best thing not happening will only be significant if a person has decided that a perfect outcome is the only acceptable option. Rather than simply hope for the best, they have decided that the optimal conclusion is the only one they can handle.

'What if' worries can also be brought on by something that happened in the past, either recently or some time ago:

- What if my presentation yesterday wasn't received well?
- What if that joke I told last week offended my friend?
- What if my friends thought I talked too much at the dinner and I am boring?
- What if dropping the ball in the cricket final last month means my team thinks badly of me?

While these thoughts are about a past event, they produce fears about the future. The 'what if' worries that arise are often to do with what other people thought of us in the moment, and a concern that this will have an ongoing effect on us.

'What do I do now' worries

'What do I do now' worries involve needing to resolve a dilemma but being unsure of the action you should take. You might think that the course of action you choose is critical, and a mistake will have significant repercussions on you or another person. This dilemma makes some people overly dependent on others for their views and advice. Some clients tell us they completely stall because of their indecision. They dwell on the problem to work out the ideal solution, rather than simply doing what they feel is the best option at the time. Others tell us they refuse to think about the problem and try to put off making a decision because it makes them too stressed.

People who can't tolerate uncertainty in the face of a dilemma want to do something quickly to take away the discomfort of sitting with doubt. They may look for ways to procrastinate rather than taking any form of useful action to alleviate their worrying thoughts, or they may jump in and make a hasty, premature decision to dispel their uncomfortable feelings. Sometimes they simply act on impulse because confronting and dealing with their worry seems way too difficult.

Many parents become troubled by 'what do I do now' questions because raising their child well is extremely important to them and they want the actions they take to be the 'right' ones. It's understandable that some become preoccupied with their parenting choices – no wonder there are so many social media sites devoted to parents canvassing others to find out what to do in situations involving their child. These sites feature questions like, 'My child's teacher has been so tough lately. What should I do?' and 'My child's grandparents are indulging them too much. Should I say something or leave it be?' Deciding the right thing to do each time is fraught for these parents, and they often look to get assistance from others. (We talk later about when social media canvassing is useful, and when it is not.)

The current parenting environment makes it easy to fall into the trap of believing there is only one 'right' way to parent and that the 'wrong' actions could lead to poor outcomes for your child. This unnecessarily increases pressure on parents and makes each parenting decision a little more fraught than it should be.

The notion of false absolutes can take hold as early as prenatal classes, which can introduce the idea that there is a right (and wrong) way to give birth, or a right (and wrong) amount of time before a parent returns to work. We've worked with many parents who have had to make difficult but sensible decisions, such as returning to work when money is tight. Unfortunately, they can be plagued by unnecessary guilt about the potential effects on children of going to day care too early because parents made a so-called wrong decision, even if it was the best decision for them, given their circumstances.

For parents, 'what if' questions can easily turn into 'what do I do now' worries when the subject is their child. When their child gets in the car after school and says they think they didn't do well on their numeracy test, a parent's 'what if' worry ('What if my child continues to do badly?') may produce fears of pessimistic outcomes (their teacher will think badly of them, they might fail their schooling, they'll likely be a failure in life). The parent may then try to solve the problem immediately by impulsively booking their child into an expensive coaching clinic, which will be a financial stretch for the family but promises good results. It's no surprise many of these tutoring services are located close to schools for all those worried and desperate parents to see as they drive past contemplating their 'what do I do now' worries!

Recall that the child simply said they *thought* they hadn't done well; it is not yet established whether that is the case. But parental fears of the possible outcome can produce an immediate urge to act to pre-emptively take control of the situation. Some parents try to solve the problem straightaway, rather than waiting to learn whether there is an actual problem or not. It's understandable and caring, but it might turn out to be completely unnecessary.

Remember that with all 'what do I do now' questions, you have the option to do nothing. The parent who anticipates their child's poor performance on their exam might do nothing. And doing nothing might produce a new set of 'what if' worries. 'What if I do nothing and they continue to fail and it is all my fault?' 'What if I do nothing and then, later on, they can't get a spot with an experienced tutor?' (Yes, we agree, it seems sometimes parents can't win.)

Step 3 – Deal with your 'what if' worries

'What if' worries often relate to fears that you have made or will make a terrible error and that you won't be able to cope with the fallout. When you walk away from a difficult conversation with your manager, you may think that they are now predisposed against you. 'What if they thought the way I voiced my opinion was rude, and now they don't like me?' If you can't find your favourite t-shirt, you may think, 'What if I've left it behind somewhere and I've lost it forever?' If a child is worried about their place in a group assignment, they might think, 'What if my friends think I am not contributing equally or usefully?'

Remember that 'what if' questions are problematic because a person is tussling with whether or not to react to what they imagine will be possible negative outcomes. If worry is your habit, you have probably trained the pessimistic part of your brain to become muscly and strong enough to beat up any belief that you can comfortably contemplate uncertain possibilities and safely wait until you know their outcome. 'I don't know the answer yet so I will have to wait' will always be beaten by the 'it's going to be a disaster unless I can pre-empt and control this' heavyweight champion.

But you can train up your wait-and-see-what-happens muscles, so they have the power to go up against their do-something-immediately sparring partner. Here's how to do that.

Ask yourself, 'When will I know for sure what happened?'

Answers to your 'what if' worries are only discovered when the outcome actually occurs. So the first essential step for responding to a 'what if' worry is to ask yourself, 'When will I know if this thing I fear has actually happened? Or simply, 'When will I know for sure what happened?'

The point in time when you think you will find out depends on several circumstances. If you are worried about what you said to your manager, and you interact with them a few times a week, you might think, 'I'll know after seeing my manager another couple of times; either they'll smile and invite my opinion, or they won't. I'll probably know by Friday next week.' If a teen is worried about whether their contribution to their group assignment has been sufficient to do well, they may think, 'I'll know in about two weeks after we've submitted, and the results are handed back.'

All events have a timeline. While you might wish to know the outcome of your worry as soon as possible, in some circumstances your answer will lie far in the future. It might take a year to find that t-shirt when you are going through another pile of clothes. You will only know if your career choice was the best one for you after spending some years working in that field weighing the pros against the cons – it may even take until the time you retire. But that is still a timeline, and we want you to commit to determining a likely end point for your persistent 'what if' worries. Anxiety often pressures us to take away our uncertainty as soon as we can, but choosing the earliest possible end point does not help – we become more desperate and upset when we haven't learnt the outcome of our worry by the time we set our hopes on.

> *Choose the latest realistic time*
> *you will know the outcome of your worry;*
> *don't be tempted to make it improbably early.*

Think of this process as drawing out a timeline so that your feelings will be stirred only when you know the final outcome of the worry, instead of letting potential conclusions constantly play on your mind. When the worry pops back into your thoughts, simply recall its timeline and the point at which you will know how it ends. It might help to write down the worry and the timeline with its end point because you can refer to it if the worry returns. This will also remind you that no one else can know the outcome of a 'what if' worry before it happens either, so it removes the urge to seek reassurance from others as well.

Determining a 'what if' worry's end point also helps you to pin down what the scary component of your fear would look like in reality. You do this when, to fix your end point, you work out how you would know if your feared outcome has eventuated. If you have had a vehement disagreement with a friend about a legal case in the news during what was intended to be a friendly catch-up, and you still feel agitated on your way home, you may have a range of 'what if' thoughts, even though your overall feeling is simply general unease. What if your friend now decides to exclude you from their birthday celebration next month? What if they no longer like you at all? What if they have changed, and you are losing your connection with them?

Noting your 'what if' thoughts clearly helps you to work out the specific concerns that now have you worried. If you note several 'what if' worries (most people find they have more than one), determine specific timelines and end points for each one. You will know whether you have been invited to the celebration by the day of your friend's birthday, and you'll know about the state of your friendship by mid-December once you have seen them at their birthday party, the play you both have tickets for, and your Christmas party – three catch-ups give plenty of opportunity to tell whether the friendship remains strong after the argument.

By spelling out each timeline and end point, you fold up each worry and put it in a metaphorical envelope where it may be re-examined if necessary. This way you contain the agitation that was simmering inside each 'what if'.

Relax your body

You may not be aware that you hold tension in your body while you battle your worries. The tension most likely arises because, in the back of your mind, you can't quite work out whether to focus on the fear (given the outcome isn't actually a problem yet) or ignore it. Many people don't notice muscular tension when worrying because anxiety itself commands much of their attention and they can become preoccupied with their troubling thoughts.

Reducing tension in our bodies is always worthwhile, and particularly beneficial when you are feeling worried. Try the following options to respond to muscle tension by relaxing your body. Choose the one which works best for you.

> **Visualisation**
>
> This brief exercise involves some creative thinking. Start by imagining the bad scenario of your 'what if' worry as though it were a painting. Picture your missing favourite t-shirt lying covered in footprints on the floor of the gym changeroom where you might have dropped it. Or your workstation daubed in red graffiti by your boss who is still not happy with you for voicing your opinion. Pay attention to the physical effects you feel as you create the picture in your mind, then mentally place the image on the area of your body where you notice the strongest reaction. Allow the reaction to sit in your body, make space for it and breathe around it. Take as long as you need, but you will most likely find you can complete this in less than five minutes. Create a new image each time; it doesn't matter exactly what the image is, as long as it represents the scenario that is bugging you in the moment.

Tense-relax exercise

This body scan and tense–relax exercise will only take two minutes. Scan your body from head to toe and pick a muscle that you notice is tense. It may be your shoulders, or in your chest or your neck. Try not to choose a part of your body that has suffered an injury; you're looking for an area that is healthy yet carries a degree of tension you can feel. Now imagine the pendulum of a grandfather clock swinging this way and that. When the pendulum swings one way, increase the tension in the muscle you have chosen and hold it for 15 seconds. As the pendulum swings the other way, deliberately relax your body to release the tension for 15 seconds.

Whole body relaxation

Lie down or sit in a location with some space around you and point your fingers and toes while stretching all the muscles in your arms and legs. Really feel the stretch and hold the tension for five seconds. Take a breath in, then relax the muscles as you breathe out, allowing your fingers, toes, arms and legs to soften and relax. Keep relaxing those muscles for a further 20 seconds.

Shoulder and neck pull

Our shoulders are often affected when we are anxious; this is particularly exacerbated when we spend extended periods sitting at a desk or carrying a toddler. A quick, effective relaxation exercise is to pull your shoulders back and hold the tension there for a minute. Really notice the tension in your shoulders. Now gradually let your shoulders relax, letting the tension go bit by bit with each breath out. Now pull your chin towards your neck without allowing them to actually touch. Hold the tension, wait five seconds and release. Slowly let the tension go with each breath out. Feel your chin and neck totally relax and allow that feeling to stay for ten seconds without resuming any new activity.

Practise powerful distraction

Determining the end point for your 'what if' worry and relaxing your body will often be sufficient to take the heat out of your troubling thoughts. But if your worry is still particularly frightening, you may need to allow yourself some time in powerful distraction as your next step.

Powerful distraction refers to activities that you usually take pleasure in or find comforting, such as going to visit a friend whose company you enjoy, heading to your favourite art gallery, or working on an engaging task. Treating yourself to one of these activities when you feel weighed down by worry will relieve the pressure of your anxious thoughts. This is different to procrastination, where you put off or stop doing a task because you don't feel like doing it. This is purposeful distraction to overcome an overwhelming feeling.

> *The kindness you show to yourself*
> *when you engage in powerful distraction*
> *is genuinely needed, not simply preferred.*

Write your worry story

If determining your worry's timeline, relaxing your body and practising powerful distraction are not enough to stop your worry bugging you, move on to this step.

Writing your worry story involves facing the outcome you fear by thinking it through in a realistic way. You choose the potential outcome you are fearful of and write about the experience of facing it.

Because the outcome is uncertain, there are always several possible ways for 'what if' worries to end. A person who is concerned about their boss being unhappy with them might worry about a range of potential negative outcomes, from the manager telling them they were rude, to the workplace becoming uncomfortable, to being put on a performance improvement plan, to being moved to a different department, through to being fired. The fact that every story has more than one potential outcome mirrors the uncertainty that prompts us to worry.

Don't attempt to cover every outcome when you write your story. Despite the number of possibilities, a worry story contemplates one outcome only. Choose the 'what if' which is troubling you most – 'What if I am fired from my job?' – and write down what happens emotionally and practically from start to finish when that outcome eventuates.

In this exercise we ask you to work through the logical coping consequences of the event occurring. Your story commences with the initial worry coming true – 'I am fired from my job' – and you tell the narrative by working through what would likely happen and how you would cope.

It's important for you to write your story showing yourself coping. We ask this not because we are playing Pollyanna, but because, in most situations, people do cope. This is not to say that you won't feel angry, disappointed or miserable if your feared outcome actually happens, nor that times won't be tough. But you will learn to adapt and cope.

If you are in any doubt here, think about tough things that have happened to you in the past that you got through. The time you didn't get into the university course you wanted, the time you broke up with that special person, the health condition you had, or the time a beloved pet died. These times are never pleasant or easy. But, over and over, people cope.

Going to the trouble of writing a worry story and facing what you fear prompts you to examine your potential situation realistically, without the melodramatic flourishes that worry can encourage.

To begin, write down a sequence of events that is true to life, not fanciful – each step must be practical. Don't start with, 'I lose my job and I am homeless' because this is not how this would actually happen. There are many steps in between losing your job and losing your home that you need to examine; as you write them down you will realise that you can't easily make these leaps. Try to write this episode of your life in a likely enough way that it could become the script for a believable prime-time TV drama, not a fanciful soap opera where the main character is kidnapped in one week, stood up at the altar by their fiancé in the next, and escapes a zombie invasion of their city in the season finale.

As you write, remember to acknowledge and make use of your strengths while drawing on available resources: the people around you (friends, family and community), government support if relevant, or therapeutic advice and treatment. If you are in any doubt whether you would be able to cope, first write a story of a real-life difficulty you have already faced successfully. This serves as a warm-up and reminder of your coping skills; it prepares you to think through what is likely to happen when the circumstances of your current worry play out. We include a sample below of a story someone might write to remind themself of how they coped with a difficult event in their past.

As you become used to writing worry stories based on your what ifs, you will notice that you are able to logically work through your 'what do I do now' worries about the future. This occurs because when you write in practical terms about what could happen, you need to include details such as when and where you would reach out for help and how you would eventually adapt to your circumstances.

As the final step in the Einstein What When model, writing your worry story can be uncomfortable – few of us enjoy looking in detail at a potentially dark event in our future because it is not our natural instinct to face uncomfortable outcomes. However, thinking through each negative outcome is beneficial because when we examine how we would manage the difficulties likely to arise, it helps us remember and recognise our ability to cope with whatever befalls us.

How to write a worry story

Choose a 'what if' worry that is currently troubling you.

- Write your story in the present tense as events unfold. ('I get to work on Monday and am devastated to be told that I am fired from my job.')
- Write in the first-person point of view (use 'I', not 'he', 'she' or 'they') – you are telling the story of what happens to *you*.
- Begin by talking about receiving the news that your worry has come true.
- Describe in detail every step as it happens, using words like 'I feel', 'I hear', 'I see'.
- Include your feelings in the story (I feel afraid, angry, agitated, sad).
- Include the reactions of your family and friends to what happens (keeping to the present tense). ('My partner is keeping up a brave face, but I can see how worried they are about the mortgage and how we will manage.')
- Include the coping options you consider and employ as part of your story.
- Include at least three timeframes in your story, such as immediately after your worry becomes reality, months later and years later.
- Keep writing the story (in the present tense) until you reach its natural end point.
- Write in more detail at the beginning of the story as you imagine your reactions to the immediate news and during the week afterwards. As you progress through the timeframes, you may include less detail in your story.
- If any of these steps seem too overwhelming, start by writing about

a past event that was upsetting at the start, but you faced successfully in the end. This will help remind you of your coping skills. Then go through the steps above to write your current worry story.

Sometimes you may find it helps to work through your story with a trusted, sensible person in your life who is likely to be supportive. Make sure they understand these instructions so they can help keep you on track. Remember, a worry story is not worst case followed by worst case followed by worst case. Instead, it is first worst case followed by resourcefulness, adjustments and eventual coping.

If you are tempted to write a different significant negative event into your worry story, do not place it within the existing story; instead commence another worry story with that negative event. If you are writing about losing your job, don't add your marriage breaking down and the outbreak of another pandemic to that story. Write out separate worry stories following the same steps and detail how, if these things were to occur, you would adjust and cope with them.

Here are some sample worry stories which will help you write your own. We start with a warm-up worry story recounting a time when someone faced something difficult and how they coped.

A 'past' worry story – coping with the loss of a beloved pet

The day my worry becomes reality
My dog Annie is 15. She has not been well for months and needs regular appointments with the local vet. One day he tells me he thinks it is time to put her to sleep. It's horrible to hear, but I know he is ultimately being kind. I stay strong and keep it together for Annie. But the next morning when I take her to the vet and he puts her to sleep, I am overwhelmed by grief.

The first few days
I feel awful, particularly when I'm on the couch without her. I cry many tears and don't want to see anyone. I am reassured though by how many friends call to check on me.

The first few weeks
I try to hold on to what I can – I still try to walk in the mornings and evenings like I did with Annie. A few people ask me if I will get another dog, but I rebuff them because I don't believe I could face a similar loss again.

Three months later
Seeing photos of Annie devastates me at first but, over time, pictures of her increasingly make me smile because they bring back lovely memories.

Eight months later
I go on a weekend away with friends for my birthday. I realise I have not cried about her for weeks. Her loss is becoming easier.

Eighteen months later
I get a beautiful four-year-old rescue dog, Maisie. I feel strong enough to do this because even though the first months felt unbearable, I realise the sadness of losing Annie is far outweighed by the joy of the time while I had her.

Here are some examples of future worry stories to help you do your own.

Worry story – I receive a negative performance review

The day my worry becomes reality
During my performance review, my manager makes it clear I haven't met all of my objectives for the year and my team's achievements are lagging behind some of the others'. I am so disappointed – there goes that bonus I was going to use on the holiday for Jake and the kids. I tell Jake and I can see he's disappointed too. He supports me by criticising my manager, which makes me feel a little bit better. We talk about whether I should make a change or just put up with my current situation for another year. I decide to stick with it for six months before I seriously consider leaving. Jake and I tell the kids about the holiday and they whine a bit, but they don't seem as upset as I thought they'd be. I guess they like catching up with the other kids who holiday at the camping ground we have always gone to.

One week later
I'm still feeling stung. I talk to Anna and Jim at work about what happened because I know they won't tell anyone else. I contact Will, an ex-colleague who now works in a similar unit at another company. He gives me a few networking ideas.

One month later
I'm starting to feel a little bit optimistic again. I've also found out one of my colleagues didn't get much of their bonus either and I feel better now I know I'm not the only one.

Three months later
I put some of the networking ideas into practice and present at one of our regional meetings where I get some good feedback.

Six months later
I'm feeling less negative. My career is still one step behind where I had hoped it would be, but I'm better at focusing on what the company is looking for in my performance. I have an ear out for other opportunities.

Two years later
I've moved companies. My new job has its ups and downs, but I've stopped thinking about that disappointing performance review – it feels like eons ago.

Worry story – I injure myself while training for a half marathon

The day **my worry becomes reality**
My knee seizes up in the middle of a training run. I can't even walk home. I call my sister Ella, and she picks me up. I see my physiotherapist and it's my knee that's injured. Again. It's only three weeks out from the half marathon. I feel gutted. The physio refers me to a surgeon who says surgery is not necessary at this point, but I need to rest my leg for two months. I feel so annoyed and frustrated – I hate not being able to exercise properly.

During the first couple of months
I sometimes feel frustrated and angry. I use my time productively by reading more books and doing the exercise I can, but I'm worried about losing my fitness. My family are very supportive so it's not quite so bad as I imagined. I feel less fit, but I see the physio once a week and make an effort to do all of the exercises she says are needed for my recovery.

After three months
I start to see an improvement. I've gone back to yoga and Pilates and taken up cycling. I still can't run though.

After twelve months
I'm running again but not the distances I was. I've learned to accept that my knee's never going to be quite the same, and I've had to give up my dream to run a marathon. This was disappointing but I have found other goals, and my weekly exercise is more social.

Worry story – my husband loses his job

The day **my worry becomes reality**
Patrick calls to tell me they can't keep him on at work in the current economic situation.

> We have been worried that he would lose his job, but now I can't believe that it's actually happening. I know we're not the only ones going through this – everyone in hospo is affected – but this doesn't make it any easier. I'm genuinely scared. I start to have sleepless nights and I'm tired and cranky at times. I'm afraid Patrick won't get another position at his professional level. He seems calm and has already applied for a few jobs and put the word out among his hospo friends.
>
> *One week later*
> Patrick and I re-do our budget. We can stay in our home, and the kids can stay at their schools. We've had to cancel our holidays, but so have lots of people. We decide we don't need our second car and are quite happy to sell it.
>
> *Three months later*
> Patrick picks up some casual work and gets a range of irregular shifts. He likes having more time at home with us, particularly in the evenings. He's become more involved with the kids and homework supervision. I am offered extra hours marking HSC exams, and with Patrick at home more, I can snap them up. So my income has gone up slightly which has helped offset the rise in our mortgage repayments.
>
> *Two years later*
> Patrick has had a career change and he's retraining as a carpenter. I remember the time he lost his job as very stressful for both of us, but we got through it in the end. And it gave us more time together as a family when that was important to all of us.

Step 4 – Deal with your 'what do I do now' worries

'What do I do now' worries are more straightforward to deal with than 'what if' worries. They are dilemmas that involve making a decision in order to move forward. The difficulty is that anxiety doesn't open our minds up to contemplate a full range of options to help us make good decisions. Our desire to be free of our worry can prompt us to quickly choose an option to get a fast resolution, even though it may not be helpful at all.

> *Instead of making immediate but unhelpful decisions,*
> *take a calm and deliberate approach*
> *to solving 'what do I do now' worries.*

It's critical here that you do not determine your course of action impulsively or in haste.

Weigh up your objectives

Once you have recognised a 'what do I do now' dilemma, start thinking about the objectives you want your solution to achieve. Imagine your child is passionate about learning dance. In November, their school announces it will stop offering Dance as an elective in Year 8 at the close of the year. You are upset because your child is now bitterly disappointed to learn they cannot study Dance the following year. What do you do now?

You may wish to make your views clear to the principal because the Dance program was one of the factors that led you to choose this school and you want your child to continue their education there. You may also see the situation as an opportunity to show your child how flexible and resilient they can be.

To decide how to proceed you will need to choose which is most important to you: making your views clear about the withdrawal of the subject, or showing your child the importance of being adaptable in the face of change. The action you subsequently take to solve your 'what do I do now' problem will depend on which objective you most want your solution to demonstrate.

Your teen can also face such dilemmas. They may want to reduce their swimming training commitments to give them more time to take part in the school musical this year, but they also want the team to think well of their commitment to the sport and still be in with a chance to make the representative team. In this case, they need to clarify whether it is team membership and sporting achievement or being involved in a mix of extracurricular activities that they value most.

You can see how our 'what do I do now' problems or worries rarely have simple, straightforward solutions. Often the only possible outcomes are suboptimal and imperfect. Reflect on your values and think about what will be *most* important to you in the outcome (expressing disappointment or demonstrating flexibility when confronted with change; being in the musical or having the best chance of sporting accomplishment and meeting team expectations). During your deliberations, you might also want to talk to one or two trusted people who will not pressure you with their opinions about what they think your goal should be.

Imagine a situation where Sam does not get on with their manager. They like their workplace and the type of work they do, but it seems that the most interesting work is always allocated to a colleague, leaving Sam feeling dissatisfied and undervalued. When Sam starts to define what they want to achieve, they begin by thinking about what they would like above all else. Perhaps they think, 'I want more of my preferred work to come my way,' or 'I want my workplace to see me as capable and willing.' Or they might think, 'I want to have it out with my manager and let them know that I see what they are doing and it's not okay.' While Sam might feel a childish urge to have a go at their manager or start sniping at their colleague's efforts in the tasks they are given, they would do better to think sensibly about all the available options.

What's important here is to look at your big picture objectives in your workplace or home life. When Sam weighs up their objectives, they are deciding whether to stand up for themself in the moment or prioritise their ongoing relationship with their manager and more effectively demonstrate their skills. After thinking these through, Sam will be in a better position to choose which matters most to them and subsequently go on to determine an action in line with this choice.

Consider a parent who asks themself 'what do I do now?' about their Year 8 child's lazy attitude towards their homework assignments and correspondingly low marks. When they think about what is most important to them, they might decide they simply want their child to reach their potential at school, or they might decide on specific marks they want their child to attain. While each of these objectives might ultimately deliver the same result, achieving them is likely to involve different actions. Getting the desired marks might involve the parent continuing to organise their child and assist them to complete their homework to the required standard. Reaching their potential might involve building the child's self-regulation and responsibility and allowing them to face the consequences of their choices without the parent's constant coaching and cheering. When the parent has carefully considered their objectives and chosen the one which is most important to them, they will be well placed to choose the actions that will produce their preferred outcome.

The parent might also need to acknowledge that their child's motivation is separate from their own and they must take this into consideration when deciding what the best outcome would be (together with how much homework enthusiasm is likely in a child in Year 8). These factors will help them come to terms with the fact that there is no ideal outcome in which all their wishes will be easily met. (If there were, the parent wouldn't have a 'what do I do now' dilemma that they need to solve!)

Brainstorm your options

Once you have decided on the most important objective you want to achieve, it's time to consider your options for how to proceed. Brainstorming involves thinking of all the possible actions you could take. We recommend you consult a few trusted people with a range of experiences to get a varied mix of opinions. Be careful when choosing people to talk to. Don't involve those who are likely to tell you exactly what to do or pressure you to take an action that simply mirrors their own response to a similar situation. Now is not the time to talk to the bossy sibling, the know-it-all neighbour, or the friend who is occasionally a little jealous. Instead, choose the friends, colleagues and family members who are good listeners and supportive of you doing well.

Sam, whose problem is being overlooked at work, could consult someone they trust in a different department in the company, a colleague who mentioned having similar difficulties a year ago, and a TAFE or uni friend they keep regular contact with. It's important that Sam does not restrict their consultation to only one person, and also that they don't speak about their dilemma to every person they bump into. It's best for them to be selective and canvass ideas from several people they think have relevant experience, are wise or sensible and willing to listen and offer their view, but who will not pressure them to follow the advice given.

The parent with the lazy Year 8 student could talk to their own parent or sibling, another trusted parent at the school, or their child's classroom teacher. Alternatively, they might look to a trusted source on the internet, such as a university page or Triple P, or reread a section of a parenting book (such as Judith's *The Bonsai Student*) specifically on the topic of schooling and homework.

Don't speak to people who take an unhealthy interest in your problem. By this we mean people who, once they know you have a dilemma, are likely to call you night and day because they are invested in your choice of outcome. Ideally the people you choose to consult are those who can contemplate your concern with you without the need to take a starring role to help you sort it out.

Don't forget that you also have the option of doing nothing. Not taking action and leaving the situation as is can always be considered a possibility.

Evaluate your options and act on your choice

This is where you evaluate the pros and cons of each option. After this, decide on your preferred course of action and complete it.

If you do seek help at this stage, refrain from leaning too heavily on the advice you receive at the expense of your own deliberations.

> *If you simply do what someone tells you to do,*
> *you are at risk of not truly owning your actions.*

It's important that you evaluate your potential actions and implementation steps yourself, without assistance. That's because if you accept a solution another person suggested and it doesn't work, you can easily absolve yourself of responsibility and blame them for the unsatisfactory result. (This is the same problem many parents face when they tell their child how to solve one of their problems and then get blamed by the child when the solution doesn't work out.)

Making the decision yourself also means you can take pride in solving your dilemma and become more confident in your decision-making skills. This makes you able to purposefully move forward in life, knowing that you can capably face what happens. Even if in hindsight your decision ends up being the wrong one, you can still learn from it and not pass on all culpability to the friend or co-worker who gave you their advice.

Let's get back to Sam being overlooked at the office. Having sought some advice from sensible confidants, Sam now needs to work through their decision alone. They need to take some time to think about their options, comparing the pros and cons of each before deciding which ones are feasible. Then Sam needs to select the one (or combination of several) which most closely meets what they want to achieve and implement it. If it doesn't work, then back to the drawing board they go.

Despite seeking advice from others, Sam will essentially arrive at their choice on their own two feet. This will build Sam's autonomy, confidence and sense of ownership when they approach problems and implement solutions in future.

And the parent with the lazy Year 8 student has listened to selected advice, worked through the pros and cons, and decided to take on the solution offered by their child's classroom teacher to allow the child to experience the consequences of their lazy choices – detentions and low marks. The parent believes this will be enough to nudge their child into putting more effort into their schoolwork while they take a wait-and-see approach for a term to see if this has the desired effect. (Trial and error are valid means of working through dilemmas.)

Once you have carefully made your decision, act on it. Make sure you continue to make sensible choices while carrying out what you have decided to do. If your decision is to ask your sibling to help pay for your parent's birthday celebration, don't immediately make the phone call at 9.30 pm on Monday evening. Plan the best time and way to take the action you have decided on.

Stay calm prior to acting on your choice. If you find yourself dwelling on the potential fallout of things not going well, work out the timeline of when you will know if this action has worked out for the best as we have described. If all else fails, go into a 'what if' worry story.

Review and repeat as required

Your responsibilities don't end once you have acted. To truly become better at dealing with worries and making good decisions, you must do a forensic sum up of the outcome you achieved. Review how successful you were in implementing your choice and what happened as a result. If your action has not worked to your satisfaction, you may need to go through the brainstorming, evaluating and implementing steps again to make a new choice and act once more.

We learn from the outcomes of our actions whether we judge them to be successful or not. This further develops our resilience and decision-making skills.

> **A sample 'what do I do now' worry and solution**
>
> My child, Morgan, has just received the lowest score in the class for her Year 7 Maths exam. I am overwhelmed by 'what if' questions: What if she is simply not applying herself? What if I have sent her to a school that is too academic for her ability? What if she does badly all through high school? What if she has learning difficulties that haven't been picked up yet? What should I do?
>
> I write down these worries and realise that while most are 'what if' worries, I also have a 'what do I do now' worry that I need to deal with. I have a real concern about doing the right thing, so I write down: 'what do I do now to help Morgan with her Maths?'.

Weigh up your objectives

I need to work out whether my most important objective is for Morgan to get good results in Maths or for her to simply apply herself sufficiently to get results she is capable of and not fall further behind her classmates. I was good at Maths at school and consider it an extremely important skill to have. I also enjoyed Maths and learning in general, and I'd like Morgan to experience this too, but I'm not sure how much attention to give to it. I can't assume Morgan is motivated to study enough to get the marks I did; maybe I should simply let her follow her own interests. I have a conversation with my sister. After weighing up the objectives, I decide the most important one to me is to do what I can to ensure Morgan does not slip any further back in Maths.

Brainstorm your options

I consider the people whose opinions I will seek to help me decide what to do. There's Morgan's dad, a friend who used to be a high-school teacher, and a parent I recently met at the school who has a daughter in a higher grade.

From my discussions, I set out a list of potential actions to consider.

- Do nothing and trust Morgan will be okay because she was doing quite well in Maths last year.
- Arrange a meeting with the Maths teacher as soon as possible to ask what she thinks Morgan needs.
- Wait two weeks until parent–teacher night and speak to the Maths teacher then.
- Sit with Morgan to check on her understanding of her Maths homework every night.
- See if I can arrange a cognitive assessment for Morgan just in case her Maths result is a sign she has other problems.

Evaluate your options and act on your choice

I think through my options, keeping in mind that my most important objective is to try to ensure Morgan doesn't slip further behind in Maths. I decide to sit with her when she does her homework to check on her understanding of the work she is doing. When I try this, Morgan tells me I am babying her, and we have an argument. I realise my decision goes against her need to develop her independence.

I re-evaluate my options. I decide to wait for parent–teacher night since it's only two weeks away. If my 'what if' worries start to feel too much for me in the meantime, I will write a worry story about the one that concerns me most. I prepare some questions to ask the Maths teacher on parent–teacher night so I can get the most out of the time available.

> On the night, the Maths teacher says Morgan works well in class and asks relevant questions. She says quite a few students found the exam difficult and that their first exam in high school can often be challenging. She suggests we wait until the next exam to see if Morgan has problems that need to be followed up. I feel reassured and am happy to follow this advice.
>
> ***Review and repeat as required***
> I am pleased with the choice I made because I now know Morgan is engaged with the subject and working well in class. I'm also pleased I didn't unnecessarily incur the cost and potential emotional upheaval for Morgan of a cognitive assessment because it looks like it won't be needed. Given my decision-making process helped me eventually choose a course of action that resulted in a positive outcome, I decide to do the same in future if similar problems crop up for Morgan or my younger child, Timothy, when he gets to high school.

How to help your child with persistent worries

Just as your child is unlikely to come home excited about doing their chores and homework and getting to bed on time, they will probably have little enthusiasm and patience for listening to you tell them how to deal with their worries and eagerly doing everything you say. This is particularly true if your child is a tween or teen who has been known to do the occasional eye roll at your sage advice.

They may not be looking to you for a solution in any case. Many children, tweens, and some teens are very good at telling their parents of their fears and worries. But they are not so good at then allowing the parents to help or teach them how to resolve their concerns. Yet many parents continue trying to tell their child exactly what they should do. This is always an act of love; parents see the problems and they want their child to overcome them and avoid any potential long-term difficulties which could occur. But – and it is a significant 'but' – as you know from your own childhood years, most children won't listen unless they are truly motivated and willing to put in the hard work to solve whatever is bothering them.

If people don't think they have a solvable problem or aren't really invested in solving their problem or positively dealing with their concerns, the stirring speech is often wasted. The receiver of 'helpful' advice may even resolve to do everything *but* what they are told to do to assert their independence.

Sometimes, even in therapy, people have difficulty taking advice from a psychologist to solve the exact problem they have come to get help with. They may be reluctant to give up the subtle benefits their situation offers, or they may be unwilling to do the hard work of altering their familiar but unhelpful coping behaviours (as we explained in chapter 8 about secondary gains).

So that you don't waste your time or lessen your child's desire to resolve their worries, avoid delivering the motivational speech, because our experience has shown that most children will not want to act on your advice. Others may overly rely on parental assistance and fail to adequately develop their own problem-solving skills as a result.

There is a more effective response you can take. First, do as we suggested in chapter 13 to discourage anxiety in your child by teaching them how to manage their day-to-day challenges. When they express typical hesitations or concerns – worry about exams, concern about their chosen free-dress-day outfit, or fears that their friend sitting with someone else at lunch means the friendship is over – make the following steps your base response.

> *With any fear or worry they express,*
> *your first steps are to name their emotion,*
> *empathise with them and normalise their feeling.*

Be positive about their ability to cope with whatever the outcome turns out to be, and talk about their past resilience and strength in facing less than ideal circumstances. Make sure they feel heard, but don't extend this conversation to the point where it could amp up their emotions.

If they remain nervous – dwelling on their concern about the foolish thing they said in yesterday's class, their nerves about next week's cheer squad competition, or fretting that their outfit for the school dance is not cool enough – move on to the strategies we describe below.

These are all low-key conversational techniques. Don't get out the butcher's paper and whiteboard pens and make a big deal of helping them solve their concern. That approach will not go down well with them, and you risk becoming so much the 'problem-solver' that you end by doing all the work. You simply want to support them to become more confident and capable at facing their future fears or dilemmas somewhat independently.

When your child comes to you with a concern, listen to them and then ask them to name what it is they are actually afraid of. This helps them to identify their worrying thoughts and classify them. As you now know, their problem will likely fall into one of two types – what if something happens or what do they do now.

Help them deal with their 'what if' worries

'What if' worries are usually about something bad happening, predicted failure, or concern that a past action might have been embarrassing for them or somehow wrong. It might be that they are afraid they will have no one to talk to at the party before their friend arrives, that they won't play well in the final on Saturday, or that the candidate speech they gave last week wasn't good enough for them to be made school captain next year. Several 'what ifs' can occur in any situation.

Respond to these concerns by saying that it sounds like they are worried because they don't know what will happen in the circumstances they describe, or what the result will mean for them. Then ask them when they will know the outcome of their worry. When will they know if there's someone at the party to talk to? When will they know if they played well in the final? When will they know if their school captain's speech was successful?

Coach them through the process of determining the timeline for when they will know what ends up happening; push them to consider the latest possible end point (not the earliest). Of course, this will only be once their friend has arrived at the party or even when the party is over, or after they have played the final, or when the school captain appointments are made. Explain that they will not necessarily know in the next day or week; if they are concerned about their career choice or future success, they may not know the outcome of their worry until their 16th, 21st or even 50th birthday.

Social anxiety is usually composed of a raft of 'what if' worries and therefore responds well to this technique. If your child is socially anxious, every time they try out a new activity or participate in a conversation with unfamiliar people, they will face fears of failure. When your teenager attempts to work out when and how they will know whether their conversation with the potential new friends they met at last weekend's party went well, advise them it will usually take a few weeks, based on whether the others smile at them and choose to include them in conversations when they meet them again. Remind your tween or teen that they will cross paths with the others several times before they'll know if they will become friends. This helps them work out for themself whether this will take two weeks, a month or longer. Normalise the experience of forming friendships as slow and gradual; give them some examples of gently developing friendships of your own to help dispel any impatience they feel.

Once your child determines when they will know the result of their concern, encourage them to calmly await the outcome without dwelling on it conversationally, particularly with you. There is no point seeking reassurance in the meantime because no one else can know what will happen either.

If they feel troubled while waiting, encourage them to do a beneficial self-soothing activity where they focus deliberately on something purposeful that relaxes them, such as listening to or playing music they enjoy, taking the dog for a walk, or scrapbooking to allow time to pass. Ensure they go to school and have opportunities to socialise. Continuing to engage in life will boost their mood and help them lose their preoccupation with a worry. If they try to block their worries with screen use instead, they are most likely to lose chunks of time and become frustrated and upset. Distraction via screen activities is rarely a helpful way to respond to a worry. The exception to this may be a family movie night or trip to a cinema.

If your child wants to continue talking about their worry, simply ask them again when they will know what happens in the scenario they are concerned about. Be calm and patient but place a limit on the discussion: don't reward them with your eagerness to dissect their concern whenever they want to download. Say something like, 'You've worked out when you'll know the outcome of this, why not just wait till then rather than waste time worrying now?'

Remember you are not doing a formal brainstorming session with them. You are asking questions that redirect them to what they need to do now, rather than overly encouraging them to come to you for endless downloading or constant reassurance which will not help their coping skills.

Your conversation could go something like this:

> Theo: I'm worried I'm going to fail the Maths exam.
> Parent: Well, that's totally understandable. You're studying some thorny stuff right now.
>   [This should be a sufficient response. But if Theo pushes on . . .]

> Theo: But what if I fail? How am I going to get into Vet Science?
> Parent: Whoa ... hang on. Before you go down that path, let's take a step back. When are you going to know the outcome of this exam?
> Theo: What do you mean?
> Parent: When are you going to know for sure if you failed?
> Theo: When the results come out, about a week after the exams.
> Parent: Well, if you fail, I guess you'll either repeat the year or try and do well in first year Science and then see if you can transfer across. But you'll only know whether it will come to that on the 17th December, so it seems to me that it would be a better idea to think about that only if it happens then. In the meantime, what can you do?

If your child goes on to turn the conversation against you, proceed to give the conversational equivalent of a shrug.

> Theo: You clearly don't understand my stress.
> Parent: Look, I know it matters a lot to you, and you'll know on the 17th of December, but it seems to me you either focus on your worry or focus on your study and doing everything else you need and want to do. I know what I'd do – but it's up to you how you approach this.

Help them deal with their 'what do I do now' worries

To help your child overcome the negative feelings produced by 'what do I do now' worries, similarly show them that you have heard their dilemma and empathise with them. You can also encourage them to either develop a plan of action or make a deliberate decision not to do anything.

Their discomfort usually arises from not knowing the best action to take. When their birthday is coming up, they may be worried whether they should invite 15 friends for an afternoon celebration, or simply have their two best mates over for a movie, pizza and a sleepover. When they think their friend has been mean recently, they may worry whether they should say how they feel or leave it be. When their co-worker at their part-time job is not pulling their weight on shared shifts, they don't know whether they should speak directly to them or to their supervisor.

Resist all urges to tell your child what they should do. If you tell them what to do and it doesn't go well, they can blame you and absolve themself of all responsibility (even though choosing to take your suggestion is their decision). Eventually they must learn how to solve their own problems without you doing all the work. Your effort is best invested in helping them learn how to help themself.

If they raise their 'what do I do now' worry with you, we recommend the vent-and-problem-solve strategy. Allow them to vent briefly and show them you have heard their concern by naming their emotion, empathising and normalising their feeling. Remind them that doing nothing is an option to consider. If they continue to bring their dilemma up with you, encourage them to think of a range of achievable actions and outcomes, to think these through and discuss them with a few trusted friends, relatives or perhaps a teacher or their coach.

While they can talk to you, it is also beneficial for them to seek other opinions, so they don't become too dependent on you or anyone else in particular to solve their dilemmas. The people they choose to consult for a friendship dilemma could include yourself, their school buddy who is a few years ahead of them, or their socially adept older sibling. For a work situation, they might talk to their aunt who works in hospitality, or their co-worker who is on different shifts. Remind them that they are seeking opinions and ideas here, not prescriptive instructions. Canvassing these suggestions allows them to broaden their perspective and also creates a wider group of people they can consult in future. This will be of great assistance to them.

This is how your conversation might go:

> Taylor: I'm really worried that Selena isn't going to pull her weight in our group and we won't do well. She hasn't replied to any of the emails yet.
> Parent: It sounds like you are nervous about this performance – that's understandable. Drama is important to you, huh?
> Taylor: Yes, but what am I going to do? If she mucks it up, then we're all in trouble.
> Parent: Have you thought about what you could do?
> Taylor: I have no idea.
> Parent: Is there anyone you can think of who might have some good ideas on what to do?
> Taylor: What do you think I should do?
> Parent: I can offer you one opinion, but I think you need to get ideas from a few people. There's probably not one perfect answer but it's a good idea to think it through. I know things have changed since I was at school back in the ice age.
> Taylor: Haha. I might ask my stupid sister – she's Captain Fairness.

> Parent: Yup. Anyone else who might have some good ideas?
> Taylor: My junior coach at cheer might know, she's studying drama at uni now. Maybe Elicia, who had the same problem last term with Carissa.
> Parent: Sounds good. Chat to them all and then decide. I'm sure they will all have some good ideas.

Your child then needs to think through the suggestions they gather from their discussions with respected confidants and make their choice. Remind them to choose an option in line with the values they feel are important to live by. If they want to be considered a good friend, this might be their dominant value when weighing up options in the midst of friendship difficulties. Let them talk through what they are considering with you if they wish but don't judge the ideas they have gathered or become defensive of your own ideas – be curious about their choice rather than directing them to one conclusion.

After your child has taken time to decide and act, follow up with them to see if they feel their decision was wise in retrospect and ask them what they learnt from it. Remind them that there is rarely a perfect decision, and the best we can generally hope for is to become better at making these choices over time. You may have to encourage them to stay open and accepting of the likelihood that they might not know the ultimate outcome of their choice for some time. Sometimes bad decisions end up being good decisions and vice versa.

Let's look at an example. Your child is worried that they will suddenly miss you at their friend's sleepover. To respond, you might ask when they would know if that outcome happened. If they say they'll know on the night of the sleepover but would be worried about what to do if it happened, encourage them to think through their options.

One way to direct your child's thoughts toward helpful ones when responding to a 'what do I do now' worry (or even 'what will I do if the worst happens') is to ask them to think about what they would feel most proud of in retrospect, considering the traits they want to show the world. They might like to think of themself as brave for facing the sleepover or applying to be class captain and delivering their speech. This will help them choose solutions that favour facing the potentially difficult situation and being proud of their strength and resilience. You might say, 'What would you like to say about yourself the next morning after the sleepover? How do you think you would you feel the next day if you didn't go?' and 'What could you do if you think you need to come home midway through the night?'

The ways you can use these ideas are endless
once you accept that your role is not to solve their dilemmas
or take away their concerns.

Instead, you are asking them to think their actions through, to sit with the uncertainty that worries bring up and seek a range of solutions. It is important to be relatively calm about their discomfort while they wait for others to give an opinion or make their decision about what to do. If you can do that, you are modelling composure to your child and practising it yourself. Trust your child to be able to work though these steps and come out more confident and capable on the other side.

If you need more support

You now have the tools you need to understand and redirect your anxiety and to help your child manage their fears in a way that encourages them to develop their problem-solving skills. But we acknowledge that some readers might feel a need for more support. Please register on this book's website (www.raisinganxiety.com) if you would like to be notified when we release additional online resources and workshops to help you master and apply the worry steps.

If you believe your child is significantly affected by anxiety (or if you feel you are overly anxious) or if your situation is complex, you are best to seek therapeutic assistance. We discuss the best ways to do this in the next chapter.

Dr Einstein's **What When** Model to Redirect Anxiety

Your World
daily life, social media,
email, news cycle

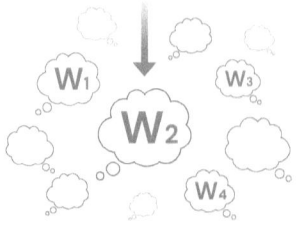

Step 1: *Identify your worries*
Step 2: *Classify your worries*

WHAT IF?

1. **WHEN will I know for sure?**
2. Relax your body
3. Practise powerful distraction
4. Write your worry story

WHAT DO I DO NOW?

1. Weigh up your objectives ⎤
2. Brainstorm your options ⎦ in consultation

3. Evaluate your options and act ⎤
4. Review and repeat as required ⎦ independently

Note: Please read this chapter to understand the nuances within the model (© Locke & Einstein, 2024)

CHAPTER 15

Seeking professional assistance

Therapy can be very effective when its goal is to help your child learn to manage and overcome their anxious tendencies. This chapter shows you how to make sure professional assistance will genuinely improve your child's wellbeing.

If you have followed the approach and techniques we have described, yet anxiety remains a problem for your child, you may choose to seek individual professional assistance. Before you begin, it's helpful to understand what to reasonably expect from therapy.

'Hole' and 'ladder' therapies

Think back to our discussion in chapter 8 about psychological gains and anxiety where we described the two types of benefit therapy can offer: immediate and longer-term relief. Immediate relief is primarily therapist-assisted conversation that allows a person to feel better right away. It typically involves encouraging them to talk through the problematic situation they face, such as their stress about their work, their grief at the loss of a parent, or their feelings about their partner's recent infidelity. The discussion might also include more minor irritations of their week, such as the tension that arose from the argument about work schedules they had with their co-worker on Tuesday, or the frustration they felt when their family failed to clean the kitchen before the barbeque on Saturday.

Most of us experience relief when we are able to unburden ourselves to someone objective who actively listens when we freely speak our mind and say things we might not be prepared to say to friends and family.

Immediate relief doesn't only come from chat. When treating a child, a therapist might remove a feared outcome or task that feels overwhelming by, for example, writing a letter to their school asking that the child be allowed to have some extra time for their assignment or deliver their history talk to their teacher instead of in front of the class.

The second type of benefit – longer-term relief – involves a therapist assisting their client to take steps to overcome their problem. They help people face difficult situations and slowly guide them toward improving their mental health as much as possible. Therapists do this by giving clients strategies that have been shown through research to help people in similar circumstances. They might show someone who is stressed by their job how to set up a clear demarcation between work and home, help them avoid work on the weekend, organise their day more efficiently, and put in better boundaries with the manager who has a habit of contacting them at all hours. If a person's recent quarrel is typical of the conflicts they have with their family, a therapist might teach them better ways to communicate at home so that every minor dispute doesn't turn into an argument.

Another way therapists help people overcome their difficulties is by teaching them how to accept what they cannot change. Therapists do this by using psychological techniques like cognitive re-structuring, which shows clients how to think helpful thoughts and learn to sit more peacefully with past events, or activity scheduling, which encourages clients to shift their daily mood by participating in pastimes they previously enjoyed.

We believe it's helpful to think of the types of therapy that produce immediate and longer-term relief as 'hole' therapy and 'ladder' therapy. When a person comes to a therapist they are usually in a hole – of anxiety, stress, grief, depression, procrastination, or a difficult relationship they don't know how to mend. They are stuck in their hole, and it might feel so deep they can't see any way out.

At first, the therapist will question the client about their difficult situation to determine the extent of its effect on them, how and when it started, and any techniques they have already tried to improve or overcome it. Once a client feels heard and the therapist fully understands their situation, truly helpful therapy moves on to the ladder stage where the therapist gives their client ways to climb out of the hole of their situation and freely move on with their life. The therapist will show anxious clients how to face or become more realistic about their fears, and to slowly start to do what is difficult for them so they become better at facing challenge more confidently.

Climbing a therapeutic ladder is often hard work – sometimes even harder than remaining in the hole of a difficult situation – because it can be frightening, and the effort to change can feel tougher than the discomfort of remaining stuck. By nature, we tend to choose the familiar over the new. But when we deliberately choose to take different actions than we have in the past, we are more likely to climb out of our hole of despair and into a life where we are no longer held back by our old thoughts, fears or other people's expectations.

False ideas of 'good' therapy

In our opinion, some popular ideas over the last decade or two about the purpose of therapy have resulted in mistaken notions of what 'typical' and 'good' therapy entail. This is particularly true for anxiety treatment for children and adolescents.

We find that many people think anxiety psychotherapy involves a client talking to their clinician about their recent worries or challenges and the therapist responding with immediate support by listening, empathising and soothing. For example, consider a teen, Elise, who seeks treatment for her anxiety. The simplistic popular view of therapy imagines Elise tells the therapist about tricky situations she faces, such as the friendship fight that arose when she felt she was not being listened to in the group science project last week, and her fears about the speech she has to give in the English class next Tuesday. The therapist helps Elise by empathising with her over her friendship difficulty and offering to write to her school recommending that she gives her speeches only in front of the teacher for the rest of the year to save her from her fears.

This approach to therapy does exist. We call it 'hole therapy': the client tells the therapist about their difficulties inside the hole of their anxiety, and the therapist absorbs themself in examining the client's plight, then offers sympathy and a temporary escape from their pressing concerns. We see problems arise when every session is exclusively devoted to this immediately soothing approach because the therapist can become the client's one-sided confidant in conversations focused solely on their problematic feelings. This can become a child's or teen's preferred way of downloading challenges encountered within their family or school week. The problem is that this situation won't ever be replicated in real life, and over time, parents and school friends can seem unsupportive in comparison to the therapist who listens attentively, always agrees with them, and never interjects to talk about themself. Indeed, this approach may have encouraged Elise to think her friends in the science group were not supporting her when they simply wanted to listen to everyone's ideas, not just hers.

In addition to offering empathy and escape, Elise's therapist might help her problem-solve individual challenges that arise for her each week or fortnight, which also provides immediate relief and reassurance as to what she should do in tricky situations. If this becomes a child's or teen's preferred method of dealing with their dilemmas, it means their problem-solving is only done with or by the therapist, because the therapy does not teach them to develop their own skills in problem-solving and overcoming anxiety, nor does it encourage them to do this independently outside therapy. Worse still, the therapist's excusing letters might allow clients like Elise to continue to avoid her upcoming fears, and so keep them stuck in the hole of their anxiety where they are not expected to face challenge or resolve daily dilemmas.

Don't get us wrong. Daily or weekly downloading is important in people's lives. We need to discuss the events of our days and weeks with people who care about us – but this is best done with our empathetic family and friends (particularly the wise ones), rather than a therapist. If a person doesn't have this kind of support, they may benefit from the assistance of a therapist to help them build a supportive network in their lives through strategies to make friends and mend relationships with members of their family (or detach from them if they will always remain problematic).

Additionally, if a client or a close family member has a pervasive developmental disorder, such as autism, or a serious health problem like Crohn's disease, they may well benefit from therapeutic support that allows them to talk through their concerns and feelings about what may essentially be an unchangeable situation. This is not to say that therapists can't give some longer-term ways of alleviating their circumstances to some degree. For example, carers are often not good at caring for themselves. A therapist can encourage them to obtain respite assistance, maintain an exercise schedule alongside other self-care activities, and alter any unhelpful thoughts they have, such as ideas that they have somehow created their situation themselves or that they need to be caring for their loved one continually, without a break. A teen whose parent has a personality disorder can't do a lot to get out of their situation while they live at home, but a therapist can help them establish better boundaries and manage their parent's behaviours in a way that keeps their relationship as healthy as it can be.

But therapy that provides relief in the short term can also emphasise approaches that allow a client to feel immediately better but are not helpful in the long term. Grounding strategies, such as breathing or counting techniques, are extremely popular, but they are not effective treatments for anxiety if they become a client's new safety behaviours. These are actions that a person latches onto to feel safe. When we consistently resort to grounding strategies, we do not learn that our anxiety can be survived on its own, without the substitute of another action. The teen who is advised to focus on controlling their breathing rate by lowering it has likely not been coached to try increasing it in order to learn that the physical feelings they experience when hyperventilating are not dangerous (interoceptive exposure therapy). Surviving uncomfortable sensations means letting them come and go as they arise, rather than trying to control or eliminate them while facing the situation that produces our fears. (We talk more about this in the next chapter.)

Hole therapy can last for a long time – sometimes for years. That's because it is ineffective: although it *feels* like it is helping, it does not provide long-term treatment. The client leaves sessions feeling immediately relieved, possibly even happy after talking through their issues and being heard. The initial feeling of release that comes from being listened to and agreed with can make therapy feel effective and keep the client booking sessions. Parents who see their child feeling better for a day or two may feel encouraged to keep paying for more sessions. But this kind of therapy doesn't require the teen to learn and use skills in the time between sessions as a necessary condition for continued treatment. These skills may include the courage to ignore and outlast anxious feelings, the confidence to speak up and the tolerance to listen in group projects, and the ability to face typical challenge without the need for extensive therapeutic downloading or ongoing special considerations.

This approach can also produce a larger problem when children or teens and their loved ones start to think their anxiety cannot be treated successfully because they are receiving therapy and the anxiety remains. Everyone concerned can start to think that the child or teen will need therapy for the rest of their life while simultaneously believing that their anxiety is untreatable.

We have become increasingly concerned in recent years that people see a diagnosis of anxiety as permanent. We believe this stems from widespread misunderstanding of the nature of anxiety and some typical approaches or expectations of hole therapy. It seems this has been produced by a perfect storm of parenting and teaching approaches which place too much importance on being extremely responsive to children and teens at the expense of expecting them to step up to increasing challenges as they become older. We believe that just as parents have been caught up in overparenting as we discussed in chapter 2, some therapists have been inadvertently swept into an approach that prioritises a client's comfort in and out of the therapy room. As a result, there is a widespread expectation that therapy will not require a client to do the hard and initially uncomfortable work between appointments of overcoming their problems via evidence-based strategies.

Hole therapy ostensibly looks to be an approach of great care, but it actually holds clients back from achieving the improvement they seek. This is why we prefer ladder therapy, which discourages exclusive reliance on the safe therapeutic space as an ongoing support, and instead helps the client to get out of their hole. Good ladder therapy teaches clients to manage the ups and downs of life with specific skills like problem-solving, assertiveness and the ability to successfully interact socially. The therapist remains warm and supportive, but they encourage the client to do the work they need to do.

We understand that it is often easiest to give a client (or anyone) what they think they want and that therapists can be tempted to adopt techniques characteristic of hole therapy that quickly bring relief and allow their clients to feel better within their session. We are aware that clients often prefer what they see as a 'kind' approach and can push back against therapeutic approaches which demand more of them. We are all human and, if given the chance, many of us would choose the sympathetic personal trainer who gives massages and doesn't make us sweat too much over the one who puts us through a more vigorous workout. Similarly, we may prefer the sweet therapist who primarily listens to us download the problems of our week and then solves them for us. It's understandable why some people favour these types of professionals over the ones that make us do the hard work to achieve what we want. We also acknowledge it can be difficult for a professional to push back on what the client says they want and insist on a therapeutic approach that teaches them the proven techniques they need.

We know that good therapy, particularly good anxiety treatment, must be targeted assistance that actively improves a client's life to the point that they no longer need regular sessions. It supports them to believe that their situation can change and motivates them to put in the effort to implement strategies that move them out of their difficult situation. It also encourages them to climb the steps of the ladder out of that hole into the wonderful world above ground.

How to help your child climb out of their anxiety hole

The first step toward moving a child out of an anxiety hole is to make that hole less cosy and rewarding. Take out the rugs and the comfy chair; turn off the central heating. The strategies we have featured so far in Part B are all about making sure the hole doesn't continue to be a satisfying place to be stuck in.

Another way to make the hole less comfortable is to offer empathy without reprieve. There are times when parents, schools and even therapists inadvertently keep a child stuck in their anxiety by lowering their expectations of them and making allowances for them. Some schools now give special consideration to anxious children by giving them extra time to complete tests or letting them do their exams in a room separate from everyone else; sometimes there are more students in these special rooms than the main exam room. But to ultimately overcome their fears, all children should learn to cope with life as it is likely to be presented to them. Anxious children may need to be coached and assisted to slowly face the same expectations as their more easy-going peers. Be empathetic about their circumstances but ensure that any allowances given to your child are not a permanent reprieve. Your aim is to encourage them to climb out of their anxiety hole and face the next set of challenges they will inevitably meet at school, university or their workplace with renewed hardiness because they now have some experience in facing similar challenges.

Put our suggestions into practice for a month to see if they encourage improvement in your child's anxious thoughts and behaviours. Re-read some chapters if you wish to check you are on track. If you do not see signs of the changes you are looking for after a month, or you find it difficult to carry out the recommended actions, we suggest you seek therapy, particularly if your situation is complicated by additional factors, such as a recent divorce or significant health problem. Therapy is also likely to be helpful if your child is neurodiverse or has been diagnosed with a comorbid diagnosis.

What to consider when you seek therapy for your child

There are aspects of receiving professional assistance which will help you have the best chance of turning your child's situation around. When you seek therapy, we recommend you take the following points into consideration.

Participate in therapy with your young child or tween

We are not fans of children younger than 12 years old attending anxiety therapy without their parents. Children – particularly those younger than ten years old – are unlikely to be able to absorb and remember to do what a psychologist has suggested to them some days ago. And many children younger than ten don't have the self-regulation skills to do what they *need* to do as opposed to what they *want* to do. When a young child or tween has treatment for anxiety, we generally recommend that parents are involved in their therapy sessions.

When parents participate in their child's sessions, they are able to coach the child when coaching is warranted. Their presence also gives them the knowledge to avoid inadvertently rewarding their child's anxiety at home and guides their actions to support rather than oppose the psychologist's recommendations. Knowing what the psychologist has said to their child also helps offset parents' worries that they may be 'doing the wrong things' when their child has an anxiety diagnosis. We have both had experience with young clients who adjust what they are told in therapy when reporting back to their parents. 'Judith says you are babying me, and you should let me go to the party on a school night.' 'Danielle thinks you should get off my back about doing my homework.' Miscommunication and misunderstanding are less likely when everyone is on the same page, and therapy usually proceeds more smoothly. There is also less likelihood of a child becoming stuck in 'hole therapy' when parents are present at discussions with the therapist.

Our only caveat here is when children receive school counselling. In our experience school counsellors primarily see children for solution-focused short-term work for issues such as friendship challenges. This type of therapy typically encourages the child to move forward and is less likely to become rewarding for them.

Make sure your child is motivated to overcome their anxiety

There is no point in sending someone to a psychologist if they don't believe they have a problem. If your child thinks their current choices are okay or they don't experience any negative consequences from them, they will likely lack sufficient motivation to do the necessary hard work of improvement.

Imagine Chloe, a 13-year-old who is always on her phone or tablet making TikTok videos – so much so that she has little time for other productive activities, moments with her family, or actual exchanges with her real-life friends. While making the videos is a creative activity for her, Chloe's parents have noticed that she has become so obsessed and anxious about responses to her efforts that she now seems solely focused on her online presence. When a clip receives negative reviews, Chloe's mood switches to anger or neediness and prompts the rest of the family to tread on eggshells around her. Every time her parents bring up their concern about the amount of time she spends on this activity, an emotional argument results. The parents worry that anxiety or depression might be causing Chloe to be engrossed by her time alone with her screens, and they arrange for her to see a therapist. This sounds sensible, but in this scenario, it is likely that only the parents see the child's use as problematic. Chloe herself probably sees her parents' nagging as a problem: to her, their unrealistic expectations are unnecessarily stopping her devoting enough time to her preferred preoccupation.

Children are typically not keen to decrease their screen use. They need sufficient maturity to see its effect on them and their ability to study or socialise face-to-face. They also need the necessary motivation to do the hard work of changing their habits. If a screen-dependent child doesn't have this, therapy could prove to be unhelpful. When talking to a therapist, children naturally tend to justify why they're on their screens and would rather focus the discussion on what annoys them about their parents.

It takes a highly skilled therapist to see through children's complaints and guide them to accept that screens can be a problem and motivate them to change their habits.

In Chloe's situation, the adults are the only ones likely to recognise the problem of her screen addiction. So it is more effective for the parents to see the psychologist and learn how to set up a helpful home environment and coach her into improved behaviours. They're also more likely to do what the therapist suggests because they are the ones motivated to change the situation.

Another option is family therapy; again, we must stress that each family member needs to have sufficient motivation and similar goals for this to work. If even one person is not on board, they can have a detrimental effect on the sessions if they are surly or antagonistic.

> *Therapy has the best chance of success for the person who recognises the problem and is motivated to change it.*

If your child does not see that they have a problem, discuss your situation with the therapist before you start and get their suggestions on what to do with an unmotivated child.

How to raise the idea of therapy with your anxious child

To encourage your child to see a therapist – particularly when they are a teen – you need to raise it in a way that is palatable to them. Find an opportunity when everyone is relatively calm, and you have sufficient time to have this conversation.

Mention that you don't think they are handling their worries in a way that is helpful for them and give a few examples. Talk about your concerns in a measured way without blame. Focus on how you believe their choices are affecting them, not their impact on you. After you present your views, ask, 'What do you think?' Listen to what they have to say with empathy and respond positively to them.

If they agree to attend therapy, tell them you could go together to a psychologist to ensure that you are both doing what you can to change the situation, particularly if it involves family disharmony and unhelpful habits. Tell them therapy will help them change the way they are reacting, and that the therapist will help everyone to support each other. Say that it might involve some hard work at first, but that they have a chance to improve their life, and the skills they learn will help them for years to come. Check if they agree or not.

If they reject what you have said – 'it's not an issue' – park the conversation for a while. Raise the idea again when their anxiety is apparent, such as when they want to avoid a test or after-school activity, or when they worry excessively before an assignment is due. When this happens, use the strategies we suggested in the previous chapter for solving 'what if' problems. If this doesn't help them feel better about facing their upcoming challenge, wait for a time – say until the next evening – and bring up your concern again. Tell them that their fears seem to be having a significant effect on them, and that you think a psychologist could help them reduce this.

Remember this conversation is best when slow cooked, not microwaved into an instant solution which they agree with right away. Show patience here.

If your child reacts by blaming you for their problems – 'I wouldn't worry so much if you were less annoying and just let me do what I want to do!' – react with something like, 'I don't think that is the cause.' Then leave it be and try again later, as above.

If your child doesn't agree to attend therapy and you are already implementing the strategies we have suggested in previous chapters, but this hasn't changed your situation sufficiently, you will need to be the person receiving individualised professional assistance. Therapy can assist you to coach your child into better behaviours or work out ways to reduce the effect on your family if your child's anxiety prompts them to behave badly.

In this case, we suggest you see a therapist without mentioning it to your child. They will worry or think they have done something wrong if you tell them their behaviour has caused you to get help. We also suggest that you be the one to get psychological help if your child has compliance or behaviour problems. In our experience, parents are better placed to adjust the home environment to encourage their children to behave better – and most times parents have greater motivation than children to follow treatment.

How to find a good therapist

The easiest way to find a good psychologist is by speaking to your regular doctor about the difficulty you or your child or teen is facing. Doctors often know of psychologists in their area they can recommend. Another way is to look up the professional association of psychologists in your country. In Australia, we have a 'Find a psychologist' page on the Australian Clinical

Psychology Association website and another on the Australian Psychological Society's website. On these, you can type in your issue of concern and your location for a list of registered psychologists you could contact.

Just because a person says they are an expert on their own webpage doesn't mean they actually have the qualifications, expertise and experience to help you. There are many words anyone without training or registration can freely use to describe themself. Be wary of terms like 'expert' or 'counsellor' or 'therapist'. Some training in psychology, such as a brief course in neuroscience or even a PhD in a non-clinical psychological area, doesn't necessarily enable someone to treat people's problems if their studies have not involved training in appropriate treatment methods. This is typically achieved by obtaining a master's degree in psychology, or several years of supervised training in a clinical area for those with a bachelor's degree.

We are both clinical psychologists and stand by our master's degree qualification as one of the best to train professionals in using proven best practice treatments. This is not to say that other psychologists and online programs can't add value; the kind of professional psychological service you use will depend on your budget and location.

What is critical is that your chosen therapist has professional registration with the Australian Health Practitioner Regulation Agency (Ahpra) in Australia, or the relevant licensing and certification board in your country. Registration and certification usually depend on a person completing the required initial training and accruing a specified number of supervised practical hours. Ongoing registration depends on continuing to maintain and undergo required training and supervision. This ensures that registered professionals are equipped to deliver best practice treatment and will do no harm.

You can look up any practitioner on your state or country's agency or registration website to confirm they are appropriately qualified. We say you should be wary of taking any psychological advice from someone not registered or licensed by their state or nation, as their guidance could misguide or harm. Just because the technique they came up with ended up working in their home doesn't mean it will work for you.

How to make sure therapy is likely to work for you

When you are looking for a psychologist, we believe it is best to prioritise seeing the right one for you. To do this, check the expertise of the therapist, and perhaps have a brief conversation with them about your situation and their experience in treating people with difficulties similar to yours, before going on their waiting list. In our experience, a clinician who specialises in working with a particular age group and type of presentation, such as teen social anxiety and worry, will understand the nuances of treatment for those problems and has a greater likelihood of successfully helping clients overcome the issue. Sometimes you might pay more per session but be able to improve your problem in fewer sessions, so more expensive therapy may still offer value for money.

Of course, if your child is at risk due to thoughts of self-harm or suicide, we recommend you have a clear plan in place for supporting them to get help. (The same goes for yourself if you have such thoughts.) The steps to prepare this plan are noted in our Q & A in the next chapter. If you haven't been able to get your child into therapy, and they express a clear intent to hurt themselves, immediately reach out to a suicide prevention service like Kids Helpline, or take your child to the emergency department of your nearest hospital and get urgent assistance. Don't wait for an appointment to free up; get help now. (If your child is already in therapy, your therapist will prepare this plan with you.)

Check which type of therapy your psychologist offers

Since Judith created the terms 'hole therapy' and 'ladder therapy', asking a psychologist if they do ladder therapy is likely to draw a blank look. But there are ways you can determine whether the approach they take will be likely to properly address and treat your child's anxiety (or your own).

Talk to the therapist about the type of treatment they propose and ask if it is evidence based (that is, if the treatment they use has been shown by empirical evidence to work). Remember that effective therapy aims to help a person improve their situation to the point where they can get on with their life without needing to continue to see the psychologist. When a client immediately feels better after their therapy sessions but needs to book in every week or fortnight to continue to feel this way, they are not receiving effective treatment.

Ask the psychologist about the typical treatment time for the issues you need addressed in yourself or your child. You are looking for them to say something like, 'I usually find my teen clients learn to manage their anxiety within six to ten sessions.' This does not mean your treatment will take a similar number of sessions; the psychologist will need to assess your child's or your own specific situation. If your situation is complex because of ADHD, autism or past trauma, therapy is likely to take longer.

Establish your expectations acknowledging any known limitations. Be upfront with the therapist and let them know your budget in advance. If they can't help you improve your situation within your available time or money, they will tell you and potentially suggest other ways for you to receive help.

Be aware that therapy needs to be regular enough for meaningful change to occur within and between sessions, and usually needs to happen weekly or fortnightly, particularly at the start. Seeing a psychologist once a month is about as effective as seeing a personal trainer once a month: therapy is unlikely to achieve improvement if sessions are irregular or spaced too far apart. Some important research has been published that finds spacing sessions out to once a month can make some clients' problems worse over time. The general recommendation is for an intensive beginning, followed by regular sessions to ensure treatment gains are maintained before therapy is stopped.

Make sure you have the time available to make the most of any therapy. It is never ideal to start when you or your child are so busy you don't have time to devote to applying new skills and doing 'homework' between sessions. Start when you and your child have sufficient time and energy to devote to doing all that treatment requires. If you are too busy now, wait until life is a little freer for both of you. Or prioritise therapeutic progress over other aspects of your lives.

Obtain a referral for Medicare-funded sessions

In Australia, Medicare-funded therapy sessions have been a blessing for many people who previously couldn't afford to see a psychologist. Australians can obtain a Medicare refund on sessions with a registered psychologist when referred by their general practitioner (GP). The refund covers part or all of the cost, depending on the psychologist's fee.

To obtain a referral, people must visit a GP for an assessment of their concerns, after which the GP may prepare a mental health treatment plan (MHTP) which allows them to obtain a Medicare rebate on their treatment sessions. People may access these sessions for anxiety, depression, adjustment issues, conduct disorder and sleep problems, among other concerns. Typically, the plan suggests a particular psychologist to treat the problem.

After the psychologist has treated the person for up to six sessions, they must write a letter to the referring GP. This letter details the progress and success of treatment so far and suggests whether a further four sessions are warranted. This allows the GP to determine whether the chosen approach is proving to be helpful. Some improvement should be evident after six sessions; if not, a different psychologist or approach might be warranted. A further four sessions may be needed to achieve improvement or to build on gains achieved already.

Therapy under any Medicare plan must be evidence based, such as Cognitive Behavioural Therapy (CBT), which helps a client change their thoughts and behaviours to be more helpful to them, or Interpersonal Therapy (IPT) which helps to resolve a client's interpersonal difficulties and improve their problem-solving or communication skills. All evidence-based therapies give the client proven strategies and encourage them to develop the insight to be able to accept or change their situation. They are much more than 'talk therapy', which can amount to the client simply chatting about their week.

Medicare-funded psychology sessions are a valuable part of the health system but there are potential improvements which could be made in regard to children's mental health and parenting problems. If parents attend their GP to get support for their six-year-old who appears to be troubled by anxiety, the parents will not receive a MHTP unless they have a clinically diagnosable disorder themselves, such as their own anxiety. Because of this, it is more likely that the child is referred to the psychologist under an MHTP, even though they are likely too young to benefit from seeing a psychologist.

The most effective solution would involve the psychologist helping the parents coach their young child, but this is less likely to happen when the client wants the sessions funded through a MHTP. Moreover, to access the refund, the child must attend four of the initial six sessions, where they hear every strategy discussed with the parents (and likely argue with them if they are of an age to understand the conversation).

It is false economy if a client gets a refund when their therapy is ineffective or risks worsening an anxiety problem. This can happen if a child is allowed to vent and exaggerate all their anxieties or grievances each week for little more than kind attention from the psychologist in return. We encourage you to make sure any Medicare-assisted therapy is genuinely overcoming your or your child's concerns; otherwise it is a waste of time or money.

Be prepared to do the work required to improve your situation

We have both had clients who tell us they are motivated to improve their situation and overcome their anxiety. However, when it comes to doing the necessary work, some stall and 'forget' to do their between-session tasks or wish to keep talking about the hole rather than climbing the ladder out of it. At this point, a therapist can try to motivate them to do the work and help them overcome any obstacles to this. If this fails, they re-evaluate whether it is the right time for the client to overcome their problem and whether they are sufficiently motivated to do the hard work required.

Likewise, if you know your child is not completing the tasks designed to help them outside their appointments, we recommend you review their treatment plan with the therapist and talk to your child about what they need to do. If they continue to neglect what they are assigned to do and stay stuck in their current behaviours, you are best to cease treatment for the time being or try a different therapist. There is no point in persisting with therapy that isn't working and isn't inspiring your child to do the work required.

Stay within the time limit for your treatment

A psychologist will need to get to know you and/or your child, assess your situation and identify the potential for improvement in your child's or your own anxiety. Then therapy should move into the active stage of changing behaviours and altering unhelpful ways of thinking.

Children or adults being treated for anxiety should begin to feel some improvement in the first couple of months. Sometimes it takes longer, particularly if they are neurodiverse, have experienced the trauma of a deeply disturbing experience, or face an ongoing challenge, such as a parent's diagnosis of a terminal illness or their own diagnosis of a chronic condition. If this is not the case for you, and you have not seen any improvement after several months, discuss this with the psychologist to determine how best to proceed and develop an agreed plan for what to do next.

When your child is already seeing a psychologist

If your child is currently seeing a psychologist, there are ways to know whether their treatment is going well. Useful indications include:

- Your child is starting to improve the way they manage their anxiety. They are getting back to being the person they were before anxiety

began to affect them, and they no longer need constant reassurance from you.
- Your child's moods and compliance no longer affect your family as much as they did. Their anxiety is not seen as a justification for poor behaviour, and you are part of the team that is helping them manage their occasional bad moods in a way that they will eventually be able to do for themself.
- Therapy does not excuse them from their responsibilities as the main way of helping them. Even if your psychologist requested they be allowed not to attend the school camp or sit their exams in a special room at the start of their therapy, your child now has a clear plan to help them to eventually face these events without these considerations.
- Your child does not threaten to 'tell their psychologist on you'. There is no sense that the psychologist is their ally in an ongoing war with you. Rather, everyone is on the same team and working toward helping your child overcome their anxiety. The flip side of this is that you do not feel you need to walk on eggshells around your child, fearful that you will be blamed for all their difficulties in the therapy room.
- Family harmony is improving because of therapy. The psychologist has helped you help your child, but not to the point where this is detrimental to you or your family. They have not requested that you put up with your child's bad moods at the end of the day – 'Oscar has held in his feelings all day and it is understandable for him to take it out on you in the evening.' Nor have they requested that the family make excessive special accommodations for your child, such as asking the rest of the family to do all of their chores in their final year of school, or letting them storm around freely if they are upset.
- Your child likes your psychologist but might occasionally feel challenged by some parts of their therapy and does not always like the work they are assigned to do. This indicates that their psychologist is sufficiently caring but also sufficiently demanding of your child to do the tough stuff necessary to improve their situation.
- Therapy is time limited, and you are aware of approximately how many sessions your child is likely to need. Be concerned (in the absence of a life-threatening or pervasive disorder) if your child has been seeing the psychologist fortnightly or monthly for a year or two, and therapy is primarily seen as ongoing support.

If your child's therapy is not progressing in this way, speak to the psychologist or have your child speak to them about the improvements they see so far and what else needs to be done. Ask how long the psychologist thinks treatment will be necessary and how many sessions it usually takes to improve the issue to the point that no further treatment is needed. If the answers are not helpful or hopeful, speak to your GP about your concerns; sometimes school counsellors can help too. Ask if they can recommend a psychologist they know to be effective in treating the issue in children.

We are both psychologists and we believe in our profession and the people in it. We encourage you to work with your psychologist to make sure you are getting the best out of therapy.

The right professional assistance will help your child start to live their life unconstrained by treatable problems. Make sure you avail yourself of your psychologist's knowledge and expertise to get your child out of the anxiety hole and into the real journey of life – above ground.

CHAPTER 16

Frequently asked questions

Now you've read almost everything you need to know to set your child on the right track to living their life without undue fears and worries. Nevertheless, you may still have some questions. Here are some we are often asked, together with our answers.

My child regularly refuses to go to school. What can I do?

Without a doubt, school avoidance or refusal is becoming more common. While the impact of COVID is likely to be the primary cause, there are other contributing factors, including many children's preference for using screens at home over going to school, and some children's reduced ability to confidently face challenge.

Before you can successfully address school refusal, you need to understand your child's main concern about school. This will help you know whether you need to remove the obstacle preventing them going to school or the reward for staying home. To do this, you must ask your child why they would prefer to stay home.

Their avoidance might be due to a specific anxiety. They may be worried about the health or safety of someone else at home (you, your partner or a pet) and feel the need to stay with them to keep an eye on them. Or your child might have a fear of germs at school, a reluctance to go to the school toilets, a fear of facing tests and exams, or be afraid they won't find a group of friends in the playground.

If any of these anxieties are the cause, they need to be addressed in a way that enables your child to face them. A clinical psychologist can help them do this with targeted and effective treatment.

Your child may have less serious concerns that make them want to avoid school. They may have social difficulties with another student or a tricky relationship with a teacher, perhaps brought on because your child has been reluctant to put sufficient effort into their schoolwork or talks too much in class. Their sticking point might be the journey to and from school if they encounter a group of rambunctious older teens on the bus. Discuss their concerns with them, then use the problem-solving technique in chapter 14 to work through how they will overcome the particular barrier that is keeping them away.

Your child might prefer to be at home because they are trying to avoid specific challenges like PE lessons, a cross-country race, sports day, a test or class presentation. Check with their school to find out whether these are scheduled on the days your child wants to stay home.

Be careful not to inadvertently reward them for staying home by permitting screen use on those days. School days spent at home should in no way be 'fun'. Make sure they do not spend this time gaming, watching videos, or any other screen-based pastime they enjoy. Be aware that they may appear to be involved in educational activities while you are in the room but switch over to their game as soon as you leave. Whiling away the hours on a screen makes time go faster, and you want their time to pass slowly so they are keen to overcome their worries or illness and return to school. Similarly, don't allow them to have special meals or to feel important by accompanying you to work where your workmates fuss over them. We understand that having a child sick at home with no screens is hard work for both parent and child, but it is important to make it clear to them that being at school offers more entertaining options than being at home.

Never allow your child to stay home because they fear being 'bored' at school. They need to experience all types of days along the scale of fascinating through to boring to be truly ready for a life that reflects this reality.

How much control over our day does my child need? Should we let them have more say in what we do?

There's nothing wrong with building some predictability into our days; your child is likely to take comfort in this too. But it is not healthy for someone to want perfect control over everything that happens. It is particularly unhelpful when a child wants to control the whole family's schedule and decide who gets the last shower or who can sit next to them at dinner.

An easy way to achieve a degree of uniformity in each day is for everyone in the family to stick to a set of routines. It's particularly useful to have unchanging morning and afternoon routines for most school days and to have weekend or holiday routines where children know the order of what will happen and what they need to do. Critical here is that the child does the tasks the parents expect them to do before they are allowed to enjoy the downtime activities they want to do. This provides them with a sense of control over the fun things in their day at the behest of their parent rather than their own wilfulness or insistence.

As they mature, children need to slowly gain more autonomy in managing their days. To help them do this, parents should deliberately adjust routines to focus on the healthiest habits they would like their child to embrace as they become older, such as completing their homework, having a shower and cleaning their teeth. Over time, let your supervision of your child's behaviour recede and slowly allow them more independence. Their school will take care of homework (and will usually deliver consequences when it's not done) but for hygiene, put some reminders in your phone to unobtrusively check the wetness of their bath towel or the freshness of their breath. Choose your schedule of reminders: it may be daily at first, then weekly, monthly or seasonally for the first year and once or twice in the following year if they are a tween. If they are younger or older than that, adjust as needed.

I have concerns about some of the things my child wants to do, such as go to parties or hang out with their friends in the shopping centre after school. Do I say 'yes' or 'no' to them?

Many parents worry excessively when their child is about to do something that carries some risk for the first time, like going to the movies with their friends or being a passenger in a car with their mate who recently got their licence. Rather than simply worry, you can prepare them well by helping them plan how to handle the new experience. This helps you determine whether your child is mature enough for the activity and that you feel confident in their ability to manage any unexpected situations that may come up. There are several steps involved.

Discuss the activity with them

Go through what they will do as part of the activity. If they want to attend a party, talk about how they will get to the party and home again. They need to be aware of what they must organise to participate in the activity successfully, such as arrange a lift or take public transport. Don't tell them what they should do: you want to develop their problem-solving skills here. Give them a few days to develop a plan, possibly in conjunction with their friends or with a sibling's input, and ask them to come back to you. You might give them a few tips, such as suggesting they get an earlier bus or train than necessary to be sure of arriving on time and getting home before their curfew. This way you increase their skill in being well prepared.

Make sure they know what to do if things go wrong

Ask them what they would do if their friend's older sibling, who was going to drive them home, appeared to be intoxicated. Or if they felt peer pressure to drink alcohol themself. Again, give them time to think through potential problems and perhaps have a conversation with friends or siblings to get further ideas for solving them. You can give them suggestions, but it's better for them to think through the possible tricky aspects of the activity and use their problem-solving skills and available resources to think of some solutions. Remember you are checking their maturity here: if they arrive at good answers after thinking deeply and consulting wise and helpful people, you will know you can trust them.

Make sure they understand your expectations of their behaviour

Be clear about the time you expect them home and your rules on potential risks at the party, such as drinking alcohol. You might also want to call the parents of the child who is having the party or insist you know who will drive your child there and back. Gain your teenager's input here: you want them to understand and agree to your rules as well as feeling you are acknowledging their maturity and trusting them to contribute to the discussion and decision-making.

State the clear benefits to them of following your rules

Tell them that if they are home by the time you specify, you will allow them to go to the next similar event. Clearly set up the consequences should they not follow the rules and explain them to your child. This is not a threat; it is so they know what will happen and can choose their actions fully aware of the consequences. Then, should they get home late, your anger or fear won't make you go overboard with an over-the-top consequence.

Clearly communicate your desire to keep them safe

Tell them you would always prefer them to call you at any sign of difficulty rather than remain exposed to risk. You don't want them to be fearful of your reaction to a situation and not call you when they are in danger. In fact, there is a view that teens whose parents have an authoritarian zero tolerance to drinking, drugs or sexual activity are more exposed to risk because when they get into danger, they are less likely to seek a parent's help for fear of their reaction.

> *Make sure your child is confident they can seek help from you when they are at risk of danger, regardless of their circumstances or choices.*

Calmly discuss the activity with them afterwards

Whatever happens, discuss the activity with them once it's done. If they broke a rule – perhaps they arrived home later than agreed – it is critical that you follow through with the consequences you discussed beforehand. Make sure you keep your temper so that your discussion is productive. Ask them what they would do to resolve the situation next time and, again, give them time to think their answer through and talk to friends or siblings to get further ideas if they need to.

My child contacts me constantly from school and texts when they are with their friends. Can I ignore them, or should I reply?

What to do here depends on several factors. If the texts are cheery 'hi, how are you going?' messages, don't be too alarmed. That they enjoy checking in with you shows you have a good connection with each other.

But if they insist on a back-and-forth exchange whenever they have any downtime, this might signal a problem. They may be not good at handling boredom and are relying on you to entertain them. Suggest that they prepare themself for times when they might be alone and bored, so they can listen to podcasts or bring books to read.

It is a problem if they regularly seek to exchange messages with you when you would expect them to be enjoying the company of others. This means they are not giving their best to their time with their friends and are instead relying on you to solve their minor problems or help them feel good through your praise and attention at any time. Perhaps this is happening because you always give them lots of what they want: parents can inadvertently be much more reassuring to their children than their friends are. Watch excessive praise or affection in your messages, as you want them to seek support and social connection from their friends when they are in their company.

Make sure you encourage their friendships. If they complain regularly about minor annoyances to do with their friends, don't triangulate by supporting them and agreeing with their comments. This may draw the two of you closer, but it distances them from their friends, which is not helpful in the long term. Support them in friendship difficulties but encourage them to sort matters out themself with the friend or friends, or to find a more congenial friendship group.

If their messages to you are complaints about minor difficulties, ignore them. You want them to make the best of the moment rather than put all their energy into complaining to you. Also ignore messages of boredom or illness sent from school. They will need to convince the school they are sick enough to come home, in which case the school will contact you. Texts or emails should not be needed.

Finally, if their messages to you are angry – trying to have the last word in an argument or berating you for not letting them have a social media account – ignore them. We can easily become quite thoughtless and cruel in online communication and use words we wouldn't say to each other's faces. Try not to participate in such exchanges, no matter how much you want the last word yourself.

And as we have said, don't regularly text or call your child when they are away from you, apart from a daily catch-up when they are with their other parent or grandparents. Allow them to enjoy their time away and catch up properly when you see them again.

My child is truly worried and stressed about their final year of school. How do I help them?

The last school year presents many challenges to students which are often needlessly amplified because of an erroneous belief that their final results determine the rest of their lives. They don't and never have. In fact, most people's working lives follow a zigzag pattern instead of a straight line from school to retirement with a single chance at one good career, only on offer when they are finishing school.

Study is important during the year to give your child as many options as possible, but they need to do other activities besides mega-study to prepare them well for the years after school. It's essential that they maintain a balanced life. They may be tempted to drop everything and just study, but this is a mistake. As well as a realistic amount of schoolwork, they need to do a range of activities to keep them in good mental health, including exercise, leisure and extracurricular activities, a part-time job, and spending time with friends and family.

If your child finds it hard to concentrate when they study, help them work through this with the 'what do I do now' steps in chapter 14. This will prompt them to focus on their values and help them reach out for ideas on how to fine-tune their study habits and manage procrastination.

If your child remains fixated on fears about their performance during the year, follow the steps in chapter 14 to help them identify and solve their 'what if' worries: 'What if I don't do well in the trials?' or 'What if I don't do as well as my friends do in exams?' Ask them to think about when they will have answers to these questions. The trials will have a specific date – say, 15th August – while the answer to the last question will only be evident at the end of the year. If their worry is 'What if my results don't get me into the right career?', they won't know if a career is right for them until they have spent a few years in the job. Remind them that many roads lead to a good life and many people who don't get their first choice at university or with an apprenticeship end up in a career that suits them much better.

How do I help my child with worries about how they look?

It's natural to feel nervous about yourself and your body as you grow up. In the tween and teen years our bodies change regularly, and most tweens and teens easily become self-conscious about their body's different appearance and changing functions, and whether they are 'normal'. These are the years when it is easy for boys and girls to become focused on parts of their body they don't like.

Such concerns are more rampant now than ever with airbrushed and curated images posted to social media suggesting that perfection is possible. It is understandable that children can become insecure about their supposed physical 'defects'.

But it is not inevitable, and you can help. Your best response when your child expresses fears about their body is to encourage them to become comfortable about how they look and focus more on what their body can do. It is important that they regularly play sport to have a better chance of appreciating their body's strength and capability as well as its aesthetics.

Don't allow them to strive for 'perfection' in their appearance. If a child in mid-primary school insists they must always have their hair perfectly braided, regard this as a danger signal because it shows they are focusing more on being 'perfect' than is good for them. Encourage them to allow themself to look less than perfect. You could start by asking them to do their own hair in the car without a mirror once a week to see what happens that day. Alternatively, have them do extra chores in return for your time spent braiding their hair; refuse to do it if they act like a diva and insist you are not getting it 'right'.

Too often we see students with anxiety allowed to have beauty procedures, such as eyelash extensions or false nails, to give them a temporary boost of confidence. This starts a vicious cycle of overdependence on needing to maintain a particular and costly standard of beauty to maintain basic self-esteem.

Schools have sensibly pushed back against this trend by establishing rules that prevent students from wearing these beauty accessories. This reduces unnecessary peer group pressure and unrealistic beauty standards. But some schools are vilified on social media for being unnecessarily harsh when they insist on enforcing the consequences of their policies on students who have broken the rules. Many schools have told us they have received letters from medical practitioners to support particular students wearing these accessories with what we consider curious expectations of benefit (such as needing eyelash extensions to do well in their academic work).

We don't agree with this. Treatment of anxiety and body dysmorphia involves removing artificial boosts to confidence such as reliance on extensions to nails, eyelashes or other cosmetic additions. We strongly believe that it's no treat to purchase these enhancements for children, nor is it helpful for health professionals to suggest them as so-called solutions for children's low self-esteem. If you regularly buy such items for your child, you buy into the idea that who they are naturally isn't good enough ... and that's just false.

What should I do if my child has panic attacks?

The most important part of responding to your child's panic attacks is to treat them as a hiccup in their life. While it feels very frightening for your child to be out of breath, their heart racing and chest contracting, these sensations feel even worse if they don't understand them.

If you think your child is not facing anything truly fearful – if they are simply walking into school or work, or getting on the bus to meet their friend – they may worry even more about their panicked reaction when they don't know why it's happening. (You may worry too.) Never fear – here's what to do.

Panic only starts to recede once we are not scared of it, and this is accomplished by simply observing and experiencing our feelings rather than fighting them. A great way to do this is panic surfing, where you imagine you are surfing up and down the waves of your panic, being there for the ride rather than fearful of it. Repeated over time, this practice reduces fear and creates courage rather than concern about your feelings.

It's critical for your child to keep going with the activity they were doing when the panic attack started (keep on 'surfing' their symptoms), even if they don't perform the activity as well as they otherwise would have. This shows them they can complete whatever they were doing, so they don't develop an unhealthy fear of panic if it shows up.

If you take your child to be treated for panic, a psychologist is likely to explain its origins (the fight or flight response) and then encourage your child to experience panic symptoms via repeated supervised exercises in the counselling room. When ready, your child is shown how to perform these exercises outside the counselling room. Over time, your child's fear of their panicky feelings will start to lessen. Once they have practised surfing their symptoms repeatedly during stressful activities, panic symptoms will stop interfering with your child's life and their fear of panic will eventually disappear.

Panic therapy should not involve grounding exercises – slowing one's breathing or counting inhalations – as they are unhelpful. In fact, there has been an almost universal misunderstanding on the value of deep-breathing exercises to ground oneself in the face of panic. While many people rely on breathing techniques to outlast panic, they can become a new 'crutch' giving a child or adult the false idea that there is something special to do to cope with panic. These people tend to believe that panic will be with them forever, but they can manage it because they have their 'antidote' of breathing exercises. While these techniques may have a short-lived place in very specific therapeutic instances, to really beat panic, you need to learn that panicky feelings cannot harm you and end up having minimal impact on your performance. Enduring them without any special accompanying technique is always the approach with the most lasting benefit for panic disorder and panic attacks which occur as part of an anxiety disorder.

My teenager avoids eye contact with adults. What can I do?

In the present era of personal devices, many children have difficulty maintaining eye contact with others. This is a problem you need to address. If your child's reluctance to look others in the eye seems to accompany social withdrawal from adults or other children, it may be a sign of social anxiety.

Talk to your child about how important it is to look in another person's eyes when they are speaking with them. Acknowledge that this can be difficult, but also explain that it is an important way for them to show respect to the other person and form a genuine connection with them. Start this from a young age so your child gets used to this expectation. Have them begin by looking members of their extended family or neighbours in the eye while they say a few sentences. Keep this private because your child might be embarrassed to learn that someone was aware they are working on this, and you would potentially reduce their willingness to try it. Once they are comfortable with extended family and people they know, move the focus to other people, such as those in shops or in the school office.

You must ensure their personal devices are put away as often as possible when your child is socialising. This makes it much easier for them to practise following a conversation by looking at the people who are speaking, rather than zoning out looking at their phone.

My child has developed a fear of vomiting. Should I be concerned?

Emetophobia is the technical term for a fear of vomiting. While no one likes vomiting, children and teens with emetophobia can start to avoid places where they know a person has vomited (a bathroom or specific toilets at school) and touching surfaces they view as contaminated. They become agitated when anyone mentions feeling ill or that they have recently been sick.

Families who are aware their child feels this way and wish to avoid any fuss or distress to them will ask others not to mention feeling nauseous in front of them. This creates a false impression that the child can and will avoid situations in which there is even a small risk of getting sick. But the only real way to eliminate a phobia is to be repeatedly exposed to triggers. This shows us that we are actually fine because it allows us to discover, from our own experience, that despite being close to sources of our fear on repeated occasions, we did not get sick. If you allow your child to avoid facing this fear, you are likely to inadvertently reinforce this phobia within your family. We recommend you seek help if you cannot manage your child's emetophobia on your own.

I've read what you say about how to manage my child's social anxiety, but they won't agree to go anywhere to use the strategy. How can I get them to try it?

Socially anxious tweens and teens often prefer to connect with others online rather than in person. This can lead them to favour online connection with people across the world over face-to-face catch-ups with their peers.

This has its problems. We know that if you tend to be socially anxious, it is easier to share private thoughts online where you can't see a person's facial expression, particularly if you hide your identity behind an alias. However, we also know that this pattern of online connection leads teens to find people's real-life company less satisfying in comparison, which in turn provides them with less incentive to get out of their room and develop their social skills in person without a screen.

Teens have many fears about what others think of them – their looks, their social success, and their identity. It's not surprising that those who are more prone to feeling socially anxious limit their opportunities to test out and broaden their 'live' social skills. Implement a rule that once your teen has a personal device, they must continue in-person activities that will stretch their social skills, such as signing up to help behind the scenes at an upcoming school production, participating in a social justice project with face-to-face meetings, or volunteering on the weekend at a charity that appeals to them. Help them find a regular activity that involves working on a common goal in person with others.

I've heard about hierarchies and behavioural experiments. Are these needed to overcome anxiety?

Exposure hierarchies and behavioural experiments are two of the most well-recognised elements of treatment for tackling phobias, social anxiety and panic disorder as part of Cognitive Behavioural Therapy (CBT) treatment. The hierarchy is a step ladder of activities which trigger a person's anxiety in an aspect of their life they would like to change, such as their fear of talking to people in real life. The therapist asks their client to list activities which bring on anxious feelings on the steps of a ladder, from least distressing (on the bottom rung) to most distressing (on the top rung). The client then assigns each step a number as a fraction of 100 which measures the level of anxiety the activity causes them to feel. Here's an example of a step hierarchy for a young adult who is anxious about talking to people they don't know at university:

> 90/100 Sitting next to someone in a lecture and asking them if they could share contact details in case we miss a class (most distressing)
> 70/100 Sitting next to someone in a lecture and asking them if they like the class
> 50/100 Asking someone in the lunch queue at university the best place to buy good coffee on campus
> 40/100 Asking someone what the time is or if there is a post office on campus
> 20/100 Walking up my street early in the morning and smiling to people as I walk past (least distressing)

Once the client has constructed their ladder, some CBT therapists develop a 'behavioural experiment' for each step on the hierarchy of activities. The therapist asks the client to predict what would happen if they were to carry out each task and the likelihood of something bad occurring as a result. They might predict that if they were to give a speech, 50% of the time they would make a terrible fool of themself, or they may imagine that if they were to ask someone they liked to lunch, their invitation would have a 75% chance of being rejected.

Let's look again at the anxious university student who wants to become more comfortable talking to others on campus. Let's call him Alex. For the activity on the bottom rung of his ladder, Alex predicts that the person he greets in passing will ignore him 50% of the time. Because of his anxious prediction, it's likely that Alex usually walks past others with his head down, avoiding eye contact and without acknowledging them.

The therapist sets Alex the task of 'smiling at a stranger as you pass them on the footpath on your morning walk'. This constitutes the first experiment that Alex will do as 'homework'. Each time he performs this activity, Alex notes whether the person walking the other way acknowledges his smile or not. After smiling at people 12 times during his morning walks, Alex has a useful measure of what actually occurs as a result of that activity.

Let's say Alex receives a pleasant response on 10 of the 12 times he smiles at a person in passing. (Our experience says this is likely.) Alex can now see that his initial prediction of being ignored 50% of the time was an overestimate and that being ignored on two out of 12 times doesn't affect the rest of his day (or even his morning walk). This is a better way of examining and challenging a deep-set fear than telling someone they are wrong to be fearful or sharing your own more positive experiences.

Activity hierarchies and behavioural experiments are powerful methods of changing a person's beliefs and behaviours by inviting them to experience frequent challenges, face uncertain outcomes and consolidate a new point of view through repeated reflections. With consistent and steady application, the client can slowly climb their ladder, commencing at the bottom and progressing to the goal at the top. This way Alex is likely to overcome his reluctance to greet others and ultimately feel comfortable enough to initiate conversations and fully engage socially at university.

For someone with social anxiety like Alex, a therapist is likely to combine this approach with social skills training. For someone with panic disorder, a therapist could construct behavioural experiments introducing panic surfing for activities and places the client currently chooses to avoid. For someone with a cockroach phobia, a therapist would work with them to construct a hierarchy around looking at and progressively approaching cockroaches.

This is a well-established way of slowly overcoming fear. There's nothing to stop you trying it out yourself, although if your fears significantly affect your wellbeing, you may prefer to do this with the support of a psychologist or targeted online anxiety program.

Can I write more than one worry story for any worry?

More than one worry story can be written for any worry. Doing this will give you an indication of the potential number of outcomes that may result from a single worry. These stories are an important reminder that we catastrophise unnecessarily and that fixating on a single negative outcome is futile. They show us that we underestimate our resourcefulness because we will usually cope with whatever ends up happening. You don't have to write worry stories for all of the potential outcomes of your problem; select the most likely scenarios to think through and tame your worries. Do this if the step of working out the timeline of the outcome has not sufficiently allayed your worrying thoughts.

What do I do if my child exhibits cutting behaviours or self-harm?

Deliberate damage to oneself without intent to suicide is known to psychologists as non-suicidal self-injury. It usually involves deliberately cutting one's skin with something sharp like a knife, razor or protractor. Some people cut superficially; others cut deeply enough to form scars or require medical help. Self-harm is similarly destructive behaviour that can include attempts to end one's life.

Widespread misperceptions about these behaviours mean some people don't get much-needed help. Cutting and self-harm are not typically done purely for attention, nor are they only done by teenage girls. Research indicates that some people begin self-harming in their twenties, and that males and females do it in equal number.

Young people say they self-harm for a range of reasons connected to strong feelings they experience at the time. They may cut themselves to release the intensity of these feelings, to let others know that they need help, to show themselves that they do indeed feel pain, or to gain a sense of control. Many say that self-inflicted pain helps them not to focus relentlessly on the thoughts or feelings which devastate them. Most psychologists believe the behaviour stems from difficulties with emotional regulation and coping with psychological distress.

Research shows that around 22% of adolescents and young adults have engaged in self-harm. It's often associated with puberty, when young people are negotiating peer group issues, changing relationships with parents, undeveloped skills in regulating their feelings, and the impact of hormones and maturing brains. While it may seem as if more people self-harm today than in the past, the evidence doesn't back this up. It is likely that our increasing willingness to talk about this behaviour leads us to think it is happening more often.

Use of social media is not necessarily a trigger for self-harm or cutting. While it can bring on overwhelming emotions for some young people, others find social media gives them a sense of community and support, which helps them feel better when they're upset. Indeed, there are some online communities specifically set up to encourage people not to engage in self-harm. But we also cannot ignore the evidence linking excessive use of social media to incidence of depression in young people: the more time they spend on social media, the less they are likely to be seeking genuinely fulfilling relationships offline. So we cannot conclude that using social media is helpful compared to other pursuits.

What should you do if you find out your child is self-harming? Get help for them as soon as you can: take them to a doctor, school counsellor, psychologist or psychiatrist.

Your initial response must be calm and non-judgemental – make sure you keep your strong feelings in check because it's easy for parental fear to quickly turn into anger. Don't take your child's behaviour as a reflection on you personally and don't assume their actions will inevitably lead to thoughts of suicide. If they bring their harmful behaviour to your attention, thank them for telling you and let them know they've done the right thing. Don't worry that discussing self-harm with your child will prompt them to do it again. Your concern is more likely to encourage them to accept the help they need.

Counselling with a clinical psychologist will teach them ways to cope when their feelings seem overwhelming. Mindfulness techniques, which develop people's ability to be present in the moment and calm themselves down, are known to be helpful. Therapy also helps young people prone to self-harm learn to cope with their difficulties through improving their communication skills and learning how to avoid building their emotions to the point where they need an extreme release. One of the most well-established treatments for self-harm is Dialectical Behaviour Therapy (DBT). It helps a person try a range of strategies to build their capacity to tolerate difficult feelings and calm their emotions through self-regulation.

Is distraction a useful technique for coping with anxiety?

We often hear people say that distraction helps them deal with uncomfortable feelings like anxiety or sadness. And an almost universal suggestion for a sure-fire way to distract ourselves from our troubles is to engage in something mindless and immediately pleasant. We go out and buy things to feel better, be it at the department store or the bakery, or get out a packet of chips and turn on the video game. On occasion, using this approach is no big deal.

There is absolutely a time and place for distraction, but it is not ultimately helpful if we distract ourselves every time our mood strays into tricky territory. This is especially so when our chosen distraction is a dopamine-inducing activity that requires little effort on our part to lift our spirits (eating salty snacks or chocolate, online shopping or binge-watching a favourite show) or if our distraction actually removes the need for us to face the challenging tasks which we feel glum or worried about (abandoning our study or assignment altogether in favour of scrolling social media). In the latter, distraction becomes avoidance. Instead of learning to cope with tricky feelings, we choose to evade them. For example, adults with a preference for social avoidance often look down at their phone instead of looking at others in what could be an awkward conversation.

When we permit children to immediately distract themselves from worry by buying them something special or letting them turn to their devices, we stifle their development of self-regulation and resilience. This makes it harder for them to face temporary challenge. The short-term gains they receive from distraction or avoidance of difficult feelings come with a likely long-term cost of depleted essential skills.

Some distraction *after* doing the hard work of taming your worries can be helpful, but we prefer 'in life' activities such as meeting up with another person and discussing each other's day or participating in an offline activity like playing a sport or taking your dog to the dog park, rather than zoning out watching YouTube. In chapter 14 we showed the value of determining when you will know the answer to your burning 'what if' worry. Once you have completed this work, doing something pleasant that distracts you while you wait for your answer can be beneficial. But only when the hard work of taming your worry precedes the distraction.

Be careful not to confuse distraction with first-line treatment for depressed mood which involves deliberately scheduling pleasant activity. For children or adults who are depressed, scheduling fun or previously enjoyed activities is important. If your child or teenager is feeling down, support them to carry out healthy activities – a bush walk, bike ride, trip to the ocean, balanced exercise or constructive hobbies – to lift their mood. If your child is genuinely depressed, seek therapeutic assistance for them. (We do not specifically address depression in this book.)

I am worried my child may have suicidal thoughts. How can I be sure they are safe?

This is an ongoing concern for many parents. There are signs to look out for that can help you detect when your child may need support.

Be aware of significant changes in your child's social group. Children draw great comfort from their peer group; they gain an important sense of belonging and support from their buddies. Losing contact with their friends, changing friendship groups, or fighting with a close friend can cause a child to experience an overwhelming reaction they may be unable to manage on their own.

Pay attention to changes in your child's behaviour. You can expect your child's personality to alter slightly as they move from childhood to adolescence. It is also natural for them to become more concerned about their peers' opinions than yours. Changes to your family's day-to-day life may prompt your child to react in different ways. But sudden or extreme changes in their behaviour may be cause for concern. If your child suddenly becomes particularly withdrawn or angry, or they no longer want to do activities they enjoyed only weeks ago, it's best to check in with them. In a quiet moment, ask how they're faring – 'How are you going? Is everything okay?'

If they confide in you about strong feelings, give them an appropriate amount of time to talk and listen to their concerns patiently. Don't dismiss extreme declarations like 'I will never get another friend' or 'everything is hopeless'. You may think you can minimise their feelings by telling them not to be silly or that they're overreacting, but this can make them feel unheard and less likely to discuss their feelings in future.

A better way to respond is to ask questions about their situation. Try not to become emotional at what they tell you, as they are likely to stop speaking if you become too upset. You want to present yourself as a capable confidant.

If the strength of their feelings worries you, ask them how bad it has ever got for them, and if they have ever thought of doing something serious like suicide. This is a difficult and uncomfortable question for most people to ask; however, research shows that contrary to planting ideas in a child's head, talking about thoughts of suicide gives them a sense of relief and allows them to feel cared for.

If they say they have thought about suicide, let them know you have heard their distress and assure them you will work together to sort it out. Express confidence to them that their situation can be turned around with the right support and immediately start planning that support with them. Now is the time for both reassurance and action.

Praise them for the strength they have shown in letting you know how they feel and reassure them that they've done the right thing. Continue to keep an eye on them as you get the necessary help.

Kids Helpline (1800 55 1800) is an excellent first point of contact in Australia for a child who is struggling. You can also see the counsellor from your child's school who may provide direct support or recommend a local psychologist with the relevant expertise. If you, or a loved one, are at risk of current harm, you can present to the emergency department of the nearest hospital to get immediate help.

Speak to your GP and ask for a referral to a psychologist for yourself. You will need support to be strong for your child and manage your own overwhelming feelings.

All of the discussions we have outlined here are tricky and stressful, but as the person who loves your child most, you must be strong in initiating them and responding to what is said. They may turn out to be the most important conversations you ever have.

If this topic has raised emotional problems for you or caused you distress, support is available in Australia at Beyond Blue https://www.beyondblue.org.au/get-support or Lifeline (13 11 14 for 24/7 Crisis Support).

Elsewhere, the International Association for Suicide Prevention (IASP) and Lifeline International provide the 'find a helpline' website with contact information for helplines and support services in over 130 countries at https://findahelpline.com/i/iasp.

Is there anything else we need to know, Judith and Danielle?

Yes, there is. Something really important, and it is in the next chapter.

CHAPTER 17

Embrace life's uncertainty

Although anxious feelings can be challenging and uncomfortable, our experience of anxiety is typically a signal that we are about to face something important and meaningful to us.

We understand why people don't like feeling anxious. Our fast-beating heart, the fluttery sensations and nausea in our stomach, the shakiness, redness in our face or neck, and difficulty catching our breath are all unpleasant symptoms which appear when we are attempting to achieve something significant or when we are feeling vulnerable. It is as if our body lets us down at precisely the moments when it should step up and support us.

We also acknowledge that anxious thoughts niggle at us persistently. For some, this leads to ongoing feelings of tension, irritability and agitation. Others react by constantly seeking reassurance or trying to downright avoid all things challenging. Either way, we can become trapped in a cycle of unhelpful behaviours as we try to block out our angst about what the future might bring. Too often we end up tossing and turning through sleepless nights, our minds full of 'what if' and 'what do I do now' thoughts.

A child's anxieties carry a particular sting for parents who want to sweep away all of their child's challenges and uncertainties, yet are forced to watch their child struggle with their feelings. It is understandable that parents do whatever they can to make their child's anxiety go away. And when they are not able to do this, they end up feeling anxious themselves about their child's emotional state and ability to cope with life.

But what would happen if we were to think of anxiety in a different way? Instead of letting anxiety constantly whisper to us, 'Beware, you don't know what's going to happen here!', imagine if we heard it clearly say, 'You are about to do something that matters – go for it!'

We understand this won't always be easy. Embracing uncertainty goes against our instinct to seek immediate reassurance and come up with ready solutions to all of our dilemmas. Helping your child to manage technology responsibly will involve the tough work of developing new habits. Teaching your child to tame their worries takes time and patience. Encouraging your child to practise these skills often enough to make the process easier requires consistent commitment.

And it will sometimes take all your strength to resist your parental instinct to protect your child from all challenge. Allowing your child to experience occasional discomfort and insist they do the things they initially find difficult is going to be tough for you at times, particularly when you are aware of their every need via their texts and phone calls. Holding the line on how they use their screens will be a regular battle. Encouraging them to sit and develop answers to their problems instead of solving their dilemmas for them might feel uncaring and unnatural to you at first. Letting them experience a life that is not perfectly predictable but imperfectly surprising will take effort and patience before you see the value of these behaviours on your child's resilience and confidence. Watching them step away from your sheltering arms into independence will potentially be the toughest part of being a parent.

But these are the tasks we ask you to take on – with good reason. Sometimes the best moments in life are the times when we can't be sure of what's coming up – for you and for your child. The recent pandemic experience for those who had to stay home for extended periods showed us how it feels when life is too predictable. COVID brought us days that were the same. Every. Single. Day. And most of us hated it; we longed to be able to embrace a different day tomorrow than the day we had today.

Uncertainty is exciting: it urges us to turn the pages of a book, it keeps us enthralled in a good movie, it leads us to take a different road and turn the corner to take us somewhere we have never been before.

Sometimes anxiety is a signal that you or your child are on the right path, bravely stepping out of your comfort zone and expanding your horizons in the way the best journeys do.

Instead of watching your child approach the future troubled by fears of *what if*, prepare them to walk toward their challenges with curiosity, thinking *let's see*. When you and your child believe they will cope with whatever life turns up for them, this is precisely what will happen.

Life's joys, sorrows, successes, failures, lessons, moments and connections are all out there for us to experience.

So – bring it on!

Further reading

Introduction

Einstein DA (2005) *The role of magical thinking in obsessive-compulsive disorder* [doctoral thesis], University of Sydney.

Einstein DA (2014) 'Extension of the transdiagnostic model to focus on intolerance of uncertainty: a review of the literature and implications for treatment', *Clinical Psychology: Science and Practice*, 21(3):280–300.

Einstein DA (2019) *The dip: a practical guide to take control of screen addiction and reconnect your family. For parents of teenagers*, Distinct Psychology, Sydney.

Einstein DA, Dabb C and Fraser M (2023) 'FoMO, but not self-compassion, moderates the link between social media use and anxiety in adolescence', *Australian Journal of Psychology*, 75 (1):2217961, doi.org/10.1080/00049530.2023.2217961.

Einstein DA, McMaugh A, Rapee RM, McEvoy P, Ferrari MI, Abbott MJ, Mansell, W and Karin E (2023) *Targeting intolerance of uncertainty in secondary schools*, National Conference of the Australian Association for Cognitive Behaviour Therapy, Sydney.

Einstein DA and Mansell W (2016) 'The relevance of uncertainty and goal conflict to mental disorders, their prevention and management: a unifying approach', *The Cognitive Behaviour Therapist*, 9, e36.

Einstein DA and Menzies RG (2006) 'Magical thinking in obsessive compulsive disorder, panic disorder and the general community', *Behavioural and Cognitive Psychotherapy*, 34(3):351–357.

Ferrari M, Beath A, Einstein DA, Yap K, Hunt C (2023) 'Gender differences in self-compassion: a latent profile analysis of compassionate and uncompassionate self-relating in a large adolescent sample', *Current Psychology*, 42:24132–24147, doi.org/10.1007/s12144-022-03408-0.

Locke JY (2015) *The bonsai child: why modern parenting limits children's potential and practical strategies to turn it around*, Judith Locke, Kelvin Grove.

Locke JY (2020) *The bonsai student: why modern parenting limits children's potential at school and practical strategies to turn it around*, Judith Locke, Kelvin Grove.

Lykos A (director) (2023) *Disconnect me* [motion picture], Lykos Entertainment, Australia.

Polderman TJC, Benyamin B, de Leeuw CA, Sullivan PF, Van Bochoven A, Visscher PM and Posthuma D (2015) 'Meta-analysis of the heritability of human traits based on fifty years of twin studies', *Nature Genetics*, 47:702–709, doi.org/10.1038/ng.3285.

Schniering CA, Einstein DA, Kirkman, JJL and Rapee RR (2022) 'Online treatment of adolescents with comorbid anxiety and depression', *Journal of Affective Disorders*, 311C:88–94.

Part A

1. All about anxiety

Bimstein JG, O'Bryan EM, Jean A and McLeish AC (2023) 'Intolerance of uncertainty, negative reinforcement alcohol use motives, and hazardous drinking in college students with clinically elevated worry', *Substance Use & Misuse*, 58(10):1254–1261, doi:10.1080/10826084.2023.2215318.

Carleton RN (2012) 'The intolerance of uncertainty construct in the context of anxiety disorders: theoretical and practical perspectives', *Expert Review of Neurotherapeutics*, 12(8):937–947.

Einstein DA (2014) 'Extension of the transdiagnostic model to focus on intolerance of uncertainty: a review of the literature and implications for treatment', *Clinical Psychology: Science and Practice*, 21(3):280–300.

Jardin C, Paulus DJ, Garey L, Kauffman B, Bakhshaie J, Manning K, Mayorga

NA and Zvolensky MJ (2018) 'Towards a greater understanding of anxiety sensitivity across groups: the construct validity of the Anxiety Sensitivity Index-3', *Psychiatry Research*, 268:72–81.

Papachristou H, Theodorou M, Neophytou K and Panayiotou G (2018) 'Community sample evidence on the relations among behavioural inhibition system, anxiety sensitivity, experiential avoidance, and social anxiety in adolescents', *Journal of Contextual Behavioral Science*, 8:36-43.

Phang IG, Balakrishnan BKPD, and Ting H (2021) 'Does sustainable consumption matter? Consumer grocery shopping behaviour and the pandemic', *Journal of Social Marketing*, 11(4):507–522.

Taylor S, Zvolensky MJ, Cox BJ, Deacon B, Heimberg RG, Ledley DR and Cardenas SJ (2007) 'Robust dimensions of anxiety sensitivity: development and initial validation of the Anxiety Sensitivity Index-3', *Psychological Assessment*, 19(2):176–188.

2. Parenting, schooling and anxiety

Brummelman E, Nelemans SA, Thomaes S, Orobio de Castro B (2017) 'When parents' praise inflates, children's self-esteem deflates', *Child Development*, 88(6):1799–1809.

Dobson IR and Skuja E (2005) 'Secondary schooling, tertiary entry ranks and university performance', *People and Place*, 13(1):53–62.

Dogan B, Yoldas C, Kocabas O, Memis CO, Sevincok D and Sevincok L (2019) 'The characteristics of the comorbidity between social anxiety and separation anxiety disorders in adult patients', *Nordic Journal of Psychiatry*, 73(6):380-386, doi:10.1080/08039488.2019.1642381.

Dornbusch SM, Ritter PL, Leiderman PH, Roberts DF and Fraleigh MJ (1987) 'The relation of parenting style to adolescent school performance', *Child Development*, 58(5):1244–1257.

Kiel EJ, Premo JE and Buss KA (2016) 'Gender moderates the progression from fearful temperament to social withdrawal through protective parenting', *Social Development*, 25:235–255, doi:10.1111/sode.12145.

Lamborn SD, Mounts NS, Steinberg L and Dornbusch SM (1991) 'Patterns of competence and adjustment among adolescents from authoritative, authoritarian, indulgent, and neglectful families', *Child Development*, 62(5):1049–1065.

LeMoyne T and Buchanan T (2011) 'Does hovering matter? Helicopter parenting and its effect on well-being', *Sociological Spectrum*, 31(4):399–418.

Locke JY (2014) *Too much of a good thing?: an investigation into overparenting* [doctoral thesis], Queensland University of Technology.

Locke JY (2015) *The bonsai child: why modern parenting limits children's potential and practical strategies to turn it around*, Judith Locke, Kelvin Grove.

Locke JY (2020) *The bonsai student: why modern parenting limits children's potential at school and practical strategies to turn it around*. Judith Locke, Kelvin Grove.

Locke JY, Campbell MA and Kavanagh D (2012) 'Can a parent do too much for their child? An examination by parenting professionals of the concept of overparenting', *Australian Journal of Guidance and Counselling*, 22(2):249–265.

Locke JY, Kavanagh DJ and Campbell MA (2015) 'Overparenting and homework: the student's task but everyone's responsibility', *Journal of Psychologists and Counsellors*, 26(1):1–15.

Montero-Marin J, Allwood M, Ball S, Crane C, De Wilde K, Hinze V, Jones B et al. (2022) 'School-based mindfulness training in early adolescence: what works, for whom and how in the MYRIAD trial?', *Evidence-based Mental Health*, 25(3):117–124.

Mueller CM and Dweck CS (1998) 'Praise for intelligence can undermine children's motivation and performance', *Journal of Personality and Social Psychology*, 75(1):33–52.

Power TG (2004) 'Stress and coping in childhood: the parents' role', *Parenting: Science and Practice*, 4(4):271–317, doi:10.1207/s15327922par0404_1.

Roberts JA and David ME (2019) 'The social media party: fear of missing out (FoMO), social media intensity, connection, and well-being', *International Journal of Human–Computer Interaction*, 36(4):386–392, doi:10.1080/10447318.2019.1646517.

Schiffrin HH, Liss M, Miles-McLean H, Geary KA, Erchull MJ and Tashner T (2013) 'Helping or hovering? The effects of helicopter parenting on college students' well-being', *Journal of Child and Family Studies*, 23:548–557.

Segrin C, Woszidlo A, Givertz M, Bauer A and Taylor Murphy M (2012) 'The association between overparenting, parent-child communication, and entitlement and adaptive traits in adult children', *Family Relations*, 61(2):237–252.

Segrin C, Woszidlo A, Givertz M and Montgomery N (2013) 'Parent and child traits associated with overparenting', *Journal of Social and Clinical Psychology*, 32(6):569–595.

Seligman MEP (1972) 'Learned helplessness', *Annual Review of Medicine*, 23(1):407–412.

Seligman MEP, Reivich K, Jaycox L and Gillham J (1995) *The optimistic child*. Houghton, Mifflin and Company, Boston.

Smith J and Naylor R (2002) 'Schooling effects on subsequent university performance: evidence for the UK university population', *Economics of Education Review*, 24(5):549–562.

Steinberg L, Elmen JD and Mounts NS (1989) 'Authoritative parenting, psychosocial maturity, and academic success among adolescents', *Child Development*, 60(6):1424–1436.

Steiner EM, Dahlquist LM, Power TG and Bollinger ME (2020) 'Intolerance of uncertainty and protective parenting in mothers of children with food allergy', *Children's Health Care*, 49(2):184–201.

Twenge JM and Campbell WK (2009) *The narcissism epidemic: living in the age of entitlement*, Free Press, New York.

Ungar M (2009) 'Overprotective parenting: helping parents provide the right amount of risk and responsibility', *The American Journal of Family Therapy*, 37(3):258–271.

Vigdal JS and Brønnick KK (2022) 'A systematic review of "helicopter parenting" and its relationship with anxiety and depression', *Frontiers in Psychology*, doi:10.3389/fpsyg.2022.872981.

3. Technology and anxiety

Boston University Medical Center (9 December 2014) 'Mobile device use leads to few interactions between mother and child during mealtime (https://www.bumc.bu.edu/camed/2014/12/09/mobile-device-use-leads-to-few-interactions-between-mother-and-child-during-mealtime/)'.

Dugas MJ, Gosselin P and Ladouceur R (2001) 'Intolerance of uncertainty and worry: investigating specificity in a nonclinical sample', *Cognitive Therapy and Research*, 25:551–558.

Froemke RC and Young LJ (2021) 'Oxytocin, neural plasticity, and social behavior', *Annual Review of Neuroscience*, 44:359–381.

Gentes EL and Ruscio AM (2011) 'A meta-analysis of the relation of intolerance of uncertainty to symptoms of generalized anxiety disorder, major depressive disorder, and obsessive compulsive disorder', *Clinical Psychology Review*, 31(6):923–933.

Giedd JN (2020) 'Adolescent brain and the natural allure of digital media', *Dialogues in Clinical Neuroscience*, 22(2):127–133, doi.org/10.31887/DCNS.2020.22.2/jgiedd.

Holaway RM, Heimberg RG and Coles ME (2006) 'A comparison of intolerance of uncertainty in analogue obsessive-compulsive disorder and generalized anxiety disorder', *Anxiety Disorders*, 20:158–174.

McEvoy PM and Mahoney AEJ (2011a) 'Achieving certainty about the structure of intolerance of uncertainty in a treatment-seeking sample of anxiety and depression', *Journal of Anxiety Disorders*, 25:112–122.

McEvoy PM and Mahoney AEJ (2011b) 'To be sure, to be sure: intolerance of uncertainty mediates symptoms of various anxiety disorders and depression', *Behavior Therapy*, 43:533–545, 10.10116/j.beth.2011.02.007.

Radesky JS, Kistin CJ, Zuckerman B, Nitzberg K, Gross J, Kaplan-Sanoff M and Silverstein, M (2014) 'Patterns of mobile device use by caregivers and children during meals in fast food restaurants', *Pediatrics*, 133(4):e843-e849.

Rigney N, de Vries GJ, Petrulis A and Young LJ (2022) 'Oxytocin, vasopressin, and social behavior: from neural circuits to clinical opportunities', *Endocrinology*, 163(9), doi.org/10.1210/endocr/bqac111.

Tabak BA, Leng G, Szeto A, Parker KJ, Verbalis JG, Ziegler TE, Lee MR, Neumann ID and Mendez AJ (2023) 'Advances in human oxytocin measurement: challenges and proposed solutions', *Molecular Psychiatry*, 28(10):127–140.

Tolin D, Abramowitz JS, Brigidi BD and Foa EB (2003) 'Intolerance of uncertainty in obsessive-compulsive disorder', *Journal of Anxiety Disorders*, 17:233–242.

4. Friendships and anxiety

Diesendruck G (2020) 'Why do children essentialize social groups?', *Advances in Child Development and Behavior*, 59:31–64.

Mukhtar S, Mukhtar S and Mahmood Z (2021) 'A correlational approach to relational aggression: assessing individual, family and classroom variables/determinants of relational aggression among adolescents', *Bahria Journal of Professional Psychology*, 21(1):28–51.

Snethen G and Van Puymbroeck M (2008) 'Girls and physical aggression:

causes, trends, and intervention guided by social learning theory', *Aggression and Violent Behavior*, 13(5):346–354.

Voulgaridou I, Kokkinos CM and Markos A (2023) 'Is relational aggression a means of pursuing social goals among adolescents with specific personality traits?', *Psychology in the Schools*, 6(6):1663–1680, doi.org/10.1002/pits.22705.

Wakefield JR, Bowe M, Kellezi B, McNamara N and Stevenson C (2019) 'When groups help and when groups harm: origins, developments, and future directions of the "social cure" perspective of group dynamics', *Social and Personality Psychology Compass*, 13(3):e12440.

5. Sensitive children and anxiety

Gigerenzer G and Gaissmaier W (2011) 'Heuristic decision making', *Annual Review of Psychology*, 62(1):451–482.

6. Envy, FoMO and anxiety

Anderson M, Vogels EA and Nolan H (2022) *Connection, creativity and drama: teen life on social media in 2022*. Pew Research Center, Washington.

Baumeister RF, and Leary MR (1995) 'The need to belong: desire for interpersonal attachments as a fundamental human motivation', *Psychological Bulletin*, 117(3):497–529.

Baumeister RF and Robson DA (2021) 'Belongingness and the modern schoolchild: on loneliness, socioemotional health, self-esteem, evolutionary mismatch, online sociality, and the numbness of rejection', *Australian Journal of Psychology*, 73(1):103–111.

Brailovskaia J, Rohmann E, Bierhoff H-W and Margraf J (2020) 'The anxious addictive narcissist: the relationship between grandiose and vulnerable narcissism, anxiety symptoms and Facebook addiction', *PLoS ONE*, 15(11):e0241632.

Einstein DA, Dabb C and Fraser M (2023) 'FoMO, but not self-compassion, moderates the link between social media use and anxiety in adolescence', *Australian Journal of Psychology*, 75(1):2217961, doi.org/10.1080/00049530.2023.2217961.

Froh JJ, Fan J, Emmons RA, Bono G, Huebner ES and Watkins P (2011) 'Measuring gratitude in youth: assessing the psychometric properties of adult gratitude scales in children and adolescents', *Psychological Assessment*, 23(2):311.

Kross E, Verduyn P, Demiralp E, Park J, Lee DS, Lin N and Ybarra O (2013) 'Facebook use predicts declines in subjective well-being in young adults', *PloS ONE*, 8(8):e69841.

Latif K, Weng Q, Pitafi AH, Ali A, Siddiqui AW, Malik MY and Latif Z (2021) 'Social comparison as a double-edged sword on social media: the role of envy type and online social identity', *Telematics and Informatics*, 56:101470.

Przybylski AK, Murayama K, DeHaan CR and Gladwell V (2013) 'Motivational, emotional, and behavioral correlates of fear of missing out', *Computers in Human Behavior*, 29(4):1841–1848, doi.org/10.1016/j.chb.2013.02.014.

Smith D, Leonis T and Anandavalli S (2021) 'Belonging and loneliness in cyberspace: impacts of social media on adolescents' well-being', *Australian Journal of Psychology*, 73(1):12–23, doi.org/10.1080/00049530.2021.1898914.

Tandoc EC, Ferrucci P and Duffy M (2015) 'Facebook use, envy, and depression among college students: is facebooking depressing?', *Computers in Human Behavior*, 43:139–146.

Utz S, Muscanell N and Khalid C (2015) 'Snapchat elicits more jealousy than Facebook: a comparison of Snapchat and Facebook use', *Cyberpsychology, Behavior, and Social Networking*, 18(3):141–146.

Valenzuela S, Park N and Kee KF (2009) 'Is there social capital in a social network site?: Facebook use and college students' life satisfaction, trust, and participation', *Journal of Computer-Mediated Communication*, 14(4):875–901, doi.org/10.1111/j.1083-6101.2009.01474.x.

7. Self-regard and anxiety

Brailovskaia J, Rohmann E, Bierhoff H-W and Margraf J (2020) 'The anxious addictive narcissist: the relationship between grandiose and vulnerable narcissism, anxiety symptoms and Facebook Addiction', *Plos ONE*, 15(11):e0241632.

Curran T and Hill AP (2019) 'Perfectionism is increasing over time: a meta-analysis of birth cohort differences from 1989 to 2016', *Psychological Bulletin*, 145(4):410–429, doi.org/10.1037/bul0000138.

Derry KL, Bayliss DM and Ohan JL (2019) 'Measuring grandiose and vulnerable narcissism in children and adolescents: the narcissism scale for children', *Assessment*, 26(4):645–660.

Dweck CS and Yeager DS (2019) 'Mindsets: a view from two eras', *Perspectives on Psychological Science*, 14(3), doi.org/10.1177/1745691618804166.

Erler SH (2018) *The mediating effect of envy on time spent on highly visual social media and general life satisfaction in university students* [bachelor's thesis], University of Twente.

Flett GL and Hewitt PL (2020) 'Reflections on three decades of research on multidimensional perfectionism: an introduction to the special issue on further advances in the assessment of perfectionism', *Journal of Psychoeducational Assessment*, 38(1):3–14.

Hamamura T, Johnson CA and Stankovic M (2020) 'Narcissism over time in Australia and Canada: a cross-temporal meta-analysis', *Personality and Individual Differences*, 155:109707.

Hanke S, Rohmann E and Förster J (2019) 'Regulatory focus and regulatory mode – keys to narcissists' (lack of) life satisfaction?', *Personality and Individual Differences*, 138:109–116.

Horton RS, Bleau G and Drwecki B (2006) 'Parenting narcissus: what are the links between parenting and narcissism?', *Journal of Personality*, 74(2):345–376.

Iancu I, Bodner E and Ben-Zion IZ (2015) 'Self esteem, dependency, self-efficacy and self-criticism in social anxiety disorder', *Comprehensive Psychiatry*, 58:165–171.

Liu Q, Shao Z and Fan W (2018) 'The impact of users' sense of belonging on social media habit formation: empirical evidence from social networking and microblogging websites in China', *International Journal of Information Management*, 43:209–223.

Mueller CM and Dweck CS (1998) 'Praise for intelligence can undermine children's motivation and performance', *Journal of Personality and Social Psychology*, 75(1):33–52.

Pantic I, Milanovic A, Loboda B, Błachnio A, Przepiorka A, Nesic D, … and Ristic S (2017) 'Association between physiological oscillations in self-esteem, narcissism and internet addiction: a cross-sectional study', *Psychiatry Research*, 258:239–243.

Sironic A and Reeve RA (2015) 'A combined analysis of the Frost Multidimensional Perfectionism Scale (FMPS), Child and Adolescent Perfectionism Scale (CAPS), and Almost Perfect Scale–Revised (APS-R): different perfectionist profiles in adolescent high school students', *Psychological Assessment*, 27:1471–1483.

Stornae AV, Rosenvinge JH, Sundgot-Borgen J, Petterson G and Friburg O (2019) 'Profiles of perfectionism among adolescents attending specialized elite and ordinary lower secondary schools: a Norwegian cross-sectional comparative study', *Frontiers in Psychology*, 10:2039, doi:10.3389/fpsyg.2019.02039.

Twenge JM, Campbell WK and Gentile B (2012) 'Generational increases in self-evaluations among American college students, 1966-2009', *Self and Identity*, 11(4):409–427.

Twenge JM and Foster JD (2010) 'Birth cohort increases in narcissistic personality traits among American college students 1982–2009', *Social Psychological and Personality Science*, 1(1):99–106.

8. The subtle benefits of anxiety

Benito KG and Walther M (2015) 'Therapeutic process during exposure: habituation model', *Journal of Obsessive-Compulsive and Related Disorders*, 6:147–157.

Blakey SM and Abramowitz JS (2016) 'The effects of safety behaviors during exposure therapy for anxiety: critical analysis from an inhibitory learning perspective', *Clinical Psychology Review*, 49:1–15.

Choahan N (22 October 2018) 'Cure for most mental disorders 'possible', award-winning psychiatrist says (https://www1.racgp.org.au/newsgp/clinical/cure-for-most-mental-disorders-'possible',-award-w)', *newsGP*.

Havik T and Ingul JM (2021) 'How to understand school refusal', *Frontiers in Education*, 6, doi.org/10.3389/feduc.2021.715177.

Kuyken W, Ball S, Crane C, Ganguli P, Jones B, Montero-Marin, J ... and MYRIAD Team. (2022) 'Effectiveness and cost-effectiveness of universal school-based mindfulness training compared with normal school provision in reducing risk of mental health problems and promoting well-being in adolescence: the MYRIAD cluster randomised controlled trial', *BMJ Mental Health*, 25(3):99–109.

Montero-Marin J, Allwood M, Ball S, Crane C, De Wilde K, Hinze V, Jones B, Lord L, Nuthall E, Raja A, Taylor L, Tudor K, Blakemore SJ, Byford S, Dalgleish T, Ford T, Greenberg MT, Ukoumunne OC, Williams JMG and Kuyken W (2022) 'School-based mindfulness training in early adolescence: what works, for whom and how in the MYRIAD trial?', *Evidence Based Mental Health*, 25(3):117–24, doi:10.1136/ebmental-2022-300439. Epub ahead of print. PMID: 35820993; PMCID: PMC9340034.

Skeen S, Laurenzi CA, Gordon SL, du Toit S, Tomlinson M, Dua T, Fleishmann A, Kohl K, Ross D, Servili C and Brand AS (2019) 'Adolescent mental health program components and behaviour risk reduction: a meta-analysis', *Pediatrics*, 144(2):e20183488.

Wood JV, Perunovic, WQ and Lee JW (2009) 'Positive self-statements: power for some, peril for others', *Psychological Science*, 20(7):860–866, doi.org/10.1111/j.1467-9280.2009.02370.x.

Part B

10. Getting your child on the right track

Baumrind D (1965) 'Parental control and parental love', *Children*, 12(6):230–234.

Locke JY (2015) *The bonsai child: why modern parenting limits children's potential and practical strategies to turn it around*, Judith Locke, Kelvin Grove.

Locke, JY (2020) *The bonsai student: why modern parenting limits children's potential at school and practical strategies to turn it around*, Judith Locke, Kelvin Grove.

Maccoby EE and Martin JA (1983) 'Socialization in the context of the family: parent–child interaction', in Mussen PH and Hetherington EM (eds), *Handbook of child psychology*, 4th edn, *Socialization, personality, and social development*, 4:1–101, Wiley, New York.

Montroy JJ, Bowles RP, Skibbe LE, McClelland, MM and Morrison FJ (2016) 'The development of self-regulation across early childhood', *Developmental Psychology*, 52(11):1744–1762.

11. Getting technology right

Goodwin K (2023) *Dear Digital, we need to talk: a guilt-free guide to taming your tech habits and thriving in a distracted world*, Major Street, Elsternwick.

Haidt J (2024) *The anxious generation: how the great rewiring of childhood is causing an epidemic of mental illness*, Penguin Press, New York.

Islam MI, Biswas RK and Khanam R (2020) 'Effect of internet use and electronic game-play on academic performance of Australian children', *Scientific Reports*, 10(1):21727.

Kim S, Favotto L, Halladay J, Wang L, Boyle MH and Georgiades K (2020) 'Differential associations between passive and active forms of screen

time and adolescent mood and anxiety disorders', *Social Psychiatry and Psychiatric Epidemiology*, 55(11):1469-1478, doi:10.1007/s00127-020-01833-9.
- Meagher B (2017) 'Problematic mobile phone use: an emerging disorder?', *InPsych*, 39(5). https://psychology.org.au/for-members/publications/inpsych/2017/oct/problematic-mobile-phone-use-an-emerging-disorder
- Mössle T, Kleimann M, Rehbein F and Pfeiffer C (2010) 'Media use and school achievement – boys at risk?', *British Journal of Developmental Psychology*, 28(3):699–725.
- Mundy L, Canterford L, Hoq M, Olds T, Moreno-Betancur M, Sawyer S, Kosola S and Patton GC (2020) 'Electronic media use and academic performance in late childhood: a longitudinal study', *Plos ONE*, doi.org/10.1371/journal.pone.0237908.
- Riehm KE, Feder KA, Tormohlen KN, Crum RM, Young AS, Green KM, Pacek LR, La Flair LN and Mojtabai R (2019) 'Associations between time spent using social media and internalizing and externalizing problems among US youth', *JAMA Psychiatry*, 76(12):1266–1273, doi.org/10.1001/jamapsychiatry.2019.2325.
- Sanders T, Parker PD, del Pozo-Cruz B, Noetel M and Lonsdale C (2019) 'Type of screen time moderates effects on outcomes in 4013 children: evidence from the Longitudinal Study of Australian Children', *International Journal of Behavioral Nutrition and Physical Activity*, 16:117, doi.org/10.1186/s12966-019-0881-7.
- Shih P, Chiang TL, Lin PI, Lin MY and Guo YL (2023) 'Attention-deficit hyperactivity disorder in children is related to maternal screen time during early childhood in Taiwan: a national prospective cohort study', *BMC Psychiatry*, 23(1):736.
- Swider-Cios E, Vermeij A and Sitskoorn MM (2023) 'Young children and screen-based media: the impact on cognitive and socioemotional development and the importance of parental mediation', *Cognitive Development*, 66:101319, doi.org/10.1016/j.cogdev.2023.101319.
- Twenge JM and Campbell W (2018) 'Associations between screen time and lower psychological well-being among children and adolescents: evidence from a population-based study', *Preventive Medicine Reports*, 12:271–283, doi.org/10.1016/j.pmedr.2018.10.003.
- Twenge JM and Farley E (2021) 'Not all screen time is created equal:

associations with mental health vary by activity and gender', *Social Psychiatry and Psychiatric Epidemiology*, 56:207–217, doi.org/10.1007/s00127-020-01906-9.

Zhang J, Hu H, Hennessy D, Zhao S and Zhang Y (2019) 'Digital media and depressive symptoms among Chinese adolescents: a cross-sectional study', *Heliyon*, 5(5):e01554.

12. Getting your child friendship ready

Amato P (2009) 'Institutional, companionate, and individualistic marriage: a social psychological perspective on marital change', in Peters H and Kamp CM (eds) *Marriage and family: perspectives and complexities*, Columbia University Press, New York.

Laursen B, Altman RL, Bukowski, WM and Wei L (2020) 'Being fun: an overlooked indicator of childhood social status', *Journal of Personality*, 88(5):993–1006.

13. Helping your child face day-to-day challenges

Mueller CM and Dweck CS (1998) 'Praise for intelligence can undermine children's motivation and performance', *Journal of Personality and Social Psychology*, 75(1):33–52.

14. Dealing with persistent worries

Seminars for practitioners to understand and apply the theoretical underpinnings of Einstein's What When Model to Redirect Anxiety are available online at www.danielleeinstein.com.

Berry C, Hodgekins J, Michelson D, Chapman L, Chelidoni O, Crowter L, Sacadura C and Fowler D (2022) 'A systematic review and lived-experience panel analysis of hopefulness in youth depression treatment', *Adolescent Research Review*, 7 (2):235–266.

Gústavsson SM, Salkovskis PM and Sigurðsson JF (2021) 'Cognitive analysis of specific threat beliefs and safety-seeking behaviours in generalised anxiety disorder: revisiting the cognitive theory of anxiety disorders', *Behavioural and Cognitive Psychotherapy*, 49(5):526–539.

Ovanessian MM, Koerner N, Antony MM and Dugas MJ (2019) 'A preliminary test of the therapeutic potential of written exposure with rescripting for generalized anxiety disorder', *Journal of Experimental Psychopathology*, 10(2), doi.org/10.1177/2043808719841529.

Thwaites R and Freeston MH (2005) 'Safety-seeking behaviours: fact or function? How can we clinically differentiate between safety behaviours and adaptive coping strategies across anxiety disorders?', *Behavioural and Cognitive Psychotherapy*, 33(2):177–188.

15. Seeking professional assistance

Erekson DM, Lambert MJ and Eggett DL (2015) 'The relationship between session frequency and psychotherapy outcome in a naturalistic setting', *Journal of Consulting and Clinical Psychology*, 83(6):1097–1107, doi:10.1037/a0039774.

16. Frequently asked questions

Baillie AJ and Rapee RM (1998) *Panic surfing: a self treatment workbook for panic disorder*, Macquarie Lighthouse Press, Sydney.

Lamplugh C, Berle D, Milicevic D and Starcevic V (2008) 'A pilot study of cognitive behaviour therapy for panic disorder augmented by panic surfing', *Clinical Psychology & Psychotherapy: An International Journal of Theory & Practice*, 15(6):440–445.

Salkovskis PM, Clark DM, Hackmann A, Wells A and Gelder MG (1999) 'An experimental investigation of the role of safety-seeking behaviours in the maintenance of panic disorder with agoraphobia', *Behaviour Research and Therapy*, 37(6):559–574.

Thwaites R and Freeston MH (2005) 'Safety-seeking behaviours: fact or function? How can we clinically differentiate between safety behaviours and adaptive coping strategies across anxiety disorders?', *Behavioural and Cognitive Psychotherapy*, 33(2):177–188.

Xiao Q, Song X, Huang L, Hou D and Huang X (2022) 'Global prevalence and characteristics of non-suicidal self-injury between 2010 and 2021 among a non-clinical sample of adolescents: a meta-analysis', *Frontiers in Psychiatry*, 13:912441, doi:10.3389/fpsyt.2022.912441.

Webb B, Looi JC, Allison S, Bidargaddi N and Bastiampillai T (2022) 'Point of view: could social media use be contributing to rising rates of deliberate self-harm and suicide in Australian youth populations?', *Australasian Psychiatry*, 30(6):694–697.

Acknowledgements

This book is the result of our professional experiences, and we would like to thank everyone who has contributed – if you have worked alongside us, asked us a question or told us a story at a session for parents, teachers or students, or consulted with us clinically, it is likely you have made a contribution to the ideas contained in this book. We particularly thank our work colleagues and the teachers we liaise with who work so tirelessly to support children and families to reach their potential. You are a huge inspiration to us.

We also want to say a heartfelt thanks to each other. For many years we talked about formally working together, and to finally see our plan come to fruition is wonderfully gratifying. Although psychology is a practice of communication and collaboration, it can at times be an isolated profession, and to work together in a meeting of minds, complementary strengths and expertise, invigorating debate and unwavering support has a been a joy.

Our immense gratitude and thanks to our editor, Sue Webster, who has been diligent, collaborative, respectful and supportive. Her work and dedication have been incredible, and it would not be the book it is without her. You were worth the wait to get you onboard, Sue!

Many thanks to Machelle Flowers-Smith for offering her expert eye to our ideas.

Thanks also to the creative people who contributed to this book: Tess McCabe for the cover design, Darryl Nixon at Sunset Publishing, and Jamie Hanson and Giselle Haber for our photos.

Finally, and most importantly, our love and many, many thanks to our individual inner circles of family and close friends – your love and support keep us going and mean the world to us.

www.ingramcontent.com/pod-product-compliance
Lightning Source LLC
Chambersburg PA
CBHW020416010526
44118CB00010B/273